Rosie Perera

Helmut Lemke's *Crossing Frontiers* is a riveting book. I could not put it down. Told in gripping first person present, it is the story of his life from his childhood on a diary farm in West Prussia through the war years under Hitler's Nazis, the post-war hardships in Poland and a divided Germany.

With his gift of storytelling Lemke makes even the most mundane and ugly aspects of life fascinating. I came to the end of the book wishing for more. I can't wait for the sequel

Hanna French-Mish, Psychologist, Seattle Wash.

It was such a privilege to read Helmut's book.... Every student should read this - they never get the true picture from their history books. I was in tears when I read about Christa...I also appreciated Helmut's keen sense of observation of nature - that really struck me at the start of the book. To sum up, the book was utterly fascinating and touching.

Dr. Gerhard Rempel, retired History Professor - Florida, USA

Your autobiography is excellent in several ways. You write your life history honestly and with interesting attention to detail and nuance. When you tell the reader of an event important in your life, you provide a full background and panoply of persons involved directly and indirectly so that one gets a clear and interesting picture of what transpired.

Christine Wiebe

I read the book and could not put it down. I read it when I woke up and when I went to bed. I thoroughly enjoyed it.

WIEHLERCHRONIK 2000 - co-author
400 years of history of Mother's family

LEMKECHRONIK   2002
A history of father's family

Nicht mehr als ihr ertragen könnt 2004
My autobiography - German edition

Crossing Frontiers - 2006
My autobiography - English edition

Crossing Frontiers

Helmut Lemke

authorHOUSE®

AuthorHouse™
1663 Liberty Drive
Bloomington, IN 47403
www.authorhouse.com
Phone: 1-800-839-8640

Cover design: Entrance to our farm (photo 1977)
Front page: Helmut as architect, Dipl. Ing. (photo 1955)

First published by AuthorHouse   5/6/2009

ISBN: 978-1-4389-7562-7 (sc)

Printed in the United States of America
Bloomington, Indiana

This book is printed on acid-free paper.

To my children

Michael, Krista, Hanno,

their spouses

and my grandchildren

Contents

Acknowledgements:

I want to thank my children, especially Krista, who showed interest in my life story and persuaded me to write this book. I am grateful to my wife, Hildegard, for her good ideas, assistance and patience and to my sister, Magdalena, with whom I could verify some of the facts.

I want to express my appreciation to our friend, Jean, who patiently gave advice and did the proofreading.

Preface

Crossing Frontiers is my autobiography, the English version of the original *"Nicht mehr als ihr ertragen könnt"* I grew up on a farm in a small village in West Prussia, during the depression. Germany still had to pay impossible war reparations imposed on it by the Treaty of Versailles. As a result, the economy was bleak and unemployment high which gave rise to political unrest. Out of this turmoil Hitler emerged. I saw him rise and fall.

I lived through the war, being involved in the defense of my homeland on the eastern front and the difficult post war years. I undertook a dangerous journey into Soviet occupied territory in search of my mother, with the deprivation and humiliation connected with it. Finally I wrote about a more positive new beginning in East and West Germany and my student exchange year in the USA.

I wrote this book for my children who urged me to add all the details of my life story to the fragments that I had mentioned to them before. Upon request I rewrote it in English

Now, at the age of eighty, I narrate my experiences as honestly and truly as I remember them and can reconstruct them from diaries, letters etc. I am also trying to provide a glimpse into the social and political climate in Germany, as I observed and understood it at that time.

We lived in the country with no TV, no car and no telephone in our home. The basic news we read in the local newspaper and later heard it from the radio. We were dependent for our entertainment mainly on our own creativity.

People in the main cities may have experienced the political development during the Nazi time differently than I did.

Some of the events during and after the war and my responses to them I can not explain other than that God guided and protected me and gave me the wisdom and courage to face the often difficult challenges.

During the last decade, I became interested in genealogy. I researched my father's parentage and wrote the *Lemke Chronik 2002*. I enlarged and co-authored the Wiehlerchronik *2000*, which tells more about my mother's history

Helmut Lemke   Vanvouver, Canada,   February 2007

A short history of Germany
as it relates to my story

East Prussia, where I was born, was the most eastern province of Germany. In the treaty of Versailles, 1919, East and West-Prussia were separated from the German mainland. Most of West Prussia was given to Poland, creating the *Polish Corridor.* Poland now had access to the Baltic Sea.

A small part of West Prussia, *The Große Werder,* (the large lowlands) around Danzig (Gdansk) became *Freistaat Danzig,* an independent entity under the jurisdiction of the League of Nations. A small remnant of West Prussia, the *Kleine Werder,* became a part of East Prussia.

After the occupation of Poland in September 1939, West Prussia became an entity again and was connected to the *German Reich* for a short time...

By the end of the war, in January 1945, the Soviets had advanced into East Prussia, The German army unit into which I had been drafted, the North wing of the Eastern Front, fought valiantly to hold back the Russians but lacking supplies and replacements were outnumbered in manpower and armament. I was wounded in that confrontation. The Russians reached our village and raided our farm on January 25, 1945 as I later learned from my mother.

The Americans could perhaps have advanced to Berlin and further if they had pushed on but they decided to slow down and let the Soviet army, conquer Berlin and move to the Elbe River and the province of Mecklenburg.

On May 8, 1945 World War II was over. The Allied troops and the Soviet army had occupied all of Germany and had met in its middle. I was in a military hospital in Schwerin, Mecklenburg when the American troops arrived in the city. The Russians were just a few kilometers east of us, on the other side of Lake Schwerin. We did not know who would come first and occupy our hospital.

In the middle of June 1945, the Allies decided to divide Germany up into occupation zones. The area conquered by the Russians became the Soviet Occupation Zone. The rest was divided into three zones. The North was occupied by the British, which meant our hospital now was under British administration. The South went to the Americans and the part west of the river Rhein including the Ruhr District to the French. The area east of the Oder – Neisse Rivers was put under Polish administration.

In the middle of July, the Allies followed up on the Yalta agreement to divide Berlin into four Zones. Each occupying force, the Americans, the British and French became a slice of Berlin. In exchange the Western forces retreated behind the Elbe River giving the rest of Mecklenburg and Saxony to the Russians. This meant that our hospital now came under Russian occupation. Germany was divided with no consideration of its people. Shortly the Russians moved in, I started my dangerous journey home to search for my mother.

When the Western Allies got more and more distrustful of their Russian 'friends' the border between East and West was sealed; on the Russian side by a barbwire fence and later a wide plowed and mined strip of land and was heavily guarded by Russian and later East German Militia.

The western Zones were united in 1949 and the Allies established West Germany, the BRD. (Bundesrepublic Deutschland), as a buffer against the Communists in the east. The Russian Zone became East Germany, - the DDR. (Deutsche Demokratische Republik). When this happened, several hundred thousand East Germans fled to Berlin every month and were flown to West Germany or they crossed the border illegally at the risk of their lives. This exodus stopped when the Russians initiated the building of the Berlin Wall in 1961. It separated Berlin into East and West Berlin, until it was united again after the fall of the Wall in November 1989.

This united West and East Germany again and the area is now recorded on the map as"Germany". The western border is the same as that of pre war Germany. The eastern German Provinces of Pomerania, Silesia, West and East Prussia were separated from Germany after the war, along the Oder and Neisse Rivers and added to Poland.

Germany with 80 Million people is once more the most populated country in the middle of Europe. Germany and France are the senior founding partners of the European Union, which in 2006 consisted of 25 countries.

Since my emigration, I have visited Germany at intervals with my wife and later, in 1977 with the whole family. I spent one year 1988-89 with Hildegard in West Germany teaching in an Art College. We contemplated staying there. However, since we have established ourselves in Canada and have our children here, we decided to return, enjoy our retirement in our comfortable home and explore the world from our base in Burnaby.

I still have fond thoughts of my homeland, its culture, its architecture, music and literature, some of its customs and the people with whom I grew up.

Remember the days of old, think of the generations long ago
Ask your Father to recount it and your elders to tell you the tale
Deuteronomy 32:7

Germany before and after World Wars (1918 + 1945)

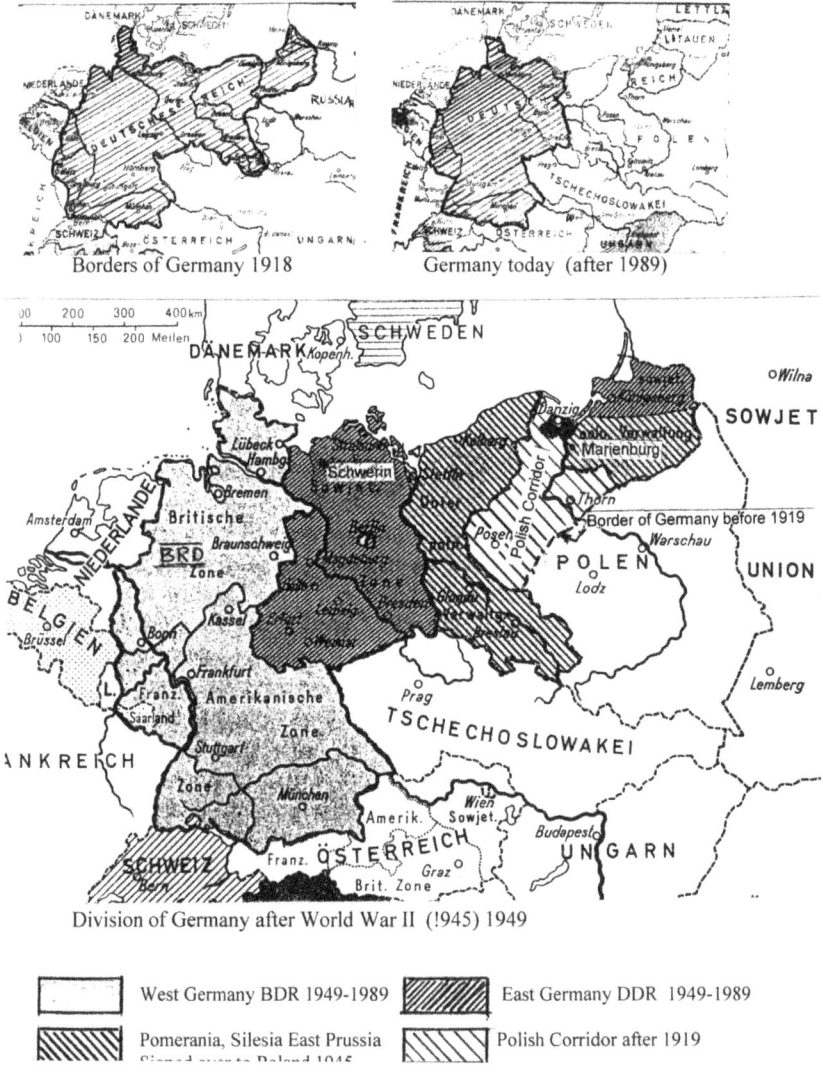

Borders of Germany 1918   Germany today (after 1989)

Division of Germany after World War II (!945) 1949

| West Germany BDR 1949-1989 | East Germany DDR 1949-1989 |
| Pomerania, Silesia East Prussia Signed over to Poland 1945 | Polish Corridor after 1919 |

Chapter One
The Beginning

The scouts had been riding for several days and halted their horses in front of the little river. They looked over the wide, flat area. "This is ideal", one of them said. "The two arms of the river encircle a vast tract of grazing land and join in the distance again. They form a natural border for a meadow where our horses can roam freely and safely."

The wind blew over the high grass. It looked like the waves on the distant lake in the background. The riders turned their horses and rode back; their white tunics flowing in the breeze exposed the black cross on the back. They belonged to the order of The German Knights (or the Knights Templar) who had finished their task in the "Holy Land" to protect Pilgrims on their way to Jerusalem from attacks of Turkish Moslem tribes. They were looking now for new opportunities and welcomed the call from the Duke of Masowia to defend the northern border of his province in Poland against the aggressive Baltic tribe of the "Pruzzen" who lived along the Baltic Sea and had been marauding his land from the north. The Knights were guaranteed by the Duke and the Pope the land that they gained from that hostile tribe. They also saw an opportunity to bring Christianity into the area.

The Knights came up from the South along the Wisla River (Weichsel). On their way, they colonized the area, built settlements and fortresses and finally reached the Baltic Sea. In 1275, they started to build their finest fortress and castle on a hill in the loop of the Nogat River and called it *Marienburg*, in honor of their patron Saint Mary. The Grand Master of the Order then moved his residence from Venice to the new castle, Marienburg.

In a few centuries, the Knights had subdued the Baltic tribes and had tried to integrate them with the settlers and tradesmen they had invited from western countries. The land was very fertile and soon flourishing villages sprang up south of the Baltic Sea.

The Knights, a religious order, became more and more involved in secular politics and the administration of a growing land base and an increasing number of people of different backgrounds and religious beliefs. This was a deviation from their original mission.

The settlers became discontent with the strict rule of the Knights and wanted to have more say in their own governance. This gradually weakened the power of the Knights and caused their decline. The Polish king took advantage of that situation and saw now an opportunity to claim some of their land for his kingdom and win access to the Baltic Sea. He got the Knights involved in a

battle and the combined Polish and Lithuanian army defeated them. In the treaty of Thorn in 1466, they lost a large portion of the land which they had colonized and ruled for two centuries.

Among those people that settled around Marienburg in the 17th century was Cornelius Wiehler, a Mennonite from Holland. The Mennonites, influenced by the Reformation, wanted to go a step further in reforming the church than did Luther in Germany and Zwingli in Switzerland. They wanted separation of state and church; they believed in baptism after a confession of one's own faith, in non-resistance, rejecting war as an option to settle conflicts, as Jesus taught them in the New Testament

This brought the Anabaptists, as they were called, into disrepute with the Catholic Church and also with Luther and Zwingli. These all tried to coerce them to recant but most of them would not. They were forced into exile, beaten, drowned or burned at the stake (this might have been the fate of one of our early forebears.)

Many fled their home country Switzerland and South-Germany. Several went to Bohemia, Holland and North-Germany. From there they followed the invitation of the Polish and Prussian kings to settle in Poland and West Prussia.

They were welcomed there because of their knowledge of building dams and cultivating wet-land that stretched over large areas in the

Wistla and Nogat river deltas. They were good farmers, known for their honesty, integrity and hard work. The Polish and, later, Prussian authorities promised them freedom of religion and, as non-violent people, absolution from military service.

A few generations later a tradesman by the name of Johann Adolf Lemke settled with his large family in the same area, in Lichtfelde. He was a blacksmith, farmer and knew how to repair farm equipment. He believed each young man should learn a decent trade in order to be able to support a family. So he trained six of his sons in his own trade and soon had a flourishing business going. He did not mind that only two sons practiced it later. One took over the family business and the other married a blacksmith's daughter and inherited her father's shop.

The well-to-do Mennonite farmer and the well-established Lutheran tradesman learned to know each other. Their families were devout Christians and founded a non-denominational Christian fellowship in their area, serving in it together as lay preachers, - and that is where *my* story begins.

Chapter Two

Our Home

We park our Peugeot Motor home off the street beside the house of our former neighbor, Cornelsen. It is a one of a kind vehicle. We borrowed it from a retired nun who had used it to transport children to Sunday school in West Germany. We tried to hide the writing on the sides of the "Bus" by putting a wide crepe paper tape over it. We thought the East German border guards would not let us pass through communist East Germany on our way to my home in West Prussia, now Poland, if the words were visible. By careful examination one could still make out the writing *"Jesus liebt Dich"* on one side, and, *"Lasset die Kindlein zu mir kommen"* (let the children come to me), on the other. We call it our *Jesus Bus.*

We all climb out of it and breathe the fresh country air. I head for the old wooden gate at the end of the fence in the back, which opens the way across the meadows to our farm. The gate hangs crookedly in its hinges and groans as I open it, but it still holds together. With anticipation I walk along the overgrown grassy path beside the straight drainage ditch which is the border between our and neighbor Peters' farm.

It is more than thirty years since I walked this path or, perhaps, I should say navigated it last in a homemade boat. The smell of the flowers I seem to recognize. There are still the same thick yellow marsh marigolds growing along the ditch, the fine pink stars of the wild carnations, which I liked so much, the long rows of the yellowish blooming chamomile along the tracks and the tall stalks of the grayish white blooming yarrow waving in the wind. Mother used to make bitter tasting tea from them against fever, indigestion and other ailments. Scattered all over the place are the cheerful color spots of the white and red daisies.

I raise my eyes again and can make out in the distance, between the old gnarled willow trees, our house with the low-hanging, thick thatched roof. There it is, still standing, the long stretched-out building I was born in fifty-one years ago. It has weathered two world wars, floods, and now the Russian and Polish occupation. It has aged visibly as I have. Patched-up with old boards and metal sheets, it looks dilapidated. My father would never have let it deteriorate to that condition.

Quickening my steps, I take the shortcut across the meadow over the narrow footbridge, which we used to take when we were in a hurry coming home from school. There is still our old telephone pole, which we used as home base when we played hide and seek. Behind it we gradually climb up a small hill on which house and farm buildings are standing. Farmland in the area of the Nogat delta was often below sea level, ours was about 1.20 meters. Therefore, houses were built on raised ground above sea level.

Here I am, this time with my whole family, transported back in time thirty-two years. Our oldest son is now the same age as I was when I was drafted for war duty.

This is my birthplace, a typical farmhouse as they were built in this, the eastern part of Germany, living quarters for men and beast all under one roof. A wide drainage canal, the *Mühlengraben*, flows on the north side of the property and separates garden and orchard from the common dirt road that leads to the main country road.

The living room and bedrooms are on the south side of the long complex, facing the garden and the open meadows behind it. A board fence keeps the animals from coming into the garden. We go through the gate, up a few steps, open the door with the rusty wrought iron lock and come into the Diele, the wide-open hall that extends to the end of the house and separates the living rooms from those of the animals. From the Diele we have access to the *gute Stube*, the living room; further on is the door to the kitchen with the wood and coal stove on one side, and the big built-in kettle on the other. We heated the bath water in it, boiled the meat from the butchered pig or calf for the preparation of the sausages and stirred the plum jam in it.

Above the kitchen ceiling, continuing through the roof, is the big brick chimney. It is accessible from the floor above and has a smoke chamber in which we used to hang the ham and sausages after the butchering.

In the middle of the house is the big tile stove, which heats the whole house. One section warms the living room, the other the family dining room. It has a big oven, accessible from the family room in which mother bakes bread, cake, apples and keeps the meals hot. At the end of the hall is the utility room with the cream separator, the butter urn, the meat grinder and the bread cutter. At the end of the hallway are the stairs that lead to the upstairs bedrooms. In one corner stands the big *Wäschemangel* (mangle, to flatten sheets after washing) with big stones as weights

From the hall opposite the kitchen, a plank door leads to the animal quarters. A few steps down we reach the water pump, which serves both man and beast. On the left of the centre passageway are the stalls for the cows, on the opposite side the stall for the horse and the storage bins. At the end on the outside wall is the door to the attached outhouse.

The next section is the barn and behind it the wagon and machine shed and at the end the equipment storage, everything under one roof. The outside walls of the house are made from tightly fitted big square wooden logs. The roof over the barn is supported by round rafters and the reed bundles are tied to them with willow switches. Reed is plentiful here along the rivers and swampy lakes.

Our farm has an additional building on the opposite side of the yard in which we keep the heifers, yearlings, pigs, chicken, geese and sheep. On top is the hayloft, a good place to hide and from the venting hole in the gable I can watch the swallows that twitter on the electrical wire just below it. Our guard dog, Karo, has his hut against that building, overlooking the whole yard. He announces visitors and howls sorrowfully at the full moon.

Beside the covered free run area for the chickens is our vegetable garden in which my mother cultivates all the normal veggies and a number of special herbs. She encourages us to eat as many fresh vegetables as possible and we know there are plenty of them, because we have to help weed the garden and keep it orderly.

Our parents had bought the farm, after their marriage in 1921, from an elderly couple, the Albrechts. Albrechts were not able to take care of the place properly anymore; it was run-down, and rats had infested the barn. Father bought a 22mm pistol sat on watch one evening and, when the rats came down the rafters, he shot six of them. That was the end of it. Father liked order and kept everything in good shape.

Our Parents

My father was a farmer but not a passionate one like my mother's brothers, the Wiehlers. He had fallen in love with a farmer's daughter, married her and they agreed, perhaps supported by her parents, to buy a farm. I think his talents and interests were in another area. Judging by the kind of tools he had acquired, he was more mechanically inclined. In my eyes, he was an inventor. If he had had the means and the encouragement from his parents, he could have become a good engineer.

Father was born in 1894 in Schönfeld, East Prussia. He grew up in the country and his father moved with his family several times before he settled in Lichtfelde and established himself as a well-respected blacksmith.

Father was the fourth of eleven children. Grandfather's principle was that each son should learn an "honest" trade from which he could make a good living and support a family. So he taught all his sons his trade, even if only two practiced it later; Max, who took over grandfather's blacksmith shop and Willi, who fell in love with a blacksmith daughter and inherited his father-in-law's business. I think grandfather did not mind.

Gustav, the oldest brother, was the entrepreneur in the family. On his own initiative, he bought himself a violin and from his own savings paid for instruction. My father joined him and both became good violin players. Most of the children were musical, played stringed instruments and had good voices. The two oldest boys developed and applied their musical talents further. Father founded a choir in the

Christian fellowship which they attended and gave lessons in stringed instruments in order to recruit players for a small orchestra.

I think he needed some balance with the hard work of a blacksmith.

At the age of twenty father had to go to war, the First World War. He served as a Medic and in the music corps. We have a photo of him on horseback with his trumpet. He never talked much about his war experiences but kept sketchbooks of his missions on the eastern front. Pages filled with sketches of officers and comrades from the cavalry and infantry attacking the enemy lines and artillery firing support; also Trenches, wounded comrades, field hospitals and peaceful field-kitchens.

Unfortunately, these valuable sketchbooks did not survive the Second World War. Russian soldiers plundering our house must have taken them or destroyed them. Only two of my fathers sketches survived, one a war scene of a dying soldier who cannot respond to the trumpet call to action anymore and another of a shepherd boy lying in the grass, dreaming.

I remember only one incident that my father mentioned about the last days of the war. His unit had been stationed in the Balkan and its last hospital train was slowly pulling out of Romania when Romanian partisans stopped it. They pushed the train unto a dead track, pulled off the locomotive, arrested the staff and were going to rob the wounded soldiers. Unexpectedly, a German armored military train pulled into the station. The commanding officer summoned the stationmaster and told him to restore the hospital train immediately, and provide water and food for the wounded. If he did not want to see himself and the station blown up, he had better comply. Orders were followed reluctantly and in a short time both trains left in the direction of Germany - rescue at the last moment.

While fighting in the marshy fields in the Balkan my father had contracted malaria and was in a military hospital for a while. When he arrived home after the war was over, he became seriously ill and for weeks his mother feared for his life. These malaria attacks with high fever returned later in his life repeatedly and caused him great physical discomfort and us the fear of losing him.

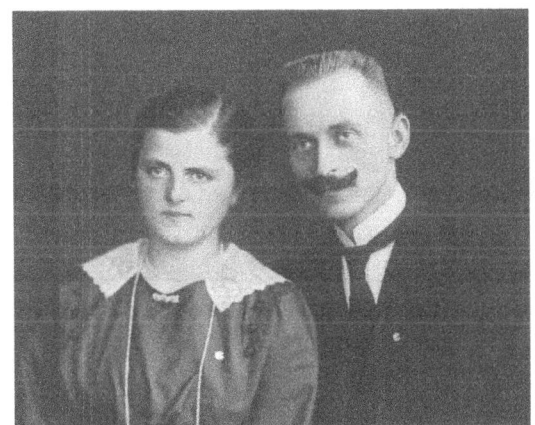

My parents Selma and Franz Lemke

Our farm 1928

Our Family 1928

My father was a tall, slim, handsome man with short blond hair and a mustache usually well groomed. He was very skillful and innovative. He found a solution for everything. He was good mechanically and in working with wood. He made a lot of furniture for the house and toys for us children. Everything had to be perfect. Father could do everything. Honesty, integrity and respect combined with a high degree of responsibility were his principles in life.

Once our neighbor and Mayor, Peters, came to father and told him, "I am ready to retire as *Bürgermeister* and I thought of you as a worthy successor, you have the potential for it". Father was too modest and felt he could not fill his shoes. Peters was the largest estate owner in the village and we had only a small farm. Father had no education beyond public school although he read a lot. He told Peters he could not do this. He would rather do what he could do better, being the first aid attendant in the village for which he was trained and had been commissioned by the health authorities.

To identify him as such and our house as first aid station, we had to fasten a big blue sign with a white circle and a red cross in it on our gable, visible from the street. As far as I remember, nobody ever came for medical help.

He was a sensitive and reserved person, did not talk much, nor did he involve me in his work and did not play often with us children. In later years, he fell into depressions. In these moods he had difficulty making important decisions and mother had to help him and encourage him.

Looking back now I assume these mood changes in my father were the result of many sensations and influences, one of which could have been the terrible images of war, which come back and haunt especially sensitive soldiers. His malaria attacks with high fever had their side effects, severe headaches, circulatory problems and a twitching in his eyes, which at times inhibited his focusing. Once it caused him to drive right into a water-filled ditch, which embarrassed him greatly and made him more insecure. Finally, perhaps unconsciously, he might have felt emptiness, not being able to find expression in his actual talents and interests, music and art, perhaps even feeling being a failure. Once I remember him standing beside me stroking my hair, looking at me with sad eyes and saying, "I think you would be better off if I were not around anymore, restricting your development.."

I did not know how to respond. Could I have changed the situation if I had thrown my arms around him and told him, "Dad, I love you and I need you to show me how to respond to the challenges of life; you know so much and I want to learn a lot from you." Although I felt that way, I could not express it at that age. I only looked at him helplessly because I did not understand how he felt and what he meant.

Mother mentioned that in his last year he had said to her occasionally the same thing that it would be easier for her and the children if he were not in the way and she would not have to care for him.

His condition gradually became worse and he seemed to see no light in the darkness anymore; he could see no way out.

On the morning of July 25, 1939, we received the terrible news from our aunt, Tante Lenchen, Mother's sister, that she had found father dead among the flowerbeds in her garden. He had shot himself. He did not want to do it at home to scare us and cause us additional burden so he had gone the two km to grandfather's house, the *Grüne Aue*, to take his life there.

Tante Lenchen and her brother, Onkel Heinrich, took care of the preparation for the funeral. When we all assembled to say good-bye to him, we were advised not to look at him again because his fine face was disfigured through the shot in the head. My sister Christa wanted to see him once more and we heard her cry when she saw him in the coffin. Elder Dirksen from the Thiensdorf congregation and Elder Heinrich Wiehler, mother's uncle, conducted the funeral in our Mennonite Church in Pr. Rosengart. Father was buried in the cemetery beside the church. I often stood silently beside his grave after our church services, praying and thinking of him.

Relatives from the area, neighbors and members from the congregation attended the funeral and some came afterwards to Grandfather's house for the memorial service. None of father's siblings from Berlin could attend but they sent consoling letters and his eldest brother, Gustav, added money for the coffin.

For me, everything was overwhelming. At first I could not grasp what had happened. All of a sudden, I, the shy little boy, received so much attention. Old and young shook my hand and gave me consoling and encouraging words. I felt important. Not until later did I become aware of the loss of my father and the emptiness in me.

At age thirteen I had now become an adult; as the only male member in the family I felt responsible for my mother, my sisters and the farm, far beyond my ability to cope with.

For Mother it was a hard blow. She must have felt sorry, perhaps even guilty, that she had not understood the severity of Father's suffering, had not been the support he had needed at that time. Could she have prevented his death?

In the society and congregations of that time, this kind of death was not honorable. Mother needed a lot of encouragement, consolation and words of comfort. Ältester Dirksen and Wiehler spoke to her and us as a family, assured us of God's love and forgiveness, and affirmed to mother that God had accepted Father. They visited us later again and gave us words of comfort. Our neighbors were helpful and understanding.

Much later, here in Canada, I learned that Father had sought help from our church leaders and from Hugo Scheffler, his friend from the youth group, who had become a preacher and later became my father in-law. Unfortunately, I found that out long after Father Scheffler had died.

For us as a family a new way of life began.

Mother also came from a large family. She was the seventh of ten children. Her father, Johann Wiehler, had increased his estate through hard work, economical operation and a simple life style, He bought small farms in the neighborhood from farmers who retired or were alcoholics and went bankrupt; those purchases added land to his estate and he became a well-to-do farmer.

The farm on which mother grew up was in the middle of fields and meadows quite a distance away from the village. She had adopted some of her father's values. His modesty and simple life style.

She was good looking, not tall, close to the earth and had a positive attitude towards life. She did her work in house, garden and field joyfully and persistently, was intuitive and had things under control. She applied what she had observed from her mother.

The basic knowledge of how to manage a farm household, how to cook and prepare good meals, to sew and knit, care for a garden and animals she gained from attending a home economics school in Elbing. The finer details, how to entertain and create a beautiful home atmosphere, how to bring up children according to Christian principles and be a helpful partner to her husband, were added later, when she spent a year as a "housekeeper apprentice " with the noble minded countess of Lagow.

On our 1977 trip back to my childhood home we traveled through the little town of Lagova, now in Poland. When I saw the tower of the castle, which I recognized from a postcard my mother had sent home, I was reminded of the time she spent there.

Mother was unimposing, caring, thrifty, innovative, and able to adjust to circumstances that were out of her control. She often acted on intuition and found unconsciously the right solution. I remember one little incident. Someone had taken the valve out of her bicycle tire and she had to push the bike home. It happened again at the same place. When school children passed by our place she saw the 12 year old neighborboy, Rudolf and called him over: „Rudolf, come here, you took the valve out of my bike, didn't you? Could you please give it back to me." He was embarrassed and pulled it out of his pocket, "and give me the one you took yesterday too." Now he thought Mom could look right through him, he hesitated a moment and then pulled out the second one. Mother thanked him for it, no long speech or chastising. He was ashamed, mumbled an excuse and left.

Sometimes, when Mother lost or misplaced something that she urgently needed, she would disappear and come back after a few minutes and go to the place where the item was, while we were still searching. We asked her how she found it so soon. She said she had prayed about it and God hears prayers and had guided her to the right place; we could do the same. No further sermon.

Our parents were believing Christians and had high moral standards; a good example for us children. Father came from a Lutheran and mother from a Mennonite family. They had met in the Jugendbund für EC (a youth group of committed Christians) in the community fellowship. Father was leader of the youth group in that fellowship and conductor of a choir and a string ensemble – guitars, lutes, mandolins and violins. He taught young people keen on joining his orchestra how to play stringed instruments. He also played the trumpet.

As a small boy I would sit in the front row of the fellowship meeting hall proudly watching my father conducting the choir and enjoying the instrumental music and the beautiful tenor voice of my uncle Heinrich.

Sometimes, at home, we could entice Father to play pieces on the mandolin for us. At Christmas he often accompanied our singing with the violin before we got our piano.

Both grandparents Wiehler and Lemke were the main supporters of that inter -denominational Christian community fellowship and were lay ministers. Later they employed a full time preacher and spiritual advisor. The first one, Abraham Harder, came from a former Mennonite settlement in the Ukraine. He had been headmaster of an orphanage in which my future mother-in- law had found refuge. He sort of adopted her and brought her out of the Ukraine when they had a chance to escape from the terror of Stalinist Russia.

Both families attended Sunday evening services, the youth gatherings, Sunday school and Bible studies in the community fellowship in Thiergart. On Sunday mornings the Wiehlers attended the service in the Mennonite Church in Pr. Rosengart and the Lemkes in the Lutheran Church in Lichtfelde. Thiergart was between these two villages.

The community fellowship was the meeting place for the young people, of which the Lemkes and Wiehlers made up half, the rest were the Boetchers, who had 21 children, the Schefflers, Deutschendorfs and Froeses. They joined as singles and many left as couples

Some of the Lemke family, the grandparents with five of their children moved to Berlin. The other four remained in the area. Father's younger brother Max inherited the family estate and stayed in Lichtfelde, Walter married one of the Boetcher girls and opened an electronics business and Emma married Ernst Froese and became a farmer's wife.

The more stable Wiehler family lived within the region. Mother's elder brother Richard inherited the family farm. Grandfather bought a smaller farm closer to the church and took three of his children with him. Lenchen and Heinrich helped on the farm and Anna became a deaconess and founded the orphanage and children's home, Sorgenfrei (without worries).

Under the Nazi party's new order, all Christian and private youth organizations were to be replaced by the state's *Hitlerjugend*. Father's youth group fell under that order and had to be dissolved while he was in military reserve training. It was a hard blow for Father because this was part of his life's work.

My Siblings and I

A number of beautiful girls were in Father's youth group and he finally decided to propose to one of them, my mother Selma Wiehler. When she had no objections, he asked her father for the hand of his daughter. They were married in October 1921; father was 27 and mother was 25. Opa Wiehler gave his daughter a hectare of land, as a dowry, to add to their newly purchased farm. Everything was in place and a year after their wedding my elder sister, Magdalena, was born. She grew up to be the one most obedient, responsible, ambitious and caring. Christa, the second, was more determined, adventurous and life-loving. I was the last one, the only son. When I made my arrival known, early in February, it was still deep winter, sometimes down to −35° C. Father may have hitched the horse before the sleigh and galloped to Thiergart, the neighbor village, stopped at the butcher's and asked if his wife, the region's midwife could come and help mother to bring me into this world. We had no telephone, no car and poor public transportation. Mail and news were delivered by courier. Everything must have gone well, and the midwife put the ten-pound baby into the cradle, crafted by my father. I think all three of us spent our first year in it.

I grew up under the loving care of my parents and the guardianship of my two sisters, who did not mind spoiling their little brother. As a toddler, they sometimes sat me on a chair, combed my hair, tied a ribbon into it and called me "Ruthchen". Perhaps they had wanted a sister or they did not quite know how to handle a brother. I usually played along enjoying the attention, except that, if it took too long, I would jump off the chair and run away. I normally got along fine with my sisters. This was not always the case between them. Magdalena as the eldest thought she had to arrange how and what to play but Christa had her own ideas and did not always want to follow. Mother often had to settle the dispute between them. But most of the time we were a peaceful bunch. On the farm, we had a lot of space in which to run around and our parents usually gave us children chores to do that kept us out of mischief.

Father had built a big brick sandbox in one corner of the garden. It was partly hidden by a big round vigelia bush. I loved to play in the clean yellow sand where I could give rein to my imagination. I would lay out a village with streets, water canals and pump house, with school, stores, farmhouses and the little river Thiene with a bridge and a motorboat on it. Or I built a farmhouse with the living quarters on one side, stables and barns forming a yard, with horses hitched to wagons or pulling a plough and cows and sheep grazing on fenced-in meadows - similar to our own farm layout.

Father had made most of the toys, buildings and equipment for the play-farm and the animals, some I got from Meister Heske, a war invalid. He had taken up the design and construction of wooden toys and I loved to watch him producing these, some he did in a simplified mass production, which I had never seen before. A very noble horse team stood out among the other toys, it was a birthday gift from relatives in Berlin.

When I was deeply involved in my play, I did not want to be interrupted. Sometimes my mother would call me to tend to my chores or have my nap, I would pretend not to hear her and hide in the sandbox. After a while, suffering from a bad conscience, I would run to Mother and attend to my tasks or be put to bed. When mother thought I had fallen asleep, I would very quietly slip out of bed and sneak back to the sandbox and play. Sometimes I could make it back to bed before she noticed I had disappeared. But she always knew whether I had slept or not.

Our garden was my paradise. Flowers were blooming almost all year long, snow bells were already looking out of the snow in early March, ready for Mother's birthday. Later in spring crocuses, violets, daffodils and narcissus, then snap-dragons, peonies, marguerites, lady slippers, hyacinths, pansies and in the fall dahlias and chrysanthemums would display their splendor. On the right of the wide garden path, dividing our garden between flowers and orchard, Father had created a round bed for roses in view of the living room window. a little further on, a row of currant bushes grew along the Mühlen-graben. From them we picked red, yellow and black currants, as many as we could eat. On the left of the path were rows of strawberries and raspberries and beside them the big hairy gooseberries for which we were known among our relatives. The garden had rich black soil and the water table was always high enough that we hardly ever had to water the plants. Scattered around the garden were many fruit trees, yellow plums, big dark purple ones and a number of Italian prune trees. They had many plums that we could prepare plum jam in the big kettle in the kitchen. Sometimes we had so many that we could not even give them away. The pigs had to help us consume them. In one hard winter, 20 of the plum trees died and after that we had no more problems using up our plums. The farm's former owner had planted quite a variety of apple trees and Father had added more, the early Grafensteins and Transparents, the striped "Onion apples" the Boskop and a good winter species, which we called "Yellow Richard". The most interesting one was the one on which father had grafted three kinds of apples, the small sweet apples, the dark red ones of which I forgot the names and the very good tasting *pound apples* each one of which weighed at least one pound or more. Many of the species are not known here in Canada.

My favorite tree was the tall "Raisin pear" tree. It was much taller than our house and I loved to climb up to the top. I had a good view from there and could even look down into our chimney. The best fruit was on the highest branches. I used to hide in it and when my sisters came into the Garden, looking for me, I threw a pear in front of their feet, they jumped because it startled them and I had my fun. The children in the village knew when the pears were ripe, they came with their bags or baskets behind their backs, and Father knew what they were up to. He invited them into the garden, took the long pole with a hook on top, hooked it over some of the pear tree branches and pulled a few times, the pears fell down and the kids gathered them quickly into their baskets and went home happily. Some years the tree produced up to 600 pounds of pears. This was the time when mother prepared special dishes of noodles or beans with pears.

The pear tree provided shade for the garden. Below it an arbor, formed by a lilac hedge, gave us a space to hide, sit, read or meditate in and enjoy the fragrance. The other side of the garden was fenced in with a sturdy board fence. In front of it, facing the entrance to the house was a spacey porch grown over with vines of honey-suckle. On a hot Sunday afternoon, the parents would drink coffee with guests or we kids play with our friends in it.

Behind the fence next to the chicken run, mother had planted the vegetable garden. We helped her to sow the carrots, radishes, lettuce and onions and waited patiently until the small shoots came through the black soil. Mother used a lot of vegetables for our meals. What we did not finish in summer and fall mother would preserve for the winter. Only broccoli, Brussels sprouts and kale we left in the garden and sometimes we had to dust the snow off before we harvested them

In these surroundings, I grew up under the care of my parents and the company of my sisters. On a farm, there are so many interesting things to observe and experience that I was never bored.

Chapter Three

Attending Public School

We can see our village school from our house. It is built like most East German farm houses, the teacher's residence on one side and adjacent to it the class room addition, both under one roof.

Magdalena started school when I was two-and-a-half years old. She likes school, is ambitious, does her homework conscientiously and usually gets good marks. Christa who attends school two years later is not that much interested in school and finds some subjects difficult.

I want to find out what school is like and accompany my sisters once in a while, so that I know what to expect.

Every two years the school photographer comes to school. On this particular day I happen to be there. The photographer smiles at me and asks, "What class are you in"? I tell him, "I am only four and don't go to school yet, I just came along with my sisters". "Well stand with them for the picture". (That photo survived and is now in the family album.)

When I ask too many questions about school, Magdalena says, "We can play school and you will see". Of course she is the teacher and Christa and I the pupils. She gives me an idea what to expect when I have to attend school. I later find out what it is like to be taught in a one-room school.

In winter, on our way to school, we slither along the frozen drainage ditches, we prefer to do this on wooden clogs as they give less resistance and go farther on ice, but we are not allowed to go to school in them, because they are not good for our feet or our reputation - only the poorer kids wear them.

We climb a few steps from the schoolyard to a foyer where we hang our coats and boots and from there a double door opens to an aisle, which divides the elementary from the high school student's sections. On the window side, which faces the garden, the grades one through four students are seated on the other side the grades five through eight students.

Our teacher, Mr. Dehnke, teaches all eight classes in one room. In one year we were forty children. Looking back, I wonder how he managed to do that. The quality of teaching we receive is very basic, which I find out, when I apply for entrance into secondary school.

Good students from the upper classes occasionally assist the teacher by supervising the lower grades. He sometimes asks me to help and I practice the alphabet with the beginner's class, show them how to form and write simple sentences or how to add and subtract numbers. This is early practice for my later profession.

Understandably, the teacher has to assign us seatwork while he teaches the other classes. When I am finished with my work I listen to his instruction to the upper classes and try to do their assignments as well, which I often can do. My sister, Christa, sits behind me. She has some difficulty with math. If in an oral test she cannot come up with the anwer, she looks at me and I wisper it to her. The teacher does not approve of that and tells me to do my own work .

In grade two I sit beside Irmgard, the daughter of a farmer on the other side of the village. She is a fun girl and we like each other, we play together, talk about and exchange our homework. After school, if she takes the shortcut across the meadows to go home, we can go together. My schoolmates call her my girlfriend and tease me about it. I don't really know what that means to have a girlfriend. Once she takes me to her home. Her parents live in a fine house with a glass entrance door and period furniture. I have the feeling they do not appreciate her bringing a boy home. Her father is also a businessman besides being a farmer. Soon afterwards, they move to the town and this means the end of our friendship

One day there is great excitement in school. A big truck comes to the school yard with lots of pipes and a large drill in the back. The men dig the ground up, put the drill equipment over it, drill a hole and push pipes down. After several days of work, they hit water. They screw a spout on the end of the last pipe and we have an artesian spring near the front entrance to the schoolyard. The water tastes good and runs continuously for years.

Another pleasant event I remember is the school's summer outing to Kahlberg, a small sea resort. In order for us to have good supervision, the teacher also invites our parents to come along. Father makes this a family affair. Mother packs a big food basket enough for the whole family and perhaps for someone else who did not bring anything. We meet at the Grunau railway station and take the train to Elbing. We walk from the station to the harbor and see the slender white steamer *Moeve* (seagull) and the newer one, the *Preussen,* tied to the dock, waiting for us. We rush up to get a good seat on the sun deck. The steam whistle blows and we move slowly out of the harbor accompanied by a flock of slim bright white sea gulls. They gulp up the crumbs, which we throw at them, often catching them out of the air. We first sail through the Elbing River and then across the *Frische Haff,* a lake divided from the Ostsee (Baltic Sea) by a very narrow land strip, the Nehrung. On it, facing the sea, lies the Baltic Sea resort of Kahlberg. We land at the south side of the Nehrung, walk across it over sand dunes through a group of snarled short pine trees and from there we have a fantastic view of the beach and the wide expanse of the Ostsee before us. That is always an exciting moment for us kids and we run down to the white sand beach. When our parents are around, they allow us to go into the water and swim. We explore the sand dunes and the beach further on or build sand castles and play ball with the other pupils. For a snack father takes us to the village and buys some bananas or other tropical fruit, which we usually do not get at home. This outing is the highlight of our school year

Not all children enjoy school. At the very end of the village lives the Schmeier family. Their son Hans reaches school age and his father enrolls him in grade one. Wild-eyed *Hänschen* looks around. Everybody and everything is strange; he doesn't like it. When his father turns around to go home he runs after him. His dad scolds him, brings him back again, sits in the back and watches him. After a while Hans notices his father has sneaked out, jumps up, protests and tells the teacher he does not like school or teacher and he is going home. Mr. Dehnke sends two of the older boys to bring him back and seats him between them they are to hold him if he tries to escape. Teaching is impossible in this situation. The whole scene is both sad and funny for us other students. At lunch hour he runs home. A few days later his father brings him back again. The same scene takes place He sits in his bench for a short time, sobs, looks around bewildered and, finally, unable to stand it any longer, screams, curses and runs out of the classroom. This he repeats a few more times until the school administrator decides that Hans is not ready for school yet.

Part of the village teacher's salary is an allowance. For our teacher it means free lodging, a barn with a cow, chicken, some land and a garden. Neighbor Thiede ploughs the field for him, where he grows potatoes and grain. For the daily chores in the stable and garden the students have to help. Some are glad if they can get out of the classroom, others hate it. Sometimes the teacher asks me to feed the cow and clean the stable when I have finished my work in class. I do it with mixed feelings

School starts in summer at seven and in winter at eight. We do not mind but for the teacher it seems sometimes to be too early. Besides being a teacher he is also *Ortsgruppenleiter der NSDAP* (village leader of the National Socialist German Labor Party). The regional meetings of the party are in the neighbor village and end sometimes with a drinking spree which can extend into the early morning hours and the teacher has to walk home. We see him from the school window staggering along the street and entering his house. Shortly after he enters, his wife comes into the classroom, tells us that her husband is not well and writes some exercises on the blackboard, which we have to do. I finish mine quickly and out of boredom and mischief I fold little paper strips and propel them with a rubber band against the neck of an unsuspecting pupil. He jumps and yowls. That causes diversion and laughter. Soon those pupils targeted, find out where these slugs come from and, when the teacher finally enters the classroom a few hours later, they raise their hands and tell him what I have done. I admit my deed and give as my reason that I had nothing to do anymore; but he calls me to the front, pulls me over the bench and gives me a good licking with the cane. That hurts and I am embarrassed because it is the first and only time I get a spanking.

Elementary School house

Pupils Helmut and Christa

Skating with cousin Walter

My parents find out and, what I did not tell, my sisters fill in. Father who usually defends the teacher and taught us to respect him, makes an exception this time, because he does not condone the teacher's lifestyle.

Physical punishment was the method to keep discipline at that time in schools and at home. I don't know if the special cane is part of the school furniture or the teacher's private property. He uses it selectively and stores it in the cupboard behind his desk. Sometimes the lazy pupils who did not do their homework and know what is coming, hide the cane, hoping they will be spared punishment. But the teacher is resourceful; he asks them to go to the yard and cut a cane from the hazelnut bushes that grow there. The clever ones cut rings into it, so that when it lands on their posterior, will splinter and become useless. Depending on his mood, the teacher may smile and let them go. Most of the time, however, they have to cut another one. Now they know the procedure and put a notebook under their trousers before they come back. We can tell by the hollow noise it makes, when the cane comes down on it.

At home our father sometimes applies the Biblical principle: 'If you don't punish your son, you don't love him. If you do love him, you will correct him'. This also is true for the daughters. I know our parents love us and want the best for us. Father does not like to apply this "principle". When he feels he has to, he does it sparingly and only after he warns us and explains the consequences of our actions. His device to correct us in this way is the *'Kloppeitsche*, a handle with thin leather strips attached at the end.

I remember one situation. We are not allowed to cross the frozen drainage ditches until the ice is thick enough to carry us. One cold, sunny winter morning Magdalena and I try the ice on the *Mühlengraben*, to find out if we can skate on it already. So we two slide along. I, the adventurous seven year old, in front. Everything is fine until I come across some circular forms of a different ice structure. I try the first one- the ice crackles; I try the second one- the ice is so thin that I fall through it. My sister comes to my rescue and pulls me out. When I arrive home I am an iceman, my clothes are frozen from the neck down. Mother pulls my clothes off, rubs me until I am warm and puts me to bed. After a while, Father comes into my room, sits down on the side of the bed and looks at me. "You could have drowned if you had been alone. Thanks to your sister you are here and I am glad. But I have warned you often enough not to go on the ice if it is not thick enough. You disobeyed". Then he lifts the bed cover and my nightgown and gives me a spanking to help me remember. I am somewhat confused and cannot quite understand why the spanking. I thought father would be happy that I did not drown as he said and would rather give me a hug.

Father also has other methods of correcting us. I like to build things and use his tools. I am supposed to ask him for permission. Sometimes I am so involved that I forget to put them back. If Father needs them and cannot find them, he calls me and asks where they are. I have to confess and he makes me recite ten times, "I shall ask for permission to use tools and put them back when finished from where I took them". That helps my memory and is not so painful.

I do not remember that Father and I built things together or that he showed me how I could improve my work. He allows me to observe him when he works. I can ask questions and he will answer and explain. I learn a lot from him that way, but he does not guide me and let me try. He does not often take the initiative to do fun things with me.

Our Neighbors

Our farm is built on a hillock in the midst of meadows and fields. It lies between two main roads, in the north the Grunauer Chaussee, which leads to the railway station. In the village Grunau we board the trains to our regional capital Marienburg in the west and the city of Elbing, going east, where we buy our bulk groceries. Our driveway south goes to the Pr.Rosengarter Chaussee, which we use to go to school, to church and to our grandparents.

Our next neighbor is the Reddig family. They own a smaller farm about three hundred meters east of us. Mr. Reddig works occasionally for other farmers to have some additional income. We have good neighborly relations with them, help each other out in emergencies and visit on special occasions, usually around Christmas when we sit around the Christmas tree and share Christmas cookies and the children show their gifts. They have three girls, Edith, as old as Magdalena, Christel, one year older than I and Dora, the youngest. The girls play more often with our girls. Sometimes they invite me, if they need another person for playing ball games or hide and seek.

On the farm, a little further on lives the big farmer Gruebenau, a tacit, almost unfriendly man. His wife once told Mother that he can be abusive and she does not have an easy life with him. Mother encourages her to be strong. We do not have much contact with him. His property borders on ours and I sometimes watch the beautiful black horses on his meadow, especially the vivacious filly jumping around her mother. If he is in a hurry, he takes a shortcut to the main road along our driveway. We don't mind but after a rain the surface of the dirt road is soft and he drives on our bicycle path beside it, cutting deep ruts into it; I don't like it, because it makes riding my bike to school difficult.

Our driveway on the opposite side ends at the road beside the Cornelsen's. Meister Cornelsen, a small man with a hunchback, works in his tailor shop. His wife and children do most of the work on the small farm. We pass by their house when we go to school and to church, and when we deliver our milk and pick up our newspaper. We drop in occasionally for a chat. The newspaper is delivered twice a week to their lawn and we have to pick it up from there. That is usually my job and for me it is more than only a courier's run. On the way I watch the stork quietly approaching the big marsh marigold leaf on which a frog is croaking. He grabs it with his long beak, carries it to the nest on the roof of our house and feeds it to his young. Walking along the water-filled ditch I look for pikes which lie still, close to the surface of the water, waiting for their prey. When they notice me, they dive quickly down into the mud.

When I pick up the paper, I hope Siegfried, Cornelsen's son, is outside. He is my age and we often roam around together. Once we decide to have a shooting match with bows and arrows. Father made me a beautiful bow from an ash branch with the proper tension and a number of reed arrows balanced with a nail at the top. Siegfried made himself a bow from a crooked willow branch no match for mine. So I have an advantage and my arrows fly wider than his. Father hears about it and says to me, Siegfried has no father anymore who can help him, let us make him a good bow. He is happy when I give him the new bow and now we are often even..

One day we have a practice with our bows and arrows again and don't notice that it is getting dark; we can't find our arrows anymore. I suddenly remember the newspaper and rush home. Father has been waiting for me and is worried what may have happened to me. When I try to sneak into the house he hears me, calls me, takes me into his room and tells me how dangerous it is for a little boy to walk alone in the dark and that it is not proper to let him wait so long for the paper. After explaining to me the seriousness of the situation, he gives me a reminder to remember it the next time, draws me over his knee and gives me a spanking – an anticlimax to our animated tournament with bows and arrows.

I sometimes play with Konrad, the teacher's son who is a few years younger than I. He comes to our place or his parents invite me to his house. They trust us and encourage a friendship.

Mostly I play by myself and enjoy it. There is always something interesting to try out or discover or I just lie in the meadow between the field flowers and look into the sky, watching the clouds as they move around creating forms that resemble some galloping steeds or dragons, dancing angels or fire birds. It is fun observing the changing forms. I can lose myself in my dreams.

As many children do, I like and respect water and wind as forces of nature. I am amazed about the strength of the storm, how it bends down big trees so that their branches almost touch the ground or even topples the old willows. I love to lean against the wind and measure my strength, testing how far I can resist.

Miller Giesebrecht lives at the east end of the village. His old windmill stands high on the dyke of the Thiene River. We pass by his place when we go swimming. On a windy day we see the huge wings turn around and around with a speed which the miller can regulate by setting the wings of the mill at a different angle, by unrolling more or less sail over the wings and of course by the strength of the wind. He explains all that to me when Father brings some grain to him to be ground to flour. I watch how the big wings transfer the wind power via a number of different size cogwheels, axles and rollers to the huge grinding stones that turn against each other, grind the grain to bran, and sift out the flour. It even has a gear to lift the heavy sacks of grain and flour.

All that inspires me to build one myself. I collect boards, cork, feathers, flywheel, rollers and leather strips and construct my own windmill. The big goose feathers act as wings that transfer the wind power over wheels, belts and rollers to a lift that moves loads and makes figures turn and jump.

From old willow trees, I collect thick bark and carve boats, long, slim steamers and wide freighters. Mother gives me remnants of white bedding material from which I cut sails and soon a little flotilla of boats driven by the wind sails along the Mühlengraben.

Water fascinates me. There is lots of energy in it and to harness it I build water wheels, which I have seen in books. I use my father's tools to cut two round plates, nail boards in between, in a star-like pattern, put an axle through the middle and hang it on a support so that the wheel can turn freely. A big water container is my creek; I lead the water through a pipe directly into the 'shovels' of the wheel until it turns. With the power it produces, I run little machines that I build with my 'Mechanics Set.' I demonstrate my inventions to my parents or sisters and they admire them or smile, without saying much.

One day Father comes home and tells us Meister Cornelsen, our neighbor, is seriously ill. He goes to visits him, consoles him, prays with him and helps out where he can. On one of the visits, he takes me along. He brings him some food and Mother gives me flowers to make his room friendlier. His room is dark and smells musty. It is the first time I have seen a man lying on his deathbed. Shortly after that visit, he dies and I see the lifeless body in the coffin. I ask Father what happens to him now, can he be dead and then come to life again and what happens when he gets into heaven?

My parents help with the funeral and later, too, when Mrs.Cornelsen is alone with the children.

A block further on lives farmer Schönwald. Their youngest son, Waldemar, is my age and we are in the same class in school. We chat with them when we bring the milk to the pick-up place just opposite to their house. Twice a day we lift the 40-liter metal milk cans unto a trestle on the roadside and the wagon from the dairy picks them up. The milk is processed into butter and cheese. Sometimes mother wants me to get a few groceries from the store opposite to the dairy. I ask the driver if he could take me along on his horse-drawn carriage and he will even let me steer the horses.

Most of the farms in our village are dairy farms. We smaller dairy farmers cannot afford to keep a certified bull for breeding, so we form a breeding co-operative. Schönwald buys a good bull for breeding and we others pay him for the insemination of our cows.

From 1936 on, the city of Marienburg sends a cooled container truck around to pick up our milk and the dairy of Mr. Fritz gradually closes.

North from us, at the end of our driveway, is the largest estate in the village. It belongs to Heinrich Peters, a Mennonite by name. He has been our mayor for many years. We only meet him in his office; father talks to him occasionally. I do not remember getting together with them as a family. But we don't have much contact with people in the village anyway. Peters is close to retirement and he wants to groom father to become his successor as the next mayor.

A few years before the war, Peters' old wooden farm buildings burned down. We could see the fire and smoke from our windows, only the old garden house at the entrance to the alley leading to the estate remained. No animals or people were hurt. Soon new brick buildings replaced the old ones including a stately residence.

Our village has no real centre. The farms of the roughly 200 inhabitants are scattered among meadows and fields, some along the roads or nestled at the Thiene dyke. At the South end of the village beside the bridge over the Thiene is the village inn, a combination of restaurant with guest rooms, a community meeting room, a dance hall and a grocery store. It is also the end station of the little motor boat, which plies between the city of Elbing along the Elbing River and the Thiene and delivers supplies to the inns of the villages located along the banks of those rivers. It also takes a few passengers on board, usually tourists from the city.

We walk about half an hour to the store. Only in an emergency do we buy groceries there. Mother has relatives in Elbing, who own a wholesale grocery store. We buy most of our supplies there. We have more choices and get better deals. I look forward to when Father goes shopping in Elbing. He always brings some special candies for us, the flat chocolate rounds with truffle on top.

To try to create some community spirit in the village our teacher, who is also the 'political leader', organizes community festivals. We start with sport competitions, running, jumping, throwing balls and playing games, the little ones have egg runs and sack hops. An exciting task is climbing up a smooth 18 foot metal pole. The one who makes it to the top, cheered by the crowd, can pick a prize that is fastened to the top. I usually make it. Some of the men join us in competing in gymnastics on the parallel and horizontal bars. We all stand in awe when the short Swiss dairy farmhand swings around the parallel bars a few times and does the *"Riesenwelle"*.

When it is getting dark everybody gathers in the community hall at the inn to frolic, some present humorous skits or one act plays, some perform tricks involving the audience and later all join in folk singing; Magdalena, my sister, accompanies on the piano and Father plays the fiddle.

Karo and the Other Animals

Karo is the protector of our house. He is a mongrel, a mixture of fox and wolf, medium size, a pale golden yellow color but he seems to lack the cleverness of the fox and the courage of the wolf. Maybe he lost those naturals instincts because he is on a chain most of the time. From his doghouse, he can survey the whole yard that he shares with the chickens. One year we had a stately, smart rooster guarding his hens, the white Leghorns and the brown meaty Rodeländer and also the small Bantam chickens, which we had for decoration.

Karo gets his food and is gulping it down when the rooster approaches him and wants to partake in the spread. Karo does not like that and growls. The rooster takes this for an invitation for a match and picks a hole in his right eye. From then on Karo respects him and moves aside when he comes. This episode ends when the rooster's fate is sealed and he lands in the cook pot.

Karo faithfully announces all intruders and guests through loud barking. Nights at full moon, he often jumps up on his doghouse and howls heartbreakingly and sometimes he responds to music that way. When I take him off the chain and want to play with him he seems not to understand what I want, puts his tail between his legs and retreats into his doghouse.

Father wants me to have a playmate. We read in the paper someone is selling a young German shepherd dog We inquire, observe the dog for a while, I befriend him and we take him home and call him Rolf. He is fun. He follows me wherever I go and is very docile. He obeys orders and returns the stick which I throw to him. He likes rolling in the grass and playing with me; he never gets enough. I make him a harness and he pulls my wagon. To yoke him with Karo and have both pull me in my carriage does not work, Karo does not pull his weight, perhaps he is too old for such a game. Rolf and I have become good friends. Unfortunately, he has one weakness. He is hyperactive and for no reason he decides to run through the middle of a flock of chicken or geese back and forth and the poor birds do not know where to hide and run, when he is around. I try to teach him to peacefully socialize with them, take a chicken on my lap stroke it and let him smell it. He stops his attacks for a few weeks but it is too tempting. After he brings me the third dead chicken, we have family counsel. We all have grown fond of him but this cannot go on. So we decide with a heavy heart to return him to his former owner. It is hard for me and I miss him.

Karo has competition protecting our house - the gander and the geese. If they are in the yard and a stranger approaches, they start to screech, flap their wings and jump at him, a funny sight. Not all of them are that vicious. They also have a soft side. Occasionally I watch when the newborn goslings break their shells and scramble out of them. For the first few days their down is so soft, when I touch them and hold them against my cheek. Soon the little ones follow their mother into the water and swim proudly behind her. The reason we raise them is twofold; one, their downs fill our eiderdowns and jackets and keep us warm in winter and the other, their meat is delicious and Mother serves us a tasty goose roast. When at the end of the war food gets scarce, we include a goose in Christmas food packets to relatives in Berlin. A goose is also very much appreciated by businesspeople when offered in exchange for rare products or special services which we will not receive otherwise.

Dairy is our main source of income. We raise Holstein cows and each one has a name and a special character. Laura is the broad shouldered, friendly one who likes to be stroked. Her calves come easily and are strong. Aster, the tall black one, is the leader. With her long bent horns, she requests respect. She is shy and nervous and not so easy to handle but she is the best milk producer. One can tell it by her huge udder. Mother usually does the milking. In summertime she goes to the meadow, calls each cow by name when it is time for her to come to the milking place. Mother waits with the three-legged milk stool, sits down beside her, massages the udder and extracts the milk. Sometimes the girls help her. I never learned it properly and did not have to stay home for milking time. I help with straining the milk into the big milk cans and cart them to the milk pick-up place.

In fall when the frost puts an icy blanket over the grass, we take the cattle into the barn and milk them inside. We usually shear their long hairy coat, when they come in, as they would be too warm in the stable and it is easier to keep them clean when their hair is short.

In the beginning of the year, the cows give birth to calves. For some it is easy and when we come into the barn in the morning we may find a new calf lying behind her mother. We take it to her and she licks it clean. The birth is not always that easy especially if the cow is overdue or if a young cow is having her first calf. In that case we have to keep watch during the night and when we see she has difficulty delivering the calf, we play midwife and help with the procedure. It is always exciting for me when Father allows me to keep watch at night for a few hours and to participate in the birthing process. I see the feet of the little calf come out first, Father puts a rope around them and I pull slowly on the rope while he guides its head through the small opening. It is a joy to see the little calf trying to stand up on its own legs and then come and suck on our fingers.

For us children this is practical sex education. In spring, we see how the bull inseminates the cow and after nine months, we help with the birth of the calf.

In March, depending on the weather, we untie the cows from their stands in the barn and let them out into the green meadows which are now dotted with many blobs of golden yellow blooming buttercups.

Calves can stand and walk a day after birth and when they are weaned, we take them out into a new environment. They jump and run in circles. Father puts a rope around their neck and guides them in getting acquainted with the new world. He leads them to the water-filled ditches; some sniff and carefully lick the water, others jump right into it. Father lets them struggle a little and then pulls them out. He lets them touch the fence, so that they do not run into it and get hurt. They have to learn like children.

When the barn is empty Father mixes a big pail with a lime solution. Each one of us gets a big paintbrush and we paint and disinfect the inside of the barn. It looks nice and bright afterwards and we hope that it kills all the unwanted bacteria as well.

When Grandfather left his estate in Sparau to his son Richard and moved to Pr.Rosengart, he kept a section of land along the river Thiene, known as "Die Aue" (the mead) and gave one hectare of it to my mother as a dowry. It is about half-an-hour's walk from our farm. On this pasture, we keep our range cattle, young one or two-year-old heifers and oxen, which we raise or buy in spring and sell fattened in fall, hopefully for a profit. Once a week someone has to check if everything is all right. I am about eight years old when Father asks me, "Would you venture to go to the Aue by yourself and look after the range cattle, you know the way, having gone there with me several times." I tell him courageously "I think I can do it," though I feel a little uneasy about it.

It is a sunny morning and father gives me exact instructions how to get there, what to check and off I go, first along our driveway to the Grunauer Chaussee past Peter's farm on the right. A little further back on the left side live Aunt Ella's parents, the Deutschendorfs. Most farms have German Shepherds or great Danes as watchdogs, which run free in their yards, so I have to be careful. The possibility of meeting them is the scariest part. The dirt road turns right along a slough with all sorts of flora growing in it. Storks with their long red legs walk through it and pull frogs out of it. The edge of the wheat field is dotted with blue cornflowers and small red poppies. I finally come to the Thiene. Now comes the exciting part, crossing the river. I untie the small boat, jump in and start to row. First it turns in circles until I figure out how to keep it straight. The boat glides through the big round leaves of the water lilies and I can spot a few in the distance. On the other side is our land. I fasten the boat to a pole, climb out of it, up the embankment and down the other side. The water level of the Thiene is higher here than the land below and flows between dams on each side. I open the gate to the meadow and some calves come running towards me and want to be stroked. I remember to count the cattle; all seventeen are there. Now I have to check the bridge over the Mühlengraben, which separates Grandfather's meadows from ours. It is open; our cattle can't cross over to his meadows. My job is done and I can go home. Walking back the road seems much longer. A weasel or water rat runs in front of me and disappears in the slough. I follow it, but it is gone. When I come home I tell Father proudly that everything is in order. He is pleased and praises me for my achievement. Now he can trust me to take over his job when he is busy with other work.

On one hot sultry evening Father is worried about our range cattle and asks me to go to the Aue and check the animals. The flies are especially bad on those hot days and irritate the cattle so that they often run uncontrolled across the meadows. By now, I have learned to ride a bicycle and the trip to our land seems much shorter. When I enter the gate to the meadow, I notice the cattle on the pasture are unruly. I count it and there is one extra. I discover Epp's young bull among them. He has jumped over the ditch and is courting our heifers. I have to chase him back across the border. It takes me a long time until I finally have him cornered between the fence and the ditch. He takes a big leap, lands in the ditch and crawls up to the bank on the other side of his meadow. That was hard work. I am sweaty and ready for a swim. The Mühlengraben is inviting, so I take my clothes off and jump into the cool water- what a relief! Grandfather's young horse on the other side gets curious and comes up to me. I clamber out of the water pat its neck swing myself on his back and we gallop along the meadow, a wonderful feeling. I pat it again as a thank you, dismount, grab my clothes, cross the river, jump on my bike and make it home just in time before the rain starts pouring down.

Life on a dairy farm has its cycles even the war does not change that much. We so much hoped war could be avoided,. Our family is very disappointed that Hitler does not keep the peace agreement which Chamberlain initiated.

At the beginning of the war not much changes in our life routine on the farm, at least not in regards to food supplies, since we produce most of the basic foods that we eat ourselves. It is a different story for household goods and clothing. Certain goods become scarce and ration cards are introduced to regulate their distribution. To become more self-sufficient we acquire some sheep. They provide us with wool and additional milk. We are supposed to deliver all the milk from our cows to the distribution centre and get some skim milk back for our household use, but sheep's milk is not regulated and for sheep's wool, we do not need ration cards. For people in the city it is different.

Grandmother Lemke finds that out and she leaves Berlin and lives with us for a while. She comes from an old sheep-herding family and knows how to handle wool. I learn how to shear the sheep and hand the wool to Grandma. She washes and dries it, combs it into fleeces, sits down at the spinning wheel and spins threads of different thickness. I love to watch her paddling that spinning wheel. She passes the thread to me and I roll it into balls. In the evening, she sits beside the big tile stove, knits and tells stories. We love it. Each one of us children gets something from her. For me she knits a thick white turtleneck pullover with a braid pattern in it, which I wear proudly to school in winter. In addition to it, she knits a toque, a shawl, socks, mittens and underwear; which is a little prickly and we do not appreciate that much, but it is warm.

Ewes usually have one or two lambs; they are so cute when they are very small and jump around their mother. We often have fun playing with them. We keep only as many as we need for wool and meat.

At the far end of the smaller barn is the pigpen with the small arched gate for the pigs to run in and out. Different from the cattle, chicken and geese, which we breed ourselves, Father buys piglets from neighbors or relatives in spring; we feed them through the summer and sell them or butcher them in the fall.

Butchering a pig is always a special occasion on the farm. Uncle Heinrich and Tante Lenchen come in the morning to help and we call neighbor Reddig over. Father brings the pig into the barn and calms it down; neighbor Reddig stands with the sledgehammer beside it and an unexpected blow with it to the forehead of the pig, renders it unconscious. Uncle Heinrich feels its artery and a quick cut with the sharp knife through artery and windpipe ends its life.

Father does not do the killing. I wonder why he feels uneasy doing it. Have painful war experiences, having seen so many of his comrades being killed, made him so sensitive? He gets the Brühtrog ready, a coffin-like watertight wooden box with two smaller sideboards extended to form handles for carrying the box. The dead pig is rolled into it and mother brings pails of boiling water. She pours it over the corpse to loosen the bristles. The men use bell-like scraping tools and remove all bristles from the skin. When we were small, we were not allowed to watch the killing of the pig, only after it was in the trough, we could watch. I helped remove the bristles from the hard-to-get-at places.

Father had fastened a pulley on the barn beam. Now he ties ropes to the pig's hind legs and pulls it up to eye level. Mr. Reddig's job is now done and he is going home. It is time for a break and second breakfast.

For me to watch the whole procedure carefully is very exciting. When I got older and father was not there anymore I participated more in the process. One year uncle Heinrich lets me cut open the belly of the pig. "Watch out that you do not cut into the intestines, you will have a mess and the meat will be spoiled," he warns me. I start below the anus, cut carefully through the fat cushion down to the front legs. When I pull the sides open I marvel at the entrails, how perfectly organized they are, placed according to their function: a tube coming from the snout to the stomach, the heart almost in the middle connected to all the other parts, the lung, the liver and kidneys. Almost devoutly I entwine all the different parts, cut them out and put them into a bowl which Mother takes into the kitchen to process them further. This is my first practical anatomy lesson.

Almost all parts of the butchered pig are used. The blood is caught in a bowl and acts as binder for blood and tongue sausage. The job nobody wants to do is cleaning intestines but when they are clean and rinsed in diluted vinegar they look rosy on the inside and we stuff them with cooked meat parts and liver for meat and liver sausages. Ears, tail and feet are cut up and mixed into jellied meat, headcheese.

We do not have a refrigerator and have to preserve the meat in different ways. Ham, bacon and some of the sausages are cured in the smoke chamber beside the big chimney. Mother roasts some choice parts and preserves them in cans or jars for quick meals. We layer the remainder of the meat into the big salt and brine barrel to preserve it for later use.

Neighbor Reddig gets a package of meat and sausage for his help. Our parents will also send a small package of meat and a sausage to needy people in the village.

When meat supplies are getting low, we will butcher a calf or lamb in spring.

We kids want to have some animals for ourselves to care for and Father allows us to buy rabbits with our own money. He builds a cage, divides it into two sections one for the rabbits to eat in the other for sleeping. At first, we buy one male and one female and soon they multiply and we share their offspring. It is always exciting to watch them give birth to young ones; some have a litter of five or six. At first the newly born ones have no hair, their eyes are shut and they have to feel their way to their mother's teats to drink. After a week or two, they are hopping around already and it is fun playing with them. The neighbors raise rabbits too and we trade with them and get different species. When we have too many for our cages, we sell them. The big brown Belgian rabbits make good rabbit roasts, but it is hard to give them up. Father checks occasionally to see if we feed our rabbits regularly and keep the cages clean. He wants to make sure that we treat them well. We are responsible for them.

I remember one sorry story about our animals. We have a cat, who is very good at keeping control of the mice in our house. If there are none left inside, she looks for them outdoors and disappears for days. One summer afternoon we hear loud meowing in the yard and see her approaching slowly limping and bleeding. We pick her up and see that all four paws are missing. She had been hiding in the high grass and did not notice the cutting blade of the neighbor's grass mower. Not suspecting anything, he cut her four paws off. Father cannot endure her misery. He gets his gun and relieves her of the pain. We do not have a cat after that for a long time.

For me as a boy the small and large animals on the farm are kind of friends. We treat them well, care for them when they are sick or in trouble. They provide our livelihood; in a way they are part of the family.

Relatives and Festivals

Driving to Lichtfelde to see our grandparents is always something special. It is a long way for us children. When we leave our driveway at Cornelsens, we turn right along the road to Pr.Rosengart; at the corner is our postal station operated by farmer Harms. We turn into the boulevard with the huge, dense chestnut trees whose tops almost grow together forming arches over the roads, and give shade during hot summer days. We continue past the village inn and store, and drive across the bridge over the Thiene towards Thiergart. On the left are stockpiles of lumber from Goldman's sawmill. A little further on the right we pass the community church hall with the long covered shelter where we leave our horses and buggies when we come for evening church services. Around the corner is the Catholic church. The Scheffler farm, where my father in-law grew up, is right beside it.

Most roads through villages are paved with cobblestones to make traffic slow down. I hate the clatter of the metal rims on the wheels of our wagon when we drive along the bumpy road and I am glad when Father takes the shortcut, the dirt road across the fields, which leads directly to Lichtfelde. If it rains, the road is too muddy and we have to take the long road through Güldenfelde, past the big farm of the Boettchers with their 21 children. Onkel Walter, Father's younger brother, married Herta, one of the older girls.

Lichtfelde was known for its brawls after drinking parties or political, usually communist party gatherings, at the time when Father grew up there and it was not safe to go alone along the street on a Saturday or Sunday night. Now it is a village like any other one.

At the entrance to the village, immediately behind the Catholic church, we drive down a steep road and make a very sharp right turn directly into Grandfather's yard. That is always a little scary. Grandfather comes out of his smithy and greets us. He is a tall, handsome man with a full beard. He lifts me, the four year old, from the carriage and welcomes the rest of the family. We go inside where Grandmother has prepared a meal for us, which we enjoy. I notice the plank floor is dusted with white sand, which I had not seen anywhere else.

Grandfather's blacksmith workshop has a certain fascination for me, a spooky kind of fairy tale atmosphere. It is dark when I come in, only a red orange coal fire flickers on the other end of the shop and throws an eerie light over the place. The silhouette of the anvil and the big hammer on it become visible. Grandfather stands beside the bellows, pulls the lever, the sparks are flying and the flames flare up, and turn to amber. I imagine this to be the place where swords and lances for heroes of the legends were hammered out.

Opa invites me to pull the lever of the bellow for him but it is too high for me. He lifts me up and with all my strength and weight, I can pull it down. He laughs. A farmer has tied his horse on the outside wall and Grandfather is going to shoe it. He hammers a horseshoe on the anvil, tries it on the horse, and adjusts it again; it has to fit like a shoe. He finally burns the hot metal onto the horse's hoof and nails it through the callous part of the hoof. Now the horse can run well on those cobblestone roads.

Grandfather is also a good bee-keeper and before we drive home we go down to the creek where his rows of bee-hives stand. We have to pass the horse stable and Harras, the German shepherd dog, barks as we approach his territory. Opa proudly shows us his bee-hives, explains the work of the bees and later fills our big stone jug full of honey. That will last us for a year.

I do not remember much more about Father's parents. Magdalena was there once for a holiday and remembers Grandfather as a patriarch, but I had just turned five when they transferred the smithy and farm to Uncle Max, Dad's younger brother, and moved with their younger children to Berlin in 1930.

Shortly before Grandfather died, they came back to West Prussia from Berlin for a visit. I can visualize the tall stately man with a full white beard, going with my father and Uncle Max over the fields, discussing the crops and approving of Father's work on the farm.

The story goes that when Grandfather died and his heart had stopped beating, the attending cardiologist brought him back to life for a short time. When he was conscious again he opened his eyes and asked the family: "Why did you not let me stay in heaven? it was so beautiful and peaceful there" He died in the fall of 1934, at the age of 75 .

Of Father's four siblings that remain in West Prussia, Aunt Emma, the oldest sister, lives closest to us. She is a warm-hearted, friendly, big woman. She has to work hard on the small farm, which Uncle Ernst and she manage. She still sets aside time to tell stories, sing and play her guitar. Their three children Irmgard, Waldemar and Hildegard, are a little younger than we are. We visit each other occasionally, Irmgard spends summer holidays with us, and we stay at their place.

Uncle Max and Aunt Ella have four children who are quite a bit younger than we are and to teenagers this matters. Father still has good memories of the old smithy, where he spent a good part of his life with his parents and siblings and we love to visit there. Uncle Max who continues grandfather's job and his hobby as a bee-keeper still supplies us with honey and his oldest son, Guenther, now a Police Inspector in West Germany, continues that tradition.

A little further away, in the highlands, live Uncle Walter and Aunt Herta with their six girls. They are much younger than we are. I have only a vague memory of the older ones from a visit at their home. It is somewhat difficult for us to get to their place. Too far to drive, we have to take the train and transfer a few times, so we hardly ever visit them.

Uncle Walter is a master electrician and runs an electrical supply store in the small city of Preußisch Holland. He is the first among the Lemke relatives to own a car. On one of his visits he surprises us; he brings a radio and installs it for us. At that time, it was quite a procedure. He had to climb on the reed roof to put an antenna up and beside it a lightning conductor. He had to ground it and when we encounter a lightning storm, we have to switch from antenna to lightening protector. I think we are one of the first people in the village who have a radio, a *'Volksempfänger'*, (a people receiver) the radio that Hitler thought every family should have and could afford. I think besides that the Nazis wanted a medium that they could use to infiltrate every home with their censored news and propaganda. For me it was a phenomenon to listen to music without seeing any musicians and listen to news without a speaker.

Aunt Martha is the only one in the family who is not married. She cannot share her heart with only one person. She is perhaps my favorite aunt and I remember her as efficient, adventurous, friendly, dependable, very generous. and with a good sense of humor. For several years, she is governess and seamstress in the Wiehler household in Sparau, helping Aunt Louischen with her thirteen children. She is circumspect, anticipates things that need to be done and does them, which sometimes causes tension between her and the more dominiering Aunt Louischen. We are often in Sparau and meet her there. She welcomes us heartily and always has something special for us.

When the older girls, Ruth and Liesel, are able to help their mother with the younger siblings, she goes on to other work. In Berlin where several of her siblings are, she learns to know engineer Hajek and he asks her to manage his guesthouse in Schreiberhau in middle Silesia. She does such a good job of it that he makes her co-owner of "Haus Hajek". She often invites me to visit her and I finally make it in my summer vacation. For me it is the first long trip alone. Mother takes me to the train station and waves me off. A few years ago I would have had to go through pass controls, in railroad cars that were locked while going through the *Polish Corridor*. Now it is German territory again. In a few hours, I am in Berlin, where I have to change trains. Tanta Martha has sent exact instructions and I get the right train going south. It is almost a full day's journey. The train rolls into Oberschreiberhau, the first of the three Schreiberhaus. I am to get out in Mittelschreiberhau but I get nervous, grab my suitcase and leave the train. Nobody is at the station to pick me up. I ask people where Haus Hajek is. They have never heard of it. I get desperate and finally someone tells me I got out at the wrong station, but he can give me a lift to Mittelschreiberhau. He shows me the house down the road. Tante Martha was worried when I did not show up but when I do, she is relieved, takes me into her arms, welcomes me and leads me into the tiny room under the high-pitched roof with a fantastic view of the mountain ranges. That will be my abode for the next three weeks. I do not have much to unpack and have not much room to put it anyway. I change and go downstairs. Tante Martha introduces me to her guests. At the holiday season, the house is fully booked. Here the shy farm boy meets professors, factory owners and lawyers from Berlin.

Being used to doing my chores at home, I ask if I can help. She shows me how to set the table and do little jobs in the kitchen. I also take the little handcart and take the luggage of departing guests to the railway station, bid them good-bye and pick up new guests and their luggage. I still have lots of leisure time for reading, writing and communicating with guests, but I have no playmates with whom I can do something adventurous. I scout around the town and its environment but Aunt Martha does not want me to go too far out alone. The only child in the house is the two-year-old Rita, the grand-daughter of "Papa Hajek", the senior owner of the guesthouse. She likes me and I play with her but this has its limits. I am fifteen. Oberstudienrat Siemens befriends me and one day he asks me if I would like to accompany him and his wife on a day tour through the mountains. I gladly accept and with a knapsack full of food and goodies and some pocket money from Tante Martha, we take off early in the morning. After a four-hour walk, we come to the first *Baude,* take our knapsacks off, eat a sandwich and rest a little. Along the main trail through the mountains are rest stations, Silesians call them Baude, a building with a small restaurant, some have guest quarters, where wandering tourists can relax or even stay overnight.

With his seventy-two years, the tall white haired retired biology instructor is quite fit and so is his friendly, quiet wife. They walk at a pretty good pace, which I like. He is quite knowledgeable about the variety of the fauna and flora of the Riesengebirgs-mountains. We have lunch in the next Baude. We order a bowl of soup and something to drink. I unpack what Tante Martha has sent along and we have a hefty meal. Some of the birds come over and want to have a share; they are quite tame, used to being fed.

After half an hour rest, we pick up some trail mix and continue our explorations. Dr.Siemens has planned the trip so that we do not have to go back the same way. At dusk, we reach home again. That walk through nature with beautiful views is the highpoint of my stay here and I thank the Siemens very much for taking me along.

Tante Martha or one of the guests arranges an excursion to the *Schneekoppe* (snowcap), the 1600 m summit of the Riesengebirge for everyone who is interested. We take the train to Hirschberg and from there a small bus to the top. The view over all the mountain ranges, down into the Czech Republic is breathtaking and gives me a glimpse into the beauty of God's creation.

The time passes fast and my vacation in Schreiberhau comes to an end. I have grown fond of the high gabled house and the whole elegant milieu around it and it is hard to say good by to lovely Tante Martha and all the guests. Two of my" fatherly friends" give me their addresses; I shall visit them in Berlin.

After the war, when I came through Berlin I tried to look them up, but one house was empty, badly damaged by bombs, the other a heap of rubble. I do not know what might have happened to the owners.

Uncle Gustav, the oldest of Dad's siblings, lives in Berlin. He worked hard to become an independent businessman representing a large Berlin washing machine and utilities firm.

He lives in a country house outside of Berlin, which has become the central meeting place for relatives. He is my favorite uncle. (After the war, he lost his house and office and all his belongings under the communist regime. He had to start from scratch again and established his own business in the West)

We get news from Berlin that my cousins Ruth and Roeschen, the two eldest daughters of Uncle Gustav, want to spend their summer holidays with us. We wonder how that will work out- the two city girls from Germany's capital coming to our modest farm.

They get their first taste of country life when Dad picks them up with horse and buggy. When they unpack, Magdalena is quite overwhelmed; they have three pairs of good shoes each and she has only one pair. Uncle Gustav sent a gift for me, a pair of sculptured horses for my farm set up; I am proud and thankful. At first, the girls ask strange questions but soon they become accustomed and help with chores, feed the chickens and get vegetables from the garden. They are creative and fearless and it is fun to be with them. Ruth does not respond too well to country life. After the first week she gets sick, we are worried and have to call the doctor – at that time doctors still made house calls. It is nothing to worry about. After two weeks, they say good-bye and leave again. We rather miss them.

Aunt Frieda's husband, Max Gaestel. visits us a few times especially during the war years. He is an official in one of Berlin's regional city halls. I remember that he enjoyed country food and usually took a few sausages and a goose back to Berlin. They have six children with some of whom we have good contact over the years.

Father's other siblings I never met again. Aunt Gertrud married a teacher, Paul Meier, in 1935. She became a strict *Adventist*, which alienated her somewhat from the rest of the family, the less exclusive Christians. We wanted to visit her as the last living member of that generation of Lemkes during our exchange year in Germany but she died shortly before we arrived.

Uncle Arthur learned the trade of a blacksmith at home. In his thirties, he developed a mental condition and was living in an institution when the new Nazi laws were issued, declaring certain people as "not fit for living" (*lebensuntüchtig*.) He died in 1941 of "head grippe", a term used by the Nazi medical institutions for people who were "euthanized"

Uncle Willi, also a blacksmith, married Aunt Grete, whose father owned a blacksmith shop in East Germany. As a self-employed trade master, he was so restricted by Communist regulations that he had to give up his independence and opt for manager of a farm machine pool on a collective farm.

We made contact with his children after the reunification of Germany in 1989.

Onkel Bruno, from whom I got my middle name, was one who did not learn his father's trade. He worked in Berlin as a special cabinetmaker. In the war on the eastern front, the Russians took him prisoner and sent him to Siberia. When he came home several years after the war was over, sick and in rags, his wife Aunt Elli is said to have refused to accept him back in that condition and he disappeared. Nobody knew where he went. Many years later Uncle Gustav read in a newspaper that a communist government employee, Bruno Lemke, had been killed in a car accident. Unfortunately, he was not able to find out if this was his brother. We do not know anything about their children.

As far as Mother's siblings go, only two married. The oldest, Elise, like Mother, married a farmer. She, Uncle Hermann and their six children, moved several times to different farms in East- Prussia. I still remember one visit with them in Behlenhof, their last farm, for cousin Elisabeth's wedding

We take the train to Pr.Holland and from there to a little country station. The road from the station to their farm is quite hilly and the carriage, in which cousin Hans picks us up, has wheel brakes that prevent the carriage from sliding into the hind legs of the horses; that is a new discovery for me, a son of the flat lands. As we turn into the yard, we drive through the gate which is decorated with garlands and flowers and so is the house.

Elisabeth is the first of our cousins to get married. Quite a few of the Wiehler clan have come and a number of the Eichlers and the groom's relatives and friends. It is exciting for me to participate but the shock comes when Elisabeth asks me to be a" bridal attendant". I have no idea what is expected of me and tell her I do not think I can do it; I am too shy and inexperienced. There are older cousins who can do it. She thinks about it but still wants me to be in the bridal party. With trepidation, I accept and lend my arm to Hildegard, the older, married sister of the groom and walk with her arm-in-arm up the aisle behind the bride in white with customary veil, and Siegfried, the groom, in army uniform, on furlough from the front lines. Hildegard is understanding, has a sense of humor and whispers instructions to me as to what to do next. Another first for me is signing a legal document. I feel quite important.

A big dinner follows the wedding ceremony. And in the afternoon, all the young people play lawn games like 'Cat and Mouse', 'Who is afraid of the bogey man?', 'Third Out' and more. The Ehritt family is very musical. The evening is filled with games, songs and instrumental music. Grandfather, as usual at family gatherings, closes with a devotion.

More often, we visit Sparau. It is easier and faster to get there. Uncle Richard and Aunt Louischen have taken over the paternal estate. Green meadows and tall trees surround the spacious brick residence and the barns. It takes me half an hour by bike to get to Sparau, a part of the village of Pr..Koenigsdorf.

I usually spend summer holidays there and enjoy the company of my cousins. During harvest time there is always a lot of activity on the farm. I am of the same age as the fifth of the thirteen cousins. Aunt Louischen counts me as one of them and assigns me the same chores that her own children have to do. Uncle Richard always asks me if I want to participate and he lets me do some daring jobs. I always have my eyes open and observe how things are done on a big farm. On one of the harvest days, he asks me to drive the long harvest wagon to the field, help to load the sheaves on it and drive the fully packed wagon back to the barn. I have to overcome some anxiety at first. At lunch, we sit together with the hired men, eat our sandwiches with them and drink the water, enriched with a dash of vinegar and sugar for better taste and thirst-quenching quality. At the end of a day of harvesting, we are quite bushed and go to bed early. In the morning, we get the horses from the meadow and have a race to see whose horse reaches the yard first. Uncle Richard is not supposed to see this, as he would not approve. After the harvest, he asks me if I want to help with the plowing. I accept, at least I will try it. I mount the saddle horse and join Rudi, his oldest son, to plough the freshly harvested fields with a team of four horses. I have never worked with four in a team and am a little afraid. Rudi tells me with a smile, "Watch me and just do as I do". Well said but not as easily done. After some practice, operating with four steeds on a plough, I feel like a pro.

In our free time, we play games in the garden and yard, 'hide and seek' or ball games, sample the fruit in the big orchard and in the evening, we play board games. Sometimes we have pillow fights with the girls or among us boys before we go to bed until Uncle Richard comes upstairs and admonishes us .

It is not easy for me to say good-bye after such involved holidays and it usually takes a few days until I have adjusted to the quietness and routine of our home.

Often Alfred, who is a year younger than I, spends holidays with us. He sometimes has problems getting along with his siblings but we two manage quite well. If the weather is sunny, we go along the ditches each one with a wire sling on a pole over our shoulder and watch pikes sitting quietly in the water. We try to move the sling from the back slowly around the body of the pike and pull it with a quick jerk out of the water. It is an exercise in patience and we have to have a steady hand. If we cannot be outside, we get my new big atlas out, find some unusual names of towns, mountains or rivers and see who can find these first on the map. We have fun and at the same time improve our knowledge of the geography of the world.

Aunt Anna, known as *Tante Annchen,* is Mother's older sister and confidant. She is enterprising and has a positive outlook on life. The two shared secrets with each other and made plans together what they would do when they grew up. They wanted to travel and explore different countries and imagined what they were like. After completing school and a period of work on the farm, Annchen and her older sister, Lenchen, went to the *"Friedenshort"* training school for female Christian workers established by the well-known *Mother Eva von Thiele Winkler.* Both aunts became deaconesses. I remember them only in their deaconess habit, the black frock and the white headpiece typical for a sister of that order. Mother, influenced by her older sisters, attended Friedenshort also for a year.

Tante Annchen takes over the orphanage and children's home, *"Sorgenfrei "* (without worry), on the river *Sorge.* We love to visit her there. We take our bikes cycle through Thiensdorf where our Mennonite sister church is, past Baalau, look down the dirt road that leads to Aunt Emma and Uncle Ernst's farm, through Augustwalde, the birthplace of grandfather Wiehler, until we come to Sorgenort on the little river Sorge. The owner of the inn has a ferry service and takes us across the river with our bikes. A short ride on the raised bank of the Sorge and we can see the big black two storey log house. The window and doorframes and the balcony railings are painted a contrasting white and glitter in the sun. The two gable boards on the north side of the house are extended and end in carved horse heads, which stick out into the sky. They are a symbol from Germanic mythology and are supposed to fend off bad spirits.

Tante Annchen welcomes us with open arms. She is such a joyful, considerate person. She integrates us into the thirteen children who run around in house and garden. Some are half- or full orphans, some with learning difficulties. She is a mother to all of them. We play with the children, swim, row the boat on the river and sing with them or listen to Tante Annchen's stories.

In the back of the house is a big vegetable garden, beside it a chicken coop and behind in the meadow grazes a cow which gives them milk and butter. They try to be self sufficient in regards to food and the older children have to do chores, which keep them out of mischief and from being bored. Sorgenfrei is a faith mission project, its operation depends on funds from foundations and patrons like my Grandfather and the Count von Hohendorf.

The "Grüne Aue" is the new farm of our grandparents. Since their retirement Mother's siblings, Tante Lenchen and Onkel Heinrich operate it with them. It is not far from our place and has become almost my second home since my father's death. We drive by there on our way to church.

Not too long ago an artesian well was drilled beside the road not far from their driveway and cool fresh water spills out of it continuously. On hot summer days, we sometimes stop there and refresh ourselves before we go on. After church Tante Lenchen or Grandfather ask us if we want to drop in, as her pot-roast is big enough for a few more people. If we have nothing planned, we accept their invitation. While Tante Lenchen is preparing dinner, we tell Grandfather what we are doing at home and in school or we accompany Onkel Heinrich into the barn and look at the new calves or piglets.

After Father's death, Uncle Heinrich occasionally asks Mother how the work on the farm is progressing and if we need some help with work that Mother and I cannot do. He would then come with his team of horses and help with bringing in the harvest or ploughing the fields afterwards. They live only two kilometers away from us if we use the shortcut via the back road that connects our villages. We, in turn, help him with his work

One Sunday after church, Grandfather wants to visit his old farm, which his oldest son has now inherited and he asks me if I want to come along. My parents give permission and we two take the shortcut over Epp's meadows where his dairy cattle and the big bull are grazing. The bull is vicious and quite protective of his herd. We have just crossed the bridge over the big ditch leading to the meadow when he spots us. He comes running towards us bellowing, scaring me stiff, stopping in front of Ggrandfather his head down, digging up the grass with his hooves and throwing it in the air. Grandfather seems calm and talks to him. "You want to show off, don't you? It is okay we do not intend to do you or your cows any harm, relax" and just walks on. I hide behind him, trembling, afraid the bull will get me. He follows Grandfather at close range for a while and then stays back. I am relieved but still shaking. How come grandfather is not afraid of him? at least he does not show it. Do adults have no fear or is it his trust in God? I do not dare to ask him.

Sometimes when we go for a Sunday visit Grandfather would ask me to hitch up the horse and he packs some vegetables from his garden, flour and meat packages onto the wagon and invites us kids to accompany him on a drive through the back roads of the village. These trips have a twofold purpose. He wants to visit the sick and poor, bringing them comfort and relief. He also combines that with telling the people about the grace of God and the love of Jesus. Several of the former farmers and laborers are alcoholics. They abuse their wives and children and leave them without means to buy food. When we come to their house, the women bring a bowl; he fills it with flour, puts some vegetables in the kitchen and leaves a package of meat with them. While he listens to the women and gives advice to the men, we are supposed to distribute Christian leaflets in the neighborhood. Some farmers have sharp guard dogs. We are afraid of them and, if they are running loose, we stick the leaflets on the gate posts and leave quietly. This mission work we do with mixed feelings.

Grandfather is honest, strict and has high morals but as he ages, he becomes more warm hearted and generous. He gifted the *"Friedenshorst foundation "* with two homes, the *Tannenhaus,* an orphanage and home for handicapped children and the *Lindenhaus,* a senior's home which Tante Lenchen managed for a while.

Onkel Heinrich, Mother's youngest brother, is junior boss. He is short, hard working, calculating. His sister Lenchen is the opposite, loving, joyful and generous. Onkel Heinrich once told her, it is good that we two work together, you are generous, I am sometimes too calculating and frugal. They make a good team managing the farm and caring for their parents. Grandfather is hard of hearing and Grandmother almost blind in her old age. They complement each other well. On a sunny day the two might sit under the big Linden tree in front of the house, he reads to her and she listens. If she hears some steps on the driveway, she will ask, "Johann, who is coming?" Grandfather has not heard anything, looks up and tells her. Sometimes she can identify us children from the sound and cadence of our steps. That always amazes me.

One of the most exciting events at the Grüne Aue is Grandfather's birthday, on July 12, a time when the whole family clan comes together. He has a lot of grandchildren of all age groups that come to congratulate him, thirteen alone from Sparau, six of the Eichlers, we three and often Tante Annchen brings a few along from her children's home in Sorgenfrei. We enjoy playing together, the older ones have contest games, play ball and the most fun is 'hide and seek'. We hide in the garden behind the red currant or gooseberry bushes, in the yard among machinery or in the barn. The goal post is the big Linden tree in front of the house. Onkel Heinrich sometimes plays with us and assists the smaller ones. When we are tired and hot we run down the driveway to the street, which is lined with cherry trees. The cherries are now dark red and ripe. Tante Lenchen gives us some money and we buy a bag full from the street vendor who picks and sells them or we pick them ourselves, which is not quite honest since he has rented the trees. Half of the cherries are eaten before we return to the house. A call for supper ends our outside activities. Tante Lenchen with the help of some women from the village has prepared a delicious meal. The older girls help setting the table with fine white porcelain dishes with the typical narrow gold rim.

When everybody is satisfied, the tables are cleared and the real birthday celebration can begin. We sing a lot, the grandchildren from the different families compete presenting musical interludes and reciting poems. Every one of us is nervous, we don't want to get stuck and embarrass the family and our mothers and we are proud if we manage a long poem without losing track and saying it with good intonation. Grandfather is especially gracious if we recite a Psalm or a key verse from the Bible. A short devotion and prayer usually concludes the celebration.

I remember fondly parties in Sparau, Grandpa's old estate. Tante Louischen's relatives, the Bartels, Neufelds, Dirksens and Dycks, join the Wiehlers, all well-to-do farmers with a number of children. House and yard are more spacious and can accommodate all of us. The older girls sit in the dining room and talk while the younger girls and we boys play wild games in the yard, barn and stables. When it is getting dark outside we go into the house and the whole gang plays parlor games. We are tired when we join the adults at the end of the day for Grandfather's closing meditation and prayer.

Birthday parties for our parents are on a smaller scale. For Father's birthday, mainly relatives from his side are invited and since it is in February, we often have up to two foot of snow on the ground and the guests come by sleigh. If the weather is too bad, we may have a rather small company. We children build snow castles outside or play inside. Mother puts out the best tablecloth and china, bakes a variety of tasty cakes and torte and prepares a splendid meal to honor Father and prove to her in-laws that she is a capable homemaker. I remember Father's birthdays as a more formal grown-up party.

Mother's birthdays are less formal. She is celebrating mainly with her own extended family. In the morning we pick snowbells and early spring flowers from the garden, put them in a vase on the table and around her table setting to indicate that she is special to us. We help in the kitchen and with the preparations for the guests, set the table and serve the meals; Mother shows us how to do that properly.

The Wiehler cousins, who are coming, are about our age and we have good playmates. The Lemke cousins are all younger except the ones in Berlin and we hardly ever see them. After an afternoon of sharing, eating and playing, Grandfather concludes the evening by saying a few encouraging words and praying for Mother and the family.

Grandfather's youngest brother Onkel Cornelius took over the ancestral farm in Grunau. The large brick house has a spacious porch on the south side and the big garden reaches almost down to the road. Tante Agnes keeps a variety of flowers blooming among exotic ornamental bushes and trees. The farm stands alone surrounded by green meadows, quite a distance away from the village. Onkel Cornelius is a big man, especially around the hips and buttocks, which, being unproportionally large, affects the way he walks. Tante Agnes is his second wife. They have no children of their own and have adopted seven, five from one family where the mother had died and the father was an alcoholic. I know them only as adults.

Every second Sunday afternoon Tante Agnes opens their house for children from the neighborhood and the church, we love to go there. She shares her faith with us by telling about Jesus' love for children, God's commandments and plan for our lives. She is a good storyteller and tells stories from the Bible and from her own life, blending in some Mennonite history. She is creative and also does crafts with us. We can play in her garden until it gets dark and before we leave, she has some goodies for us. Onkel Cornelius supports her. Both are kind and most generous. Since he cannot walk too well, he bought an automobile, one of the first of our relatives. One of his adopted sons is his chauffeur. He has built up an extended correspondence. In the war years, he keeps a file of all the young relatives who serve in the army and sees it as his mission to write encouraging letters to them.

In 1921, Onkel Cornelius and Tante Agnes invited all the relatives to their house and organized the first *"Wiehlertag"*. 168 of the Wiehler clan attended. We still have a big picture of that event.

Winter is usually a quieter season. The roads are snowed in. Nobody operates a snowplow to clear them. Horses and sleighs pack it down. We go to school, deliver our milk and go to church if the weather is not too bad. Otherwise, we stay at home. Usually we enjoy the snow. Word goes around that one of the farmers plans a sleigh ride, perhaps, as a birthday party for his children. He hitches his horse before a sleigh and drives through the village. We boys get our sleighs out and hook them onto his until we have a row of eight or ten sleighs which are pulled by the galloping horse along the road or across the meadows. The last sleighs in the row are the most desirable ones because they will swing wildly from one side of the road to the other.

On one sunny Sunday afternoon, Father has a surprise for us. He asks us to dress warmly and then takes the two sleighs which he had built for us, puts the horse before the big three seater, he, Mom and sister Christa, sit behind each other and Magdalena and I sit on the shorter one behind them. He takes the reins and off we go through the deep snow. We drive across the meadow to the road. After a while he turns left onto the raised embankment of the Thiene River. For half an hour, we drive along the winding trail on top of the dam. We have fun together with our parents. We are approaching Sparau where our cousins live. We can see the house from the distance. Soon we slide down onto the trail that leads to their house.

From December to early March, the water in the drainage ditches is usually frozen solid. We are all looking forward to the skating season. When I was six I received a pair of *"Holländer skates"* from my parents as a Christmas gift.. They look like a dragon boat with a steel bar bent up in the front and set into a wooden bed with slots for leather straps with which I can tie them firmly to my boots. Holland skates are lower and not quite as maneuverable for playing hockey as the all-metal ones. They are used mainly for long distance running and are quite common in the lowlands.

On not-so-cold sunny days, we skate to the Thiene, meet other kids from the neighborhood and play hockey or have some competitive games. We have a wide-open area to skate. If none of the neighbor children are on the ice, we skate along the river for half an hour to Sparau and visit our cousins on skates, just as we did driving in the sleigh.

One joyful event in the dark winter months is Christmas time. Father makes a wreath with fir twigs, which we hang up on the first Sunday of Advent. We sit around the table, light the first candle, sing songs and Father reads a story. The expectation grows with each additional candle that we light, until all the candles on the Christmas tree spread bright light into the darkness. We also have another reminder that Christmas is approaching - the "Advent calendar" with its double lining. Every morning we open a window on the outer surface, which exposes in succession the days of December. There is a piece of chocolate behind each window and each of us has to wait his or her turn to open the next window. The further we progress in the days, the more we get excited until we open the window for the 24th day of December.

On that day, early in the morning, Father goes into the garden and cuts a fir tree. He cuts only about seven feet off the top. The remainder of the tree will eventually grow another top from one of the branches and in about seven years will yield a Christmas tree again. So we will always have a new supply of fir trees. If the tree is not perfect, Father will add a branch here or there until all branches are evenly distributed. Then he brings it into the living room. We children are not allowed to enter the room. Father decorates the tree, then lines up all the gifts on a side table, and covers them with a white sheet so that our inquisitive eyes cannot identify them. Under the tree he places the big crèche with the figures of the Christmas story. In the meantime, Mother brings order to the rest of the house and we are eager to help. The animals receive a special portion for Christmas even the barn gets some decoration. Mother bakes the last cakes and prepares supper, usually a roasted goose with red cabbage, potatoes and fried apples. After the meal, we help to clean the table and wash the dishes, while Father disappears into the living room again.

When everything is done we are very quiet and listen until the little silver bell rings, the signal for us to enter the room with the song *"Ihr Kinderlein kommet…"*(little children come..). In the far corner of the room stands the Christmas tree with its mellow wax candles lit and the candles below in the crèche cast shadows from Mary, Joseph and the shepherds on the oxen and sheep. The tree is beautifully decorated with stars and angels and even with some edible shapes of chocolate or marzipan. The *lametta* glitters in the candlelight and the thin white strands of angel hair flow from one branch to the next. A big star enhances the top of the tree. Chairs are set up around the tree and we all sit down. Father reads the Christmas story from the Bible; we sing a number of Christmas songs together and recite poems about Christmas, which Mother selected and taught us. Father has another suspenseful Christmas story for us. At the end, he asks us what we appreciated especially during this year and we all kneel down and thank God for it. Then comes the part we have all been waiting for. The parents lift the white sheet from our gifts and we can explore and admire them. There are usually a couple of small gifts or one big one each year, like a rocking horse, a pair of skates, a violin and the best one, a bicycle. Mother had put together a *"Bunter Teller"*, a plate with all kinds of goodies, special cookies, chocolates, a marzipan heart, one orange, nuts and apples. Every Christmas we find a book among our gifts and after the celebration, we sit down, each one in a corner and read until Dad says, "It is time to go to bed". Christmas Eve is a "Family Fest" for us and we never go to church on that evening. I do not think there was any service anyway.

The next day is a big relatives' get-together in the Grüne Aue, similar to Grandfather's birthday. The parents share family news, we children play inside games and Tante Lenchen tells us interesting stories. Later in the evening, we recite our poems with some trepidation, sing several Christmas songs, make music, listen to the Christmas story and Grandfather concludes with a meditation and prayer for the families. The sleighs are waiting outside and one after the other of the guests put on their fur coats, we children are bundled up into fur blankets and all drive off into the cold winter night, heading for home.

Chapter Four

Political Situation

When I was six years of age a political movement started that brought changes to German society and had far-reaching effects in world politics.

We lived in the country, somewhat isolated from the turbulent life in the city. My father wanted to be up to date in world affairs so he subscribed to the only news paper which was delivered to the neighbor at the street twice a week and it was my job to pick it up from there about 1/2 km away. Later our world and local news were supplememted by radio.

As Mennonites, we seldom got personally involved in political activities.

Germany at that time was in a difficult situation. It was just starting to recover from the depression and paying the heavy war reparations, imposed by the Treaty of Versailles after WWI, put a great pressure on its economy. Many of us farmers were on the brink of insolvency because of the high cost for farm equipment, the high mortgage and interest rates and the low return for our farm products.

Our parents had paid off most of the debt for the farm to its former owners and we could just manage the low monthly payments that remained. We had a large vegetable garden, cattle that provided milk, butter and meat, chicken and geese for meat, eggs and feathers and downs for duvets; so we had enough to eat. Mother was knitting, sewing and mending our clothes, which were handed down from one child to the other. They were not in the newest fashion but they were clean and practical. We managed by living frugally, were content and lived harmoniously together.

On the political scene, Germany had to struggle for survival. The Weimar Republic was a young and inexperienced democratic model of government. A number of political parties arose and competed with each other to gain power. The struggle was especially heated between the National Socialists and the International Communists who wanted to unseat the Social Democrats who formed the government at that time.

On January 30th 1933 Father read in the newspaper: the'Nationalsozialistische Deutsche Arbeiterpartei', the NSDAP (National Socialist German Workers Party) - now known as Nazi Party- won the highest number of seats in the parliament in the last election and Reichspräsident Paul von Hindenburg installed the leader of that party, Adolf Hitler, as "Reichskanzler" of the German Reich, the acting Government leader.'

Hitler was autodidact. He had acquired considerable knowledge in politics and history through studying a variety of books, statements and manifestos of historians, politicians and public officials of different persuasions. He carefully observed the actions and tactics of politicians of his time especially in Austria, his home country. In their campaign speeches, several of those politicians incited the people against Jews who profited from our present misery and Communists who had caused it by starting the revolution. From listening to these political agitators, he formed his own strong opinions.

In his propaganda speeches, Hitler promised his listeners he would change the conditions of the repressive Versailles Treaty, wrestle the country from the claws of the Communists and Jews and restore the dignity of the German people. He was a persuasive orator and won the trust of ordinary people who were looking for changes to obtain a better quality of life.

We knew little about Hitler when he first appeared on the scene.. My parents were concerned about Hitler's attitude towards Jews and his somewhat radical viewpoints but we thought that our wise President Hindenburg, a Christian, guided by moral and ethical principles, would keep everything in balance. This confidence was tested when Hindenburg died in August 1934. Things changed rapidly. Hitler and his staff gradually dissolved all other parties until only the NSDAP remained. In the next election, there was only one party on the ballot and one candidate. We had to answer only one question 'do you acknowledge Hitler as the Leader of the Third Reich'. We could only make a check mark in either the 'Yes'or 'No' box. In the first election there was one 'no' vote in our village and soon everybody assumed it was the old, odd Mr. Riediger. Fortunately, extreme party members left him alone and did not molest him.

The NSDAP wanted to unite all German Christians in the new denomination of "Deutsche Christen" and installed Reichsbischof Mueller as its head but the churches did not buy that, and refused to join. The party did not dare to confront the established Catholic and Protestant churches. Only individual pastors or preachers who spoke openly against the dangerous actions of the party were taken into custody, interrogated and many of them then disappeared quietly, usually at night to keep it secret.

Hitler was more successful in dissolving youth groups, religious, political, cultural and sport clubs. He wanted to inspire young people, or subject them, to his grandiose ideas for building a great Germany and Europe, and to convince them that he needed their help in accomplishing this.

I am in grade two in elementary school when Hitler comes to power and do not understand much of what this means and how I could help to build a great Germany. But soon I will find out. In 1935, the government brings in a new regulation: All young people from age 10 to 18 are to join the political national youth organization, the HJ, short form for Hitler Youth.

The Hitler Youth organisation, already existing before Hitler came to power, was led by Baldur von Schirach whom Hitler had appointed to be the *Reichsjugendführer*, (leader of the nation's youth). He had been active in young peoples organizations, like the Boy Scouts, and believed in the goals of companionship, patriotism and high moral values and discipline. He was intro- duced to antisemitism by works of Henry Ford and Houston Chamberlain and then he came under the spell of Hitler and worked for him

For the first year, participation in the HJ is voluntary. My parents are skeptical about that and do not want me to join. Waldemar, who lives across from the school, and I are the only boys from the senior class who attend school on Saturday morning, all the others go to the HJ meetings. We two get some extra assignments or have to feed the teacher's cow and clean the stable. Sometimes the teacher asks me to do some math drills with the younger pupils.

The next year participation is mandatory, - "a birthday present to the Führer" (Hitler). As a law-abiding citizen, I obey the law and join the Jungvolk, (young people) the junior HJ, in spring of 1936. To my surprise, they elect me to be the leader of the newly formed Jungenschaft in our village, the smallest unit of the Jungvolk,. My parents have to buy a uniform for me, black pants with a leather belt, a light brown shirt and a black necktie held together with a brown leather knot. I wear a twisted red and white cord, which I tie loosely from the shoulder to a button of my shirt, to identify me as the Jungenschaftsführer.

In a way, I am proud of my position. Every Saturday morning we meet in the schoolyard for "duty" or service. We are taught to develop physical and mental disciplines. I am to show the boys how to march in formation, learn coordination and endure hardship. We sing marching songs, mainly folksongs and songs about loyalty and honor to our country and its leaders. I am also to inform them about the life, ideas and goals of the Führer, as outlined in a manual which I have to study. That part I usually keep short. We are also called upon to strive for moral values like trust, loyalty, honesty, courage and sacrificial love for our country. Some of the mottos we are to "internalize" are 'Hitlerjungen are tough as leather, hard as Krupp-steel and quick as greyhounds'.

The best part of our meetings is playing games and some are sophisticated for our age, especially the 'cross-country' games where we have to identify, approach and conquer the position of the other party by using compass and map. Some of these games take a whole day. All this, I think now, was intended to train us in military disciplines. During the war we are also trained in the use of firearms. We only get air guns and are shown how to care for them and to learn how to aim and shoot from different positions. I am responsible to teach that to the boys and to see that they follow safety instructions. Since we have no place to store the gun I take it home which gives me an opportunity to improve my target practice. Sparrows, which sit in flocks on fences and trees around the house, make good targets. I practice only when my parents are not around. Once, I could see for a moment the ballistic curve of the bullet against the sun and, from that observation. improve my accuracy in hitting the target.

One almost tragic event I still remember. I am cleaning the gun and remove the bullet magazine from the lock. Lotte, one of Tante Annchens girls who spends her holiday with us, watches me. She teases me continuously. "You can't aim and shoot, try it". I get annoyed, aim at her, which I strictly forbid my boys to do, and thinking that I have removed all the bullets, pull the trigger. However, one bullet had got stuck in the barrel and hit her below the nose. I am terrified. She cries and Mother comes and sees where the bullet has hit the bone. It is only a surface cut and Mother calms her down. I apologize and we both learn an important lesson.

The HJ is organized in smaller and larger units. The smallest, usually the boys of one village, is the *Jungenschaft,* the next one including two or three villages is the *Jugendzug* led by a *Zugführer,* identified by a green cord, followed by a *Fähnlein* and *Jungbann,* led by their respective leaders. The reorganized Jugendzug in our villages needs a new leader and I am the main candidate together with Hermann Reiman from the neighboring village. The Bannführer, who goes to the same high school as I, takes me aside and tells me "In two weeks we will select the leader and I want you to be the one, make sure you are there. I feel honored. Two weeks later Father tells me he has arranged with relatives in Brotsende to pick up some piglets and he needs me to help him. "But this is the day I might be promoted to Zugführer," I reply. He looks at me and says," This seems to be the best day for Uncle Bestvater to pick up the piglets and I think we have to go". He does not want to hurt me and this is his way to keep me from getting too involved in the HJ. The following Saturday the group asks me where I had been at the last meeting. I have a hard time explaining my absence without compromising my Father. They accept my excuse with great skepticism.

Our unit in Alt-Rosengart is shrinking and we have to join the unit in the neighbor village. The date for our meetings has been changed from Saturday to Sunday morning to coincide with or replace church services. For my parents this is going too far and they challenge the authorities. We were promised that we could practice our religion freely. All main churches have their services on Sunday mornings and that is where we will be. 'We are to obey God more than men'. I have to decide, shall I follow my own and my parents' beliefs and wishes, or obey the new government orders. This is a hard decision to make, which may have consequences.

I had just expressed to our church elder, Ältester Heinrich Wiehler, my wish to be baptized. He tells me of the preparation necessary for this step. He will teach those who desire to be baptized the basic biblical principles that govern the life and conduct of a Christian: faith, love and hope, based on the teachings of Jesus. If I believe and accept them as guidelines for my life, he will gladly baptize me. I have to make this decision on my own. The baptismal instruction starts in November and ends in June; it begins an hour before the Sunday church service. The situation becomes problematic for me because the HJ also meets on Sunday, about an hour earlier on the schoolyard, which is on the same street as the Mennonite church, about a quarter of a block before the church.. When I ride my bike to church, I have to pass the schoolyard and my comrades can see me coming along the street. I hope they will not notice me and paddle as fast as I can to pass by them. Sometimes they wait for me at the gate, stop me and tell me what my duty is. I tell them, that my parents and I go to church on Sunday morning; I cannot be in two places at the same time. They threaten me with fines for disobeying the law but they always let me pass. When my parents are with me it is easier, they just call my name and wave but leave me alone and we ignore them. I try to compensate for my Sunday absence by regularly attending the Wednesday afternoon HJ meetings and participating as much as I can in sports and games, which I am very good at. At one regional sports competition I place third among all the participants. My unit acknowledges this and is proud that I represent it so well.

Oberschule Marienburg

Normally boys of my age think of what they want to do or be after graduation. Father thinks it is natural that I should take over the farm and assume his role, but the farm is not very big and the work is hard. More land is not available in the neighborhood to increase our holdings. Mother wants something else for me. She knows that Father is a responsible farmer, but he is not happy in his job as he has other interests and abilities. Mother must have been thinking about this for some time. Our elementary school teacher had 'put a bug' in her ear. Last year he sent a letter home in which he suggested that my parents should send me to secondary school in our district town as I have the ability to continue my education. Father is not ready for this and fears we will not have the means to send me there and if i am gone, who would take over the farm.

Our schools are separated into elementary school (Volksschule) from grade one to eight and Oberschule (secondary school) starting from grade five and finishing with grade twelve. Students have to pay tuition for attending High School.

Father already has occasional periods of depression and does not have the energy and spunk to pursue new ideas. This year the teacher invites my parents for a parent teacher interview. He urges them to consider sending me to the Oberschule. The government has provided a fund to assist intelligent children from country schools to further their education in a secondary school. Father finally gives in to my mother's wish and they agree to send me to Oberschule. For me this is all new and exciting.

The day for the entrance examination arrives. Mother and I take the train to Marienburg, ask for the way to the Birkgasse and enter the big red brick building with the Romanesque arched windows and the inscription, *Winrich von Kniprode Schule für Jungen,* over the portal. Winrich von Kniprode was a famous Grand Master of the German Order of Knights who reigned in the 14th century over the newly colonized territory, East Prussia. He had his seat in the castle Marienburg.

The principal, Oberstudiendirektor Sahner, welcomes all of us young pupils, sizes us up through his monocle, tells us about the school and his expectations and informs us in an encouraging way about the examination. We go into different classrooms and, for four hours, we write tests in Mathematics, Natural Sciences and German. I am exhausted by the end. Some of the questions I did not understand, as our teacher had never covered that material and I had to guess the answers, which made me uncomfortable.

With apprehension, we wait for the results. The principal asks us into his office. Somewhat thoughtful he looks at my test results, "Satisfactory" he says, "you just made it". He looks at my elementary report card showing A's and a B, quite a difference from my test mark. "You went to a one room country school?" he asks, "Hmm, I think we will accept you on probation and hope you can catch up." We leave his office with mixed feelings. The standard in city schools is apparently much higher than in our one room school in the country. We console ourselves and Mother puts her arm around me, "You will make it" she encourages me and we take the train home again.

I have a little time to prepare myself physically and mentally for the new adventure. After Easter, I pack my school material into my new briefcase, fasten it to my bike rack and cycle to the railway station in Grunau. I take the train to Marienburg and find my way from the station to the new school. In the office are a number of new students like me. We register, get our class room number, our timetable and a student pass that enables me to purchase a student season train ticket, which I do for my return trip. I am now a "Fahrschüler", an out-of-town student. A number of us are placed in an "Aufbauklasse" an accelerated class. Because we started in the second grade of the school, we have only two years to cover the material, which the normal students cover in three. There are 16 boys and one girl in our class from different villages in the area, one of them a Willy Lemke who is not related to me. We have to work hard to catch up, because a lot of the material that we are expected to know, our teacher in elementary school has never taught us. Willy finds it even more difficult to adjust and has to repeat the first year. Originally, this "Gymnasium" was a boy's school, where students learned Hebrew, Greek and modern languages and the Valedictorian gave the graduation speech in Latin.

The first year two girls from our village, Christel, our neighbor's daughter, and Magdalena attend our High school. I have a crush on Magdalena. I try to meet her on the road and cycle together with her to the station. I do not get the wished-for response from her. The second year the girls transfer to another school where the requirements are not quite as stiff as in our school.

Every morning I have to get up early to catch the train at seven o'clock. When it rains the dirt driveway is soggy and the mud sticks to the spokes of my bike. I clean it out with a tree branch and push the bike to the paved road. In winter I have to push it through the snow. The additional four km to the railway station I can make in 15 minutes. Then I have a half- hour train ride and a half-hour walk to the school. This procedure can tire a 12-year-old boy out. I remember one episode at the beginning of the school year. We have music in the first period and as our music teacher plays "Schumann's Träumereien" on the piano, I find it so wonderful and soothing, that I fall asleep and hit my head on the bench in front of me. My fellow students grin and tease me but Dr. Seipelt plays with such devotion that he does not notice.

When I come home, I do my schoolwork, change and work in the fields and in the stable. One day, mother calls me for supper and finds me fast asleep in the hay beside the crib where I fed the cows because I was so tired from work.

In Fall, we have to dredge the drainage ditches from weeds and sods so that the water can flow freely from and to the pump house. I sharpen my scythe, go along the side of the ditch and cut the grass and flowers that have grown into the ditch, slide the scythe along the bottom to cut the roots of those tough weeds and drag them out with a wide steel-spiked rake. This requires a lot of strength. While Father was still alive he did that and I helped with a small rake to pull off some of the floating weeds. While doing that I looked out for fish that were swimming away from the disturbing rake. Theat was exciting for me. At the end of the day father would get the big net out and we would go to the places where I had seen the fish; he would push the net through the muddy water, pull it out and we find pikes, tench or 'karausch' in it.

Now I have to take over this job. One morning I get up early to cut the weeds and clean out the ditch, exhausted from the hard work I take a rest and lean on the wooden handle of the scythe. I had not noticed that wood bugs had eaten into the lower part of it. All of a sudden the handle breaks and the sharp point of the scythe jumps up, cuts through my shirt and goes right into my throat. I press my handkerchief against the wound and stagger home. Mother cleans the wound; she thinks I should see the doctor. After I rest for a while, we get our bicycles out and a fifteen minutes ride takes us to his office. Doctor Schulz examines the cut and tells me I have been extremely lucky; the tip of the scythe went between the trachea and the main artery and if I had pierced either one of them I might not have survived. He disinfects the cut, puts a band-aid over it and we cycle home again. We are still shaken about the incident when we think of the possible consequences and are very grateful for God's protection.

The economic situation in Germany is improving in the last years. Low income workers can afford buying houses in *Siedlungen* (low cost housing developments) and raise a family in their own house. The government is financing the construction of these Siedlungen. People need only a small down payment and can get an extended low mortgage, backed by the government. This opportunity improves the moral of the working families and people are proud of producing good work. The party motto is "Arbeit adelt" (work makes you noble, brings honor) The stamp, 'made in Germany', becomes a quality symbol.

The electronic industry develops the "Volksempfänger" a neat little radio that most people can afford. Citizens should have the opportunity to listen to music, cultural offerings and community events and the NSDAP is interested in having a medium to indoctrinate people with its propaganda.

Another achievement of the government that brings employment to the masses of unemployed people is the building of the '*Autobahn*', a four-lane traffic artery without cross street intersections, connecting north and south and also extending from the western to the eastern border. It is the first road design of this kind in Europe. It allows the moving of traffic and goods faster and more easily since the Autobahn does not go through clogged up cities. Also military convoys can travel quickly from one side of Germany to the other.

The engineer, Ferdinand Porsche, designs the Volkswagen. Hitler wants to make it possible for each family to own a small car. If he can mass-produce it, the manufacturer can keep the price low, under one thousand Marks.

The NSDAP, being a Labor Party, provides for workers who cannot afford holidays, free or very low cost cruises to beach resorts on the Mediterranean or Baltic Sea in the new "Kraft durch Freude" ships (strength through joyful relaxation)

We do not qualify for these bonuses. However, there is something for farmers as well. Many farmers are deep in debt because of a bad market economy. The cost for running an effective farm is high and the farmer gets little for his products. Several are close to declaring bankruptcy. The government values its farmers as 'the backbone of a healthy nation' and tries to help them get back on their feet with a new farm policy. Farms are assessed individually, to find out how much of outstanding loans a farmer can be expected to pay back. He can get easy credits with low interest rates or, if his farm is in very bad shape, the debt will be written off. The government takes over dealing with the financial institutions, which are mostly in the hands of Jewish financiers. They have to lower interest rates or cancel some or all of the loans. This gives new hope to the farmer.

The economy in general picks up. Industrial production increases and export and trade improve. This has benefit to the farmer his products are in demand and the price for it can be adjusted. The additional income he can reinvest in farm equipment, which will improve his productivity.

Father does not take advantage of this arrangement. He had agreed to pay the old Albrechts, from whom he had bought the farm, monthly payments and had almost finished paying what he had promised.

We benefit from the higher prices for our products and our economic situation improves; we can afford some "luxuries" in life again.

Mother tells me that she is seriously worried about me. She feels the strain of going to school and working on the farm afterwards is too hard for me at my age, things have to change,

The family gets together and we discuss how we can better distribute the workload. Mother wants us children to prepare for a career in life and not work on the farm. We decide to hire a farm worker but that is easier said than done. Most of the men are in the army. It is very difficult to find somebody suitable. Tante Annchen knows that Viktor, one of the older children from her children's home, had a friend, Anton, a Polish fellow with German ancestry, who might be willing to work for us. She gets his address and we contact him. He is available and comes for an interview. He claims to be a Christian and has worked on a farm. He speaks German fairly well, has good manners, kisses mother's hand, as Poles usually do, and seems trustworthy. Anton starts work the following week. I show him what he has to do and he is willing to learn and do the work under Mother's supervision and together with her.

The girls who had been helping before can now leave home. Magdalena has finished Business School and finds a job as secretary at the military airport. Christa is attending a Home Economics School and absolves her compulsory training year in the household. of the Quiring family. I can spend more time with school work. Anton has taken over much of my jobs on the farm.

Anton is a little clumsy at first but tries hard to fit in. He prays at the table and even has devotion with us and mother feels comfortable with him. Frau Gehrmann also approves of him and he is slowly integrated into our family

Frau Gehrmann, a fine, well-educated Christian woman has been living with us since the war. She had been married to a nobleman, who lost his estate after World War I. and had left her without means. After he died, she married a preacher from an interdenominational Christian Fellowship. These two headstrong people cannot get along when they are together so they decide to live separately for a while. He lives in West Germany and she with us in West Prussia . She visits him occasionally for a few weeks..

I am fourteen years old now, at the age of puberty. Mother thinks that since Father is no longer here anymore and Anton had previously been working with Christian young people, perhaps he could guide me through my awakening sexuality, or this might even have been Anton's suggestion.

Anton and I sleep upstairs each in one corner of the big gable room, the only finished upstairs bedroom, where the girls had been sleeping. After we had become more familiar, he initiates conversations, asking questions about what my future plans are, if I want to marry and have children and if I know what is involved. In order to win my trust he talks about medical preparation for marriage. He has a doctor friend who could help me find out if I am able to have children. I do not know much about it but find it interesting. He uses my innocence and interest for his own schemes to arouse and seduce me. Sometimes he is depressed and tells me I can get him out of this mood if I gratify him sexually. I become suspicious and our relationship becomes tense and estranged. He even threatens me with the police but I do not take this seriously and he never does it again. I do not tell Mother about his demands.

Anton has taken over much of the work on the farm and uncle Heinrich is willing to help if needed so Mother thinks she can manage without my help.

Summer holidays are over and traveling to school in fall and winter weather means a lot of strain and exhaustion for me. She is concerned about my health and looks for a solution. She finds out that the school I am attending also has a boarding school connected with it and tries to get a place for me there. We both go to our principal, Dr. Sahner. Mother describes our situation at home dramatically and asks if perhaps I could get into the boarding school. She promises my best behavior and effort. She is like the widow and the judge in Jesus' parable. After thoughtful consideration, he offers me a free place in the boarding school. We are both thankful and express this to him. Dr. Sahner had been a vice consul in the former German Colony in South West Africa and has a lot of experience in dealing with people. He is an upright, thoughtful and fair man and, as a high-ranking member in the NSDAP has some influence. He tells us that the government's offer to accept good students free of charge in the boarding school had expired last year but he will endorse my acceptance at least for one year.

For me a new kind of life begins. The boarding school, known as the "Schülerheim", is in a big three-storey white building, a former youth hostel. Remodeled, it now has room for about thirty boys of all ages who come from villages around Marienburg. Some come from large farms in the *Freistaat Danzig* area. They occasionally supplement the common kitchen with farm products. In those lean war years, we hungry boys appreciate that very much. Our matron, Miss Esau, a Mennonite, a stately, friendly person in her late thirties, cares for us and sees that her charges are well fed. She believes good food helps to develop good minds. She sees in us the future leaders in society and wants us to strive for high ethical values, respect, honesty and responsibility; she insists on good manners, politeness and good study habits. She treats us older ones as young gentlemen and we try to behave as such. The younger ones get a little more care and instruction. Occasionally she makes unannounced room checks and boys who have not made their beds properly find mattresses turned over when they come back from class much to the glee of their friends.

We eat all our meals in the large dining room. The tables are arranged in a T form so that the matron can see everyone. They are covered with white linen and have linen napkins beside the plates. Good manneers means, wehave to wait until everyone is served before we are allowed to start eating. If hunger drives someone to dig in as soon as he has been served, she will tell that person, loudly, so that everyone can hear, "Have a good appetite Mr. …" and he will drop his spoon in embarrassment. She then smiles at him graciously.

The older boys have their own rooms with a work desk or they double up. The younger ones sleep several in a room and do their homework in the study hall or lounge under supervision. The furniture is functional but rather Spartan.

Behind the house is a big fenced-in playground where we play soccer, basketball or have table tennis tournaments. When we want to go down-town, we have to give notice and report back.

One day Miss Esau calls me into her study; I wonder what has happened. She tells me that my sister has phoned and I am supposed to phone back. I have never used a phone before and do not know exactly what to do. She sees my hesitation, comes over to the telephone and shows me how to handle it. I get through to the military hospital and ask nervously for Schwester Magdalena. She had left her airport secretary job, has taken a nursing course and is working in a military hospital in Sandhof, a suburb of Marienburg. After a while, she comes to the phone and invites me over for a visit. She wants to know how her 'little brother' is getting along in the new environment. Our cousin Ruth works in the same hospital with her.

In the final years of the war, students and whole school classes from areas at risk or from bombed-out cities are evacuated to the quieter eastern part of the country. Attached to the east side of our building is a large unused hall. One day we hear a lot of noise, hammering and moving around next door. People are cleaning, building partitions and dividers and bringing beds, tables and chairs into the hall. We wonder what is going on there. The next day a young teacher with a class of elementary school kids from Cologne moves in. We now have to share the main shower room and toilets with them and have to eat in shifts in our dining room. We try to accommodate them and be as helpful as we can. The teacher does not want his students to mingle with us. Fräulein Esau is not too happy with this arrangement and the mess that her staff often has to clean up after them. We notice some tension between her and the teacher.

When we come back from our fall vacation, we are surprised when we ring the bell to our residence, an elderly, shorter, women greets us. I am Miss Klink, your new matron. We are shocked, where is Fräulein Esau.? We never find out what has really happened; we can only guess. Perhaps it was the disagreements with the teacher from next door; or maybe he was envious that we enjoyed better conditions than his pupils. Perhaps he found out about the extra food obtained without ration cards that some of the boys from Danzig brought from home and denounced her. We know she did not share his political persuasion. She never greeted anyone with 'Heil Hitler', as he did.

Miss Klink is the opposite of Fräulein Esau. She had been running a home for children in Chile and is more of a housemother type than a governess. We older boys can manage quite well without a mother and do not want to be treated as her "children". The little ones enjoy her. When they are homesick or do not feel well, she will take them on her lap and comfort them. We older ones resist that kind of condescension and I think she notices that too. To compensate for this, she tries to keep a tight ship. We have to obtain a signed permission slip when we want to go down-town and return it when we come back. In summertime, weather permitting, she wants us to have a morning fitness run before school, which the oldest students are to lead and they are just the ones who like to sleep in or prepare for early classes. She allows only short hot showers twice a week to save energy. I think the authorities ordered this in the last years of the war because of an energy shortage.

If someone claimed to be sick, Miss Esau would make a short diagnosis, hand us a thermometer and leave. Those who have a problem in school and want to play truant quickly rub the mercury column under the blanket until it heats up and reaches 38°, enough of a fever to stay in bed. Miss Esau would come back after ten minutes take the student's pulse and decide if the "sickness" was legitimate. Sometimes she would smile understandingly, ask the person if he is having a bad day in school today and write the required excuse slip. Not so Miss Klink, she stays at the bedside and waits ten minutes. If the person is desperate enough to rubs the thermometer under the blanket unchecked until it reaches 42°, she tells him "Get out and go to school, no cheating with me." If the person is really sick, she can be very compassionate.

Lights have to be out for everyone at 22:00 h, a new restriction for us older ones. I have a room with Benno on the third floor. We both like to read and have a pack of books from the library. We have just come to a tense moment in the story when we hear the old wooden stairs groan. Miss Klink is checking on us to see if the lights are out. It is too late to reach the switch so we pierce a needle through the wires of the desk lamp, a spark flares up and all the lights in our wing go out. She gropes her way downstairs and comes back with a candle. When she reaches the first bedroom door, someone behind the door blows out her candle. We think that is mean. She does not come up again but the next day Dr Sahner sits at the lunch table and tells us what proper behavior is. The result, a two-week curfew.

If someone gets a contagious disease, the whole boarding school is under quarantine. At the beginning, we like that. We can read, catch up on school work or play soccer or table tennis but after awhile, we get bored, especially when it is raining. We play card games, tell jokes and get a little rambunctious. Some tell about their secret rendezvous with girls behind the hedge. I get interested and ask how they get to know the girls and how they approach them. They smile and tell me I am still too young for that.

The older boys are allowed to smoke in their rooms. Someone offers me a cigarette. I take one and try it and feel grown up. I even buy a pack so that I can offer one to others. However, I cannot stand the smoke in my eyes and lungs and the bitter taste in my mouth. After a short time I think, why should I do something that I do not like, why spend my scarce pocket money on cigarettes because others think smoking is cool. I normally do only what I find reasonable and affordable. Perhaps I also have a bad conscience because none of my extended family smokes and they do not condone it. Therefore, I stop and become a non-smoker which I still am.

I had taken piano lessons when I was younger, but stopped when my piano teacher moved. Now I take violin lessons together with Wolfgang, a younger student. We do our required exercises and then he sometimes comes up to my room, where we play violin duets. We play folk or pop songs, harmonize, compose variations or jazz it up, which we enjoy. We doubt if others also do so we use my room, because it is on the third floor and is more 'sound proof.'

Now and then, we have concerts in our lounge, performed by music students or outside guests or we perform short drama pieces for Christmas or graduation. Or just for fun. There is often some entertainment going on.

Our boarding school is located on the Willenberg, a range of hills leading down to the flats of the Nogat River. In summer when it is quite hot, we run down to the Nogat to swim and cool off or we watch the steamers sailing down to the Baltic Sea.

Not far from us is the glider plane school. I can see the planes rise up and then follow with my eyes those white wide-winged 'birds' sail back and forth carried by the up draft from the hills on which I stand. Often I wish I could fly in one of them.

Our school has a very active rowing club, sponsored by our English teacher and trainer, Capt'n Gottschalk. In 1941, the 'coxed eight' of our school won the German rowing competition in its class. Members of the club are allowed to take boats out for training. In our free time, we go to the boathouse, swing a boat with a crane from the elevated boathouse down to the river and practice rowing skills to prepare for the next regatta. I take part in two of them as No.2 in a "coxed four scullers" (boat for four rowers on a rolling seat). In Bromberg, we beat our next competitor by three boat lengths, but in the Nogat regatta, we barely win with a quarter boat length.

One rowing event is quite alive in my memory. We bought an additional rowboat for our club from Elbing about 45 km northeast of Marienburg. Our Capt'n thinks it is easier to row it home than to have it delivered. I am one of the four volunteers to row it back. We board the boat on the Elbing River and row for a short distance before we turn into an obscure little creek, a tributary that connects the Elbing River with the Nogat. In places it is hardly wide enough to row with stretched out sculls. It is a beautiful sunny day. Gnarled willows stand on the banks of the creek, their branches hanging over the water forming arches, under which we quietly move through. Waterfowl are startled by these unexpected visitors and dive or fly away. The blue heron and stork look at us from a distance. We have an observational biology lesson. It is uplifting to glide through almost untouched Nature. The creek flows now through meadows on which cows are grazing and gets wider until it joins the Nogat River. Two more hours rowing up-stream and we dock at our boathouse.

When I left Alt-Rosengart to go to boarding school, I gave notice to the HJ leader of my unit that I could no longer participate in their meetings. When I came to Marienburg, I 'forgot' to report my move. Therefore, for one year nobody knew that I was not attending HJ meetings.

I usually come home for the weekend to help on the farm and Frau Cornelsen, our neighbor, sees me. One day she asks Mother, "How come my son Siegfried has to go to the HJ meetings every Saturdays when I need him and your son can stay at home; that is not fair". She was going to complain and did, but it does not help her much. Siegfried has to continue to attend and I am told I had committed an offence against party regulations by not attending the compulsory HJ meetings. I explain the situation and promise to report in Marienburg. I have more options in the city. The HJ is organized in different interest sections. The regular one, the "Streifen HJ", the political wing, from which many join the 'SS' later, the" motorized", the "equestrian", the "marine" and the "air force HJ", similar to the cadets. I am going to find out what their different aims and objectives are.

One evening I happen to be at home for the weekend and look out of the living room window at home and see some boys chasing men across the fields, beating them with clubs. I go outside and can identify them, Streifen HJ, lying in ambush for foreign laborers who have overextended their curfew. Young men and women from occupied countries were conscripted to work in factories and on farms, while German workers are in the army. They have to wear an insignia to identify them as foreigners, the Polish workers wear a yellow triangle on their chest, Czechs a purple one and Jews a yellow Star of David. Most farmers in our village do not care so much if their laborers stay out a little longer on a summer evening after work. They let them gather on one of the farms, sing their melancholic folk tunes, accompanied by a fiddle or harmonica, to forget their homesickness. Content workers are better workers. I wonder why the Streifen HJ mingles in our business and I am disgusted, seeing them taking the law into their own hands, treating foreigners, who have been working hard and want a little bit of fun in their free time, in this degrading way. I would certainly not want to join this wing of the HJ. I decide to go to the "Flieger HJ" (air force) Every Wednesday afternoon we have different activities like identifying and classifying airplanes, building model airplanes, learning how to splice wire cables and tie different kinds of knots. I also volunteer for a Morse Alphabet course, which was still in use at that time. Political and military training is on Saturdays. I excuse myself from that, because I am going home on Saturdays to help on the farm. The best part is learning to fly gliders. Occasionally we are allowed to use the facilities of the flying school on the Willenberg range, close to our boarding school, where we practice starting and landing. In the Easter holidays, my dream comes true; I have my first solo flight in a glider and get my first Glider Flight Certificate.

After a weekend at home, I am going back to school. It is Monday November 10, 1938. I walk along the "unter den Lauben" colonnade across the market place and notice a shop window broken and the inside vandalized. I take it for a break in. I walk on and see the show window of the prestigious clothing store smashed and some of the expensive dresses and suits lying on the sidewalk and another store and another office wrecked. Some of the villas have their doors smashed in and their windows broken and furniture thrown outside. I ask a passer-by what has happened, he shakes his head and walks away. Finally, someone tells me that last night, on the NS holiday, SA men and NS party members broke into Jewish businesses and homes and vandalized them. The irony is that they also vandalized a NS uniform store where I had bought my HJ uniform. As I walk by, I see the brown shirts, ties and jackets with the swastika armlet on the knocked-over shelves and on the sidewalk

I had noticed before, written on Jewish store windows "Don't buy from Jews," but I had taken these as graffiti pranks of NS extremists and did not pay much attention to it. I am shocked now to see this! German people degrading themselves and doing such abhorrent acts as to vandalize and destroy property of law-abiding German citizens and being able to get away with it. This is normally considered a criminal offence. Most people I speak to, do not understand this either. Why does nobody in our judicial or religious system, lawyers or priests confront these radicals and call it a crime against humanity, unworthy of German moral standards. But I do not do anything about it either. I am too shy and inexperienced in such matters. This terrible event is remembered in German and western history as "Reichskristallnacht". The Nazis had hoped most Germans would approve of these acts and join in throwing out the Jews but the opposite was the case, most of them were appalled others indifferent. The public persecution of Jews stopped for a while but the Kristallnacht was a prediction of the upcoming systematic persecution and annihilation of the Jewish people.

With all my activities in rowing, glider training and sports, (I fulfilled the requirements for the 'Rescue swimmers certificate' and the prestigious '*Reichssportabzeichen*') I do not spend enough time preparing for my academic subjects. The second year at Christmas Mother receives a letter from school in a blue envelope, known among students as "blauer Brief", a bad omen. My chemistry teacher warns me that I will get a failing grade if I do not improve before Easter reports are issued. Mother is disturbed and comes to my school to find out how my performance is in general and specifically in Chemistry. Dr.Amhaus assures her that she does not have to worry. This is a formality. He wants to warn me of the possibility of failing his subject if I do not work a little harder. Failing two subjects would mean I have to repeat the grade. When mother comes home, we have a talk about it. When I bring home the Easter report card, my Chemistry mark has gone up to 'Gut' (B)

Luftwaffenhelfer

In spring of 1942 the first students of my class are drafted for military service. We were a small class to begin with and now we shrink to a point that the remainder is joined with our 'parallel class'. I am the second youngest in this class now and wonder when it will be my turn to be drafted. It does not take long when several of us in the boarding school receive a letter to appear before the draft board to enlist for military service in the *Waffen SS*.

I am tall, blond, have blue eyes a good 'Arian appearance' that is what their draft board is looking for: but I do not have the correct political bias.

As far as I know the Waffen SS is a voluntary military unit, so they actually cannot draft me into it and I have no intention of joining it volutarily. I do not approve of their arrogant, smug even hostile attitude towards Christianity and what it stands for, respect, kindness, love, inclusivness. For them it is just a 'Jewish sect' unworthy of Germanic people.

I dare to defy the order and persuade my violin-playing buddy not to report either. We want to see what is going to happen, if we do not appear. I am, however, a little scared of the possible consequences. I could be arrested.

We wait a week and nothing happens but I feel a little uneasy about the whole situation. My fellow students complain I am a coward to avoid the draft.

To end it all, I decide to volunteer for the air force. I trained in the air force HJ and have a glider pilot's licence. I can sleep better again, after I have done this.

In the fall of 1942, our whole class is drafted to be*"Luftwaffenhelfer"*, (air defense helpers). We are put into army barracks of an artillery unit in Danzig. We receive special uniforms, similar to those of the air force. Seven of us form a gun crew and are trained to handle the well respected and feared 8,8 Flak (airplane attack cannon) I am assigned to be gunner No.5, the one who has to push the shells into the cannon barrel and pull the trigger. The ammunition is heavy and I am exhausted after each training exercise. It will be our job to defend the city of Danzig against the Allies air attacks when they come to this part of our homeland. Besides military training, we have two hours instruction in the main subjects of our school curriculum each day and free time in the late afternoon to keep our barracks clean, do homework or relax. Sometimes we walk along the beach of the Baltic Sea and gather amber pieces, or take the tram to go downtown. Occasionally we go to the theatre.

One evening Ulli and I are the only ones who make it through the corporal's uniform inspection, which means we can go out. We have cheap tickets for the performance of "Joan of Arc" on the third balcony. The theatre board allows soldiers to switch to seats that are not occupied in any section after the first act. We watch for those and spot two seats in the orchestra secton below.and see the continuation of Schiller's exciting drama from row five from the stage. Two rows ahead of us sit two pretty girls. Guessing from their dresses and expensive seats that they must come from upper class families. Ulli keeps an eye on them, while I am wrapped up in the action of the drama. After the performance, we follow them to the foyer, introduce ourselves and Ulli asks them if we may accompany them home, since it is late and perhaps not safe to walk alone at this time. They hesitantly give us permission. We try to make intelligent conversation until we reach their residence. Ulli wants to kiss his partner good-bye, but she turns him down. My partner does not seem quite as adamant and I, the shy fellow, get hot under the collar. The streetcar comes rattling along to my rescue. I tell Ulli this is our last chance to get back to the barracks on time and run after it, giving a quick handshake to my partner. He, a little disappointed, follows me. At the curve, the tram has to slow down and we jump on. It is the last one this night. We still do not make it on time for curfew, but the corporal on duty does not report us, we just have to clean the orderly's room.

In spring 1943, our training period is over and we are now reservists. We never had to fend off an actual air attack. We are back in school again only for a few months until it is our turn to be drafted. We receive an emergency graduation certificate, the "*Notabitu*r" without much ceremony. It will enable us to enter University when we come back from the front lines.

Not only boys are drafted, girls also have to help to 'defend the homeland' as draftees to the "Arbeitsdienst" (labor service). The 18 to 25 year old girls have to work on farms, in factories or military installations where men had worked before until they had to go to war. They assist mothers who have many children.

Our sister Christa is recruited to work in the office of a government agency.

I visit her in Graudenz. She manages to get a day off and we walk together through the park and have lunch in her cafeteria. She shares her life in the unit with me and tells me that she sometimes feels left out because as a Christian, she does not participate in questionable social activities. Some ask her about her faith, and seek her advice if they are in trouble. When we say good-bye, she hugs me and feels assured that her future is in God's hand. We do not know then, that this is the last time we shall see each other.

Later, Christa is transferred to an air force unit as communications assistant and works there until two weeks before the end of the war. She phones us that her unit will be dissolved and she will come and join us. This is the last time we heard from her.

Arbeitsdienst

In the summer of 1943, it is my turn to join the *"Reichsarbeitsdienst"*. The NS Government has been conscripting young men to work restoring the infra- structure of the country after WWI on projects like building roads, the Autobahn, bridges and cultivating swamps and wasteland. Its original purpose was to reduce unemployment for young people and introduce them to a kind of work ethic that the party felt was desirable for rebuilding Germany. People from different social levels should learn to accept and appreciate each other while living and working together. In 1935, it became mandatory for each young man between the ages of 18 to 25, to serve for half a year in the Arbeitsdienst. The organization of the Arbeitsdienst is similar to that of the army. A *Vormann* is in charge of a troop, a *"Feldmeister"* is like an officer, he commands a larger unit. We live in barracks and are trained to handle a spade the way a soldier handles a rifle.

My memory of the Arbeitsdienst is somewhat sketchy and not too pleasant. I receive an order from some government agency, to report to a small town in former Poland. At the town's railway station I meet a number of young men from other parts of Germany. A man in a brown uniform approaches us and introduces himself as our *"Feldmeister,"* gathers all of us in front of the station and asks us to line up in three rows. We march with our luggage in formation to the barracks. We wait there until a tall slim man with an aquiline nose, in the same uniform as the Feldmeister, comes out and presents himself as our camp commander. He greets us with "Heil Hitler", talks about commitment to fatherland and Führer, obedience and hard work. I think he is about to direct us to our quarters, but he orders us to regroup and march around the compound, still in our civilian clothes. I wonder what the purpose of this exercise is. He watches our performance carefully. If somebody gets out of step, he calls him out, lights into him and makes him run around the meadow beside the dirt road on which we march. Some of the young men are tired from the trip and physically not in shape. They can't handle this treatment and pass out on the grass from exhaustion.. He shouts at the ones who are still lying unconsciously beside the road, "You invertebrates, you are unworthy of being German elite. The Führer has no use for weaklings like you, but we will make strong and valuable men of you here". They cannot hear him, so he is actually talking to us. I shake my head, what a loser; he is supposed to be our leader? Does he want to show us right from the beginning who has the power and who has to submit or is it his intention to prepare us for the rigors of life without knowing how to do this effectively?. When we return from our march I look at the *Oberfeldmeister,* which is his rank, more closely and notice the round badge on his uniform, the emblem of the NS party. This explains his frequent references to the Führer.

Eight men are put into one room in the barracks. We receive our uniforms, a dress uniform, a standard one and work clothes. A few days later we are posted for sentry duty. For two hours, we have to stand with a spade on our shoulder under the window beside the entrance of the main barrack. We are not allowed to move, that is torture. When it is my turn to stand on guard, I discover a crack between the sill and the window frame under which I have to stand. I take a step back push the tip of the blade of my spade into the crack and let the spade dangle. It hangs by itself just about half an inch above my shoulder that makes standing on guard a little lighter. After an hour, I feel the difference. Some of my comrades, affected by the heat and lack of circulation and unfamiliar with such torture cannot endure that long. They collapse and are carried unconscious into the first aid room. Normally guards are supposed to change after one hour.

Every morning we get up at six o'clock, have an assembly in front of the barracks and go to work. Our job is to build the foundation of a road with shovel and wheelbarrow.

Once a week, the Feldmeister inspects our rooms to see if everything is clean and in order. Our Vormann orders a uniform check every second day. If he finds anything wrong with our uniform, if it does not fit properly, has loose buttons or shows any dirt, the whole group has to run into the barracks and change uniforms he calls it "*Garderobenwechsel*" after we have done it twice because we were not fast enough, I make a funny remark about him to my comrade. The Vormann hears it and is mad. He calls us two out, "In two minutes you will stand here in your work uniform". We smile at him. He shouts at us "Did you hear me" we reply in a friendly way, "The two minutes are not up yet, sir." He counts the seconds. After one minute, we rush into the barrack. The uniform we are wearing flies into the closet, we only hope he is not going to inspect it. In 59 seconds, we stand before him in our work uniform. He was not expecting this and even commends us and we are dismissed.

Some of our superiors are humane and fun. My buddy and I have a dispute with two *Unterfeldmeister*. I do not remember what the topic was but we know we are right and make a bet. They suggest a pan of fried potatoes because food was not too plentiful. The next morning although they know we were right, they change the rules and, in spite of our protest, they declare us the losers. They are our superiors and they are always right! We have to produce a pan of fries. We beg the cook to lend us a pan, steal a handful of potatoes, but have no fat in which to fry them. Someone suggests coffee as a substitute; it makes the potatoes quite dark. When we present our pan of potatoes, thinking we kept our deal, they look at it and say "You dare to offer us that burned stuff? You can eat it yourselves and right now." We try to get out of it, saying that was not in the bargain; but we have no choice. Not to lose face and accompanied by the cheers of our comrades we finally choke down those burned potatoes. The result is disastrous. I get a terrible stomach ache and cannot sleep all night. During the morning roll call, I feel miserable. We stand in three rows and I choose the middle row, not to attract attention. Halfway through the commander's instructions I get dizzy and ask the man on the right and left to prop me up. I sway and the eagle eye of the *Oberfeldmeister* sees it. He shouts, "What is going on there in the second row?" I collapse and they carry me to the medic's room. He continues with reprimands and an accusation: the Führer has to suffer again because I have failed him by fainting on duty. I do not hear much anymore and I don't care. I spend the rest of the day in the sick room.

The days go by with street construction, training and sentry duty until dismissal time on February 26, 1944. The last night I have terrible pain in my big toe and do not sleep very much. With great difficulty, I put my boots on in the morning. When I report to the office to get my dismissal papers, the officer asks me if I want to continue service as an instructor; I thank him for the honor but decline. I have enough and want to get out of there and return home to help Mother. I can hardly make it to the train station. When I arrive in Grunau, our home railway station, I see a farmer from our neighbor village, he gives me a ride to our driveway and I hobble the rest of the way home.

Mother is happy to see me back again even as an invalid. The pain from my big toe spreads to all joints in the foot, the knee, hips, and reaches the neck and shoulders. Our Physician, Dr. Schulz, comes, diagnoses acute rheumatism and suggests taking me to hospital. The ambulance arrives and the attendants carry me on a stretcher to the road and drive me to Marienburg. All my joints are now swollen and very painful. I cannot go to the toilet anymore, cannot use my hands and fingers and the nurse has to feed me. I often cry, I have never been that helpless since I was a baby. Four weeks I spend in hospital before I can slowly walk again. Mother visits me occasionally.

On one visit she brings me a letter from the recruiting office, I am to report for military service. I show it to the attending physician; he reads it and tells me he will take care of it. He writes a short report about my condition "Not fit for service" and puts his stamp on it. The army has to wait.

Mother, with input from Dr.Schulz and Mrs.Gehrman, decide to send me to a spa for complete recovery. Frau Gehrman who is still living with us, knows a family in Wiesbaden who would provide room and board while I am taking treatment in the spa.

For three months, I drink mineral water three times a day, endure mudpacks, get electro-stimulation treatments and salizyl injections. During the last weeks, I can take short trips into the city along the river Rhine. I enjoy its beauty and the sunshine, which helps the healing.

I am going home much happier now since the excruciating pain is gone. I am very grateful to Mother for making the sacrifice to provide this expensive treatment for me, and to Frau Gehrman who very likely initiated it and had the connections and practical know-how to help mother arrange the whole event.

It is harvest time so I do not have much opportunity to convalesce. There is not so much to do at home since we have a dairy farm. As soon as we are finished, with our harvest, Onkel Richard, Mother's brother, asks if I could help him, since his two oldest sons are in the army. I feel fit, get on my bicycle and ride over to Sparau. They have started with the wheat harvest and everybody is needed. Onkel Richard instructs me how to operate the machinery and as soon as the dew has dried in the morning, we drive out to the field. Cousin Alfred, who is two years younger than I, drives the four horses that pull the combine and I sit on top and watch that it operates properly. At noontime, we exchange horses and the new team with Onkel Richard and his younger son Richard, work the second shift. Later I help with setting up the shocks. He treats me like a partner and shows me what is involved in running a big farm. I enjoy working with him.

We have almost finished the harvest when unexpected news comes from my Mother. I have received another notice from the draft board to join the military forces. This ends my work here at the farm and, with a heavy heart, I say good-bye to my relatives. After lunch, we pray together and the family wishes me God's protection and blessing for an uncertain future.

So far, we have not personally experienced many of the hardships of the war which people in the big cities have. We follow, however, the actions of our troops from the reports in radio and newspaper. We hear about the defeat of general Paulus' army in Stalingrad, the retreat of German troops and Hitler's strange strategy on the eastern front.

Living on a farm gives us the advantage of producing most of our own food although there are strict regulations regarding how much of our produce we are allowed to keep for our own consumption, no more than other people get on ration cards, the government collects the rest. We try to follow the rules but it is difficult to control and enforce them. We send some food parcels to relatives in Berlin.

We live simply and are content with the articles we get on ration cards. If we desperately need some supplies for the farm, we can barter with a goose or a piece of ham. We have wool from our sheep and Grandmother spins and knits warm pullovers, socks and gloves. Mother can sew and patches, alters or remodels our wardrobe. Compared to people in the cities we are not destitute.

The fighting on the eastern front comes closer. We live about 20 km away from the military airport of Königsdorf, near Marienburg. The new Focke Wulf 190 fighter planes are assembled here and are tested. These fast planes often circle over our village and we wave to them.

Quite unexpectedly we get a taste of the terror of war, quite close to us. On October 9,1943 around noon, a formation of 98 British and American bombers fly over the airport and drop their bombs on it. The personnel of the airport hear the rumble of airplanes but do not imagine them to be enemy planes until the bombs fall and blow up air planes, hangars, office buildings, barracks and oil and gas supply tanks. My cousin, Irmgard, is working at the airport when it happened and describes the attack vividly. Apparently, Russian spies, camouflaged as workers, had cut the communication lines to the airport and thus shut off the warning system, The Allied planes, guided by the spies' wireless radio transmission, flew in from the Baltic Sea, and attacked the airport unnoticed and unhindered. The attack came completely unexpected and was devastating. Many people were killed and wounded. It took a while to rebuild the airport and make it operational again. Exactly a year later after the airport had been in operation for a short while, the camou flaged airport was attacked again by a fleet of American and British bombers and was completely destroyed.

Military Service

For me the reality of the war becomes very personal when I hold the draft order in my hands - the second one, signed by a high-ranking recruiting officer. I read it again; 'You have to report on the 26th of August 1944 to a military unit in Holland'. I get my travel papers and pack the few things I am taking along into an old wooden suitcase. Mother and I talk about what needs to be done on the farm and I admonish Anton to be a good support to Mother.

We have arranged with Uncle Gustav in Berlin to use him as a contact person, in case members of our family lose contact with each other.

I know it is hard for Mother to let her third child go to war. Magdalena is a Red Cross nurse in a military hospital and Christa serves as a telephone operator in an air force unit.

We have tears in our eyes when we quietly say good-bye to each other, not knowing if we will ever meet again. Mother commits me into God's hands as I leave.

In the train, I join soldiers who have come from the front going on furlough or back to the front lines. I have opportunity to find out what war on the front lines is like. Our train goes through the former Polish Corridor and all across Germany to the Dutch border. At larger railway stations Red Cross personnel or volunteer *BDM Mädel* (female HJ) hand coffee and sandwiches into our compartments and wave as we leave. Everybody is involved in some way or another to support each other to endure the hardships of war.

We disembark at a small railway station near the city of Amersfoort. A truck takes us to a military camp in northern Holland. The yellow brick barracks stand between short snarled pine trees and blend in well with the sandy soil.

I have volunteered for the air force and have applied for officer candidate training, in order not to be drafted into the Waffen SS. The only resemblance to the air force is the blue-grey uniform of the '*Luftwaffe*'; in addition, we have silver wings on a white lapel on the collar of our uniform and a black armband on the right sleeve with silver insignia,'*Fallschirm-Panzerdivision Hermann Göring*'. In reality, we are a special infantry unit. Our basic training is the same, perhaps a little stricter, depending on the standards and political leaning of the drillmasters. The treatment of the 'recruits' depends on the character and attitude of their 'superiors'. I have experienced this in the HJ, Arbeitsdienst and here in the military.

Our training for combat consists of drill in marching, fitness, hygiene and survival. We get theoretical and practical instruction in the use of different weapons to protect and defend ourselves and eliminate the enemy.

Our instructor, a young private first class, is correct, strict and treats us according to service regulations, as if he is preparing us for a parade and not for war. In the morning as fitness training, he points to a tree in the distance and we have to run around it. The three who arrive first after each round can step aside and the others have to continue. I figure I could perhaps be one of the first three but, if I don't make it, I will be exhausted for the following rounds. So in the first round I take it easy, saving my energy and in the second round I easily am one of the first three to be eliminated and this works.

In theory lessons a corporal stumbles through his presentation, making some foolish mistakes, so we correct him and crack jokes behind his back. He gets nervous and shouts at us: "Why do you grin, you bastards?" "We are enjoying your instruction, sir" we reply. He is mad but cannot do much about it .

Some Corporals on Duty are quite creative in playing tricks on us young recruits when they have room inspections. We send scouts out to other rooms to find out what he is looking for this time. When he comes to our room and asks us to open our locker, our underwear and uniform are at right angles on the shelf, so he does not pull it out on the floor. When he slides his finger over the top ledge of the doorframe, he finds no dust. He even has a word of acknowledgement for us when he leaves. One of them is known to be mean. When he sees a piece of a uniform sticking out from the locker door, he pulls it out as far as he can and cuts it off with a pair of scissors. The next morning that soldier stands at roll call with a jacket sleeve reaching only to his elbow or a trouser leg up to his knee - what an embarrassment!

Fortunately, our unit is being split up and we get a new group leader, a soldier from the front who has been wounded and is still convalescing. He treats us as future comrades, sounds tough when his officer can see or hear him but is companionable, almost fraternal, when we are out of sight. We stand around him and he shares his front experiences with us. "What they are doing with you is a waste of time, they should teach you what to expect when you face the enemy, how to respond in combat and survive". He demonstrates and practices different situations with us, which later saves my life.

Once a week we have company drill lead by a master sergeant. We march from our barracks to the sand hills. "A song" he shouts and if no one starts one within 5 seconds he makes us run with full marching gear up and down the sand hills. Sometimes he adds, "full cover," and we have to lie down behind a bush or in a dell and, if that is not fast enough, he repeats it several times during the march. If he notices someone is out of step, does not sing loudly enough, or is out of tune, he chases him around the marching company and whenever the soldier comes in front of him, he has to prostrate before the mighty sergeant and is allowed to get up when the shadow of the sergeant has passed him. He seems to take a perverse satisfaction in seeing us suffer.

When we are back in the barracks he picks on a quiet, simple-minded fellow, has him climb on a railing and shout in four directions, "I am stupid". I consider this a very strange sense of humor and an unusual way of instilling in us recruits self-confidence and patriotism.

Our sleeve band has the insignia 'Parachute and Tank Division". Our parachute training consists of climbing up a tree, jumping off and rolling over our shoulder as parachute jumpers do when they hit ground. We have no tanks, but we learn how to destroy them with the 'Panzerfaust' a small antitank missile.

We normally have little contact with the Dutch people, in fact we are forbidden to socialize with them or take anything from them. A few times boys come to the fence and whistle. I walk over to them; they want cigarettes and offer us a bag of apples or pears in exchange. I look around to make sure nobody is watching. The boys look innocent and the apples are very tempting, they remind me of our orchard at home. Since I don't smoke, I make a deal, give them my cigarettes and enjoy their apples. The boys are very happy.

Sometimes we get permission to go to town. In the tram, I observe the reaction of the passengers towards us soldiers. Some of them ignore us stoically, others offer us a seat. I normally decline smile at them and ask them to remain seated. They smile back. I am embarrassed about a few of our soldiers who act as conquerors and demand a seat. Passengers move angrily away from them.

After six weeks of training, we are considered ready for combat. On our last roll call, the commanding officer tells us to pack our backpacks and clean our rooms as we are going to be deployed on the eastern front.

The Allied forces have landed on the French beaches. After their initial heavy losses, they now advance into western Holland. We have not made contact with them. They now have control over the air space and the roads are no longer safe for traveling by truck. We have to march in smaller units. Our sergeant asks us to confiscate bicycles from the Dutch for faster and easier transport. At first this sounds all right and after the first soldiers come back with one or two bikes, I venture out to try my luck. I stand on the road and see women turning around on their bikes and speeding away when they see me, a German soldier. I feel ashamed; I cannot do it, as this would be theft. I return without a bike and join our group leader who announces,"I march, follow me". The road we are taking is littered with broken down and burned out vehicles Allied fighter-bombers fly very low over us and empty their guns on everything that moves. We take cover behind destroyed tanks or trucks. However, some of their bullets hit and kill some of my comrades. I see my first casualties. We march on through towns and villages. When some people stand by the street and look at us, we want to appear confident and in good form and sing marching songs, although we are dead tired. It is October and the weather gets colder. We march through rain and sleet, which is not very comfortable but this fogy weather keeps the airplanes away.

At night, we are so exhausted that all we want to do is stretch out under a tree, cover ourselves with a blanket and sleep. Some do this but wake up in the middle of the night, cold and wet. Our experienced group leader makes us zip our tent sections together and build a tent. In less than ten minutes, we have a roof over our head and it is dry and warm inside. We wrap ourselves in our blankets sleep soundly and awake refreshed the next morning.

After several days of marching, we reach the German border. We wait for the rest of our regiment to arrive and board a train that takes us right across Germany, from the Dutch to the Polish border. At main railway stations, Red Cross nurses hand us coffee and refreshments and wish us well. At train and street crossings, people wave as we pass by.

Our train finally reaches Radom in southern Poland about 90 km south of Warsaw. We move into a small castle on a hill, surrounded by a spacious garden and a creek flowing through the lower end of it. It must have been beautiful in past times but is now somewhat neglected. We carry straw into the halls and meeting rooms on the lower floor and make our beds. These are the quarters of the soldiers. The officers and uncommissioned officers are stationed in the bedrooms, drawing room and salons of the former Polish nobleman.

Partisans are hiding in the forests around the castle and we have to have a 24-hour guard duty around the castle. It is getting cold and occasionally light snow trickles down, that helps us to track their movements. Our training is now adapted to close combat. Our cook requisitions enough food to serve us healthy meals from the field kitchen, which keeps us in good spirits. One night I make an unwelcome discovery -- lice. In the morning, some of us sit outside on the old garden walls, pull those tormentors from our undershirts and squeeze them between our fingernails until we see our blood coming out of them. I hope the ones we cannot detect will catch a cold sooner than we will. It is a lost battle if some soldiers in the same room are not fighting these 'critters. One fellow is neglecting his hygiene completely. He sleeps in his uniform and does not wash or brush. We warn him and invite him to join us when we run down to the creek that flows through the old castle garden and wash our bare chests. We tell him, it is refreshing; we feels much better but the lice do not like it. He does not respond. We finally take action, undress him to his underpants put a blanket around him and lead him to the creek. Two of us are waiting with scrubbing brushes and laundry soap, we cut the thin layer of ice open which has formed during the night and scrub him thoroughly with soap and water, dry him with his towel, put some "beauty powder" over him and let him wrap himself in his blanket and run back. From then on there is a line-up at the creek in the morning.

The night watch notice footprints around the castle. We suspect partisans. No one may leave the compound alone or without a weapon. News filters through, the Russians have penetrated German lines and are approaching our position; we have to stop them. Our company leader, a young lieutenant, gives orders to form a defense line east on the outskirts of the village. We arrive on a large meadow, flat, without any trees or bushes for camouflage; I wonder who came up with that insane plan. It is irresponsible to put a company of young recruits, inexperienced in battle with no artillery or air cover, to fight against seasoned Russian combat troops which have all sorts of back-up armament. It is suicide and stoically I decide, if there is no alternative, I will sacrifice my life for my fatherland, not for the Führer. on this 'idyllic battlefield'.

Fortunately, before we start to dig in, the order comes to move back to the railway station. I am relieved.

A train takes us north to the border of East Prussia. It is shortly before Christmas. We take quarters in wooden barracks in an army camp and for the first time we get mail from home. The clerk calls out the names of mail recipients. I am full of joy when he calls my name,. It is a small parcel from Mother. It has arrived just in time for Christmas. In her letter, she writes that Anton, our farm help, wants to go home for Christmas, which means she will be on the farm all by herself. Magdalena still works in the military hospital in Marienburg and might get a few days off to help her. Christa is with an air force unit near the island of Usedom in the Baltic Sea, where the "V2 rockets are assembled. Uncle Heinrich, her youngest brother, has been called to the *Volkssturm*, the army of 'invalids and boys'. Opa Wiehler, at the old age of 84, has to manage the farm again from which he had retired twenty years ago. With the letter she included my favorite *"Fliegenkuchen"* (raisin cake) and a piece of homemade smoked ham. I cannot resist tasting a piece of cake and it tastes delicious. The ham I save for Christmas Eve to share with some of my comrades who did not get any mail. Mother's gift I stow away in my cupboard and lock the door before I go on sentry duty. On the way back, I pick up a few fir branches to decorate our room for Christmas. When I unlock my cupboard, I see that my cake and my ham are gone. Someone took my special Christmas gift. I ask my comrades if they have seen anybody getting into my locker, but nobody has. At least I tasted a piece of my favorite cake but it makes me sad not to savor that beautiful ham and the other part of the cake which I imagine Mother packed with loving thoughts for her son to enjoy. Since it is Christmas, a festival of love, I shall forgive the thief, but I am still angry about it.

After Christmas, we move on. In our heavy boots, we trudge quietly through the relentlessly falling snow, which makes Masuren look like a winter wonderland. The Russian troops are not far behind us. Tired from the long march we finally turn off the road into the yard of a large estate. The cook has gone ahead with the field kitchen. He finds plenty of food on the deserted farms to prepare a wholesome stew. We line up with our mess-tins and he fills them to the brim. Our stomachs filled, we now look for a warm place to rest for the night. I climb to the hayloft and find a spot between the rafters. My boots are soaking wet from marching through the snow for several days when I pull them off. I pull a pair of dry socks out of my pack, massage my tired feet and put them on, this feels good. We are supposed to sleep in our uniforms; in case of a surprise attack, we have to be alert.

I ask my buddy to join me in digging a hole in the hay; we wrap ourselves in our blankets and slide in it together. Two produce more heat than one. Some light candles, in order to read their mail again and this in a hayloft.! I am looking for a fast fire exit. We sleep soundly in our warm hay hole. When we crawl out of it in the morning and want to put our boots on, they are frozen stiff. No way can we get into them. The temperature has gone down to minus thirty. For those who covered themselves in only one blanket, it has been a cold, sleepless night.

I take my boots under my arm chute down to the cow stall below and slide the frozen boots quietly under the behind of a sleeping cow. After a short while, they are warm and flexible and I can put them on again. The water pump outside is still working but I have first to break down the ice column that has formed below. I wash my face and dry it quickly before the water turns to ice.

After breakfast, we move on again. The sergeant major spots a noble horse in the stable, a *Trakehner*. He hitches it to a dogcart and he and the lieutenant lead the way like Caesar in a chariot. The next morning he sees an abandoned new field kitchen with all its utensils beside the road. He looks at it, 'We can use that' he decides, turns to the company and calls, "I need two volunteers to guard it". I like a change from the monotony of marching, so I nod to my buddy and we step forward. He tells us to watch that nobody takes it until he can find a team of horses to pull it away. We see the company disappear, lean comfortably on the big kettle and watch soldiers pass by, some in formation like we were and some stragglers. Finally, a small group stumbles by. Their corporal sees us ,points back and tells us, "The Russians are right behind us, get out of here as fast as you can, find your unit, and let the Russians enjoy your field kitchen." We join them. After a few hours walk, our stomach reminds us it is noontime. We stop at a deserted farmhouse. A few chicken and geese are still in the coop. One of us grabs a goose and cuts its head off. I remove the feathers, cut it open and clean it out; I still remember how to do that from home. In the meantime, someone cooks the potatoes and gets the coffee ready. The mess sergeant could not have prepared a better meal for us. We think, "Enjoy life as long as you still have it".

One stands guard while the rest of us have a short snooze and we are back on the road again. Next day we find our regiment. We report to the sergeant major. He is glad we are back and makes no mention of the lost field kitchen. That was a nice break but now we are marching in formation again all day long in slush and cold rain. At one point, I get so tired, my head falls onto the backpack of the soldier in front of me. I call it sleep walking. It is my nineteenth birthday 1945. We walk through Insterburg; our aim is to reach Frauenburg close to the Baltic Sea, the birthplace of Copernicus.

We get a short rest after the long march. The staff is assessing the situation and decides we have to stop the advance of the Russian army. The plan is to take up a position on the ridge of a hill with a stand of trees beside and behind us as a cover, one regiment on the right side, ours in the middle and another on our left. This location is much more suited for defense than the one a few weeks before, in the open field. We are given a shovel and a pick to dig holes, each large enough for two men. The equipment could have come from a historical Germanic village museum. The ground is frozen stone hard and we make little progress with these tools. Fortunately, it is a starlit night and our eyes can adjust enough to the darkness that we don't hit each other. By dawn we have dug to the depth of about one meter. The hole is just deep enough to lie in, like a shallow grave but not deep enough for proper cover. We are sweating in spite of the cold and are exhausted. We rest for a while. It is quiet and we hear a cow mooing behind us in a barn.. My companion decides to get some milk since the soup carrier did not find us being in the last hole on the right wing. He comes back and fills my mess tin with milk "I am going to get breakfast "he tells me and leaves again. Smart guy, I think, he lets me alone to defend the position. It leaves me a little more room in the narrow hole. While he is gone, I search the horizon, it is light enough to discover a number of small black dots in the distance. They are moving and getting bigger. I finally identify 16 Russian tanks; that means trouble.

I raise my container to drink my last milk. A metallic click startles me, it sounds like a rifle bullet. Cautiously I look over the rim and spot two steel helmets behind a bunch of high dry grass, about one hundred meters below me. Russian soldiers have crawled up during the night and are ready to attack. The sun comes over the horizon. I look around; the regiment that was supposed to dig in beside us is gone. My hole is the last one on the right flank and it is unprotected. If the Russians survey the situation, they can easily encircle us.

I see one of my comrades jumping out of his hole and immediately slumping down. A direct shot through his head I find out later. The hole to the left is empty too. What shall I do? fire back at the two helmets below and expose my position to the enemy. Another thought crosses my mind, what if I kill them, I am a Mennonite, I would be a murderer. I don't know these enemy soldiers. Am I a coward if I leave without a shot?

The Russian tanks have come into firing range. I cannot stop them with a rifle. So reason and self preservation prevail. I gather my things together jump quickly out of my hole, run three steps back and throw myself down flat, crawl to the right, jump up again and run ten paces, as our trainer had shown us Bullets hit the ground where I had lain. I repeat the procedure until I am under cover in the barn. There I find my companion and the cow. We go into the village to the command post and report about our front line and the approaching Russian tanks. Nobody seems to have any plans for an attack or retreat.

I see a *"Panzerfaust"* (tank missile), leaning against the wall and tell the sergeant I will try it out on one of the Russian tanks. He has no objection. Very quietly, I stalk through the open woods avoiding any crackling dry branches. My rifle banging against the Panzerfaust makes a hollow sound, to avoid this, I hang it on a tree. I can pick it up on the way back. It is difficult to handle both at the same time. I am almost at the edge of the forest when I see three Russian Soldiers approaching. All of them are carrying submachine guns and have chains of ammunition hung around their necks. I envy them for their modern weapons. They come directly towards me, talking and laughing. I stand motionless beside a dry bush, any move would give me away and I have no weapon with which to defend myself. Only my eyes are moving and are following them. They pass by only twenty meters away and don't see me. I would have been an easy target for them. - God has blinded their eyes.

When they are gone, I continue to the rim of the woods and there stands the vicious T34 tank, about 25 meters away from me. I aim, shoot and the point of the Panzerfaust penetrates the armor of the tank, explodes and tears its side open. I suppose the three soldiers were the crew of that tank; now they have to find another vehicle.

I report back to the command post. A corporal and a machine gunner are just leaving for a sortie so I join them. Not very far from the blown up tank we spot another one and farther back two more. We crawl up to the first one. When they see us, the hatch of the tank opens, the crew jumps out and runs towards the tanks in the back. The gunner opens fire but they escape. Russian tank crews are afraid of the German Panzerfaust, which can in seconds convert their fortress into a coffin. I crawl closer, activate my hand grenade, rise and throw it through the open hatch into the tank. At that point, I feel a sharp blow at my head and shoulder, I faint and fall into the snow. When I gain consciousness again, the corporal is kneeling beside me; he has cut open his first aid kit, puts a compress against my head wound and bandages it. The snow beside me is red. The two men lead me to the first aid shelter, a potato cellar in a farmhouse. My head spins and my shoulder is punctured and hurts badly. The medic changes the head bandage, which is full of coagulated blood. "I can't do anything to your shoulder, you have to wait until they take you to a field hospital" and adds "You are lucky, that shell fragment cut through the heavy leather belt on your shoulder, without it you would be dead".

He lays me on the floor, covers me with a blanket and I fall into a coma.

Someone shakes me, "Wake up, the Russians are here". I slowly come to my senses and realize what has happened to me and where I am. I hear the medic shouting "All those who can walk take your stuff and get out as fast as you can the Russians will be here any moment." Still quite dizzy, I get up and hear some of the severely wounded immobile soldiers cry,"Sani nimm mich mit, Saaani…" (Medic, take me along). Those desperate cries resonate with me for a long time. What may happen to those poor soldiers? I am thankful that I can walk. As I climb the steps that lead to the road a soldier runs past, stops and looks at my bandaged head "You got it bad" he mumbles. Then he grabs his field flask, opens it and hands it to me "Here, drink this, it may get you going". I take a few gulps - good cognac! I feel some energy returning and I follow him. Russian tanks take aim at us and grenades explode around us. The soldier takes cover in the ditch. I don't care much and stagger on until I am out of sight of the tanks. A little farther down the road I see two German assault guns on tracks, its crew is getting ready to retreat with them. When the soldiers see me they shout, "Come on, get on board". They are out of ammunition for their guns and one of them is out of gas. The crew is hitching it to the first one when three Russian tanks appear on the hill and open fire. We quickly turn around and start downhill. The second vehicle cannot turn fast enough and runs against a tree. The crew jumps off, cuts it loose, puts a hand grenade into the gun barrel and blows it up, so that the Russians cannot use it against us. All of us who are sitting on the second one have to be moved to the operational one. It gets quite crowded but we all find a place. The Russian tanks come closer and take better aim. The crew of the immobile cannon asks for our grenades, ammunition and rifles. "We are going to show the Russians how far they can go", they tell us, and start towards the hill. We drive as fast as we can to get out of the reach of the Russian tank cannons.

We arrive in the next village, where they have an emergency field hospital. The seriously wounded stay here; we others are waiting for a vehicle to take us farther to the next field hospital. A farmer pulls up with his tractor and harvesting trailer and we are packed into it. It is getting dark and the roads are bumpy and slippery. The wounded groan and ask the farmer to drive more carefully. On an uphill road, he has to stop to let a military transport by. The wounded soldiers beg and curse him. "Shut off the engine to stop the jerking, we can't stand the pain". Their pleas become softer and finally die. He cannot shut off the engine; if he does, he could not start and move on again in the snow. At midnight, we reach the field hospital in a school building. A medic leads me to a straw mattress in the corridor and I doze off. Someone wakes me up and moves me on a stretcher to the operating table. The doctor asks what had happened, and gives me an injection. Several hours later I wake up wrapped in a blanket on another straw mattress in one of the classrooms. It is late in the morning. The doctor comes and checks my condition. "Your head wound was not too deep but your shoulder blade is punctured. That felt vest and heavy leather belt across your shoulder may have saved your life". He gives me the shell fragment that he had taken out of my shoulder. It is about the size of my little finger. I thank him for his work. He shakes my hand and leaves again. He looks pale and overworked.

They had to cut off my shirt and uniform jacket with the insignia, before they operated on me. The medics threw the blood soaked jacket out and with it my family pictures and letters from home and my small New Testament, bound in burgundy leather from my mother. I am sad about that loss.

I get a new shirt and jacket from the supply stockroom but I cannot put my right arm into the sleeve, it hurts too much. I walk to the other side of the room and see our company commander lying on a stretcher. He has been shot through both arms and thighs and cannot turn around by himself. It is strange to see your superior being so helpless. I go over to him and help him to change his position. We talk about our engagement with the Russians. He tells me the two assault cannons destroyed three Russian tanks and then ran out of ammunition. I mention that we lost one of the two and report about our unprotected right flank. I told him that I put two tanks out of action. He assures me, he will see that I get the Iron Cross for it, when he is up again. A smile comes to my lips, whenever that may be. The nurse comes, so I wish him well and return

We stay here for a few days to recuperate and then a truck takes us to a small harbor at the *Frische Haff, a* lake, which is separated from the Baltic Sea by a very narrow strip of land, the *Nehrung.* After three hours on a small ferry, we reach the harbor of Pillau on the Nehrung. We are taken to a military hospital in the city and for the first time we lie in real beds again but not for long. The Russian artillery bombards the city with shells for several days and we have to move again. The next nights we spend on a boat that takes us to *Gotenhafen* a harbor near Gdansk. The Red Cross puts railway passenger cars together and changes the seats into beds. We are unloaded from the boat into the makeshift hospital on wheels. In the evening, the train moves slowly out of the station. We are rolling west and our spirits rise. In the morning we reach the scenic *Tucheler Heide* (heath southwest of Gdansk), it seems so peaceful. Suddenly the train stops, - air raid alert. The train moves back into a more sheltered area. We hear the planes flying over us. I do not know how much protection the Red Cross sign on top of one of our cars will give us. Soon we move west again. At noon, the train slows down and switches over to a sidetrack to let a military transport pass. The staff uses the opportunity to serve us a lunch and change the bandages of the seriously wounded before we move on. Rumor spreads, 'the Russians have broken through the front lines and are controlling the tracks of our escape route ahead of us'. We stop again and wait for further news. A sudden jerk of the train makes us wonder what is going on. We notice the train is moving back again. Someone says we are going back to Danzig and will try to get out of Germany by boat to Denmark. This causes restlessness and tension. Some consider leaving the train and finding a way home on their own. We wait all night and the tension rises, we are afraid, some become frantic and the medical staff has difficulty calming them down.

At noon, the news spreads that German troops have pushed the Russians back and have opened the railway line again. We are moving now with full speed without interruption west towards Stettin and pass the place where the Russian troops had broken through the German lines. This was rescue in the nick of time, like someone opening a door for us to let us through and then closing it for good. The mood changes we are relieved and happy and many a prayer has been answered. We travel all night to avoid air attacks. The next stop is Berlin, where we load food and medical supplies. I have relatives living here, but there is no way of contacting them. Soon we travel through the beautiful Nature Park "*Lauenburgische Seen*" to the small town of *Ratzeburg* at the *Ratzeburger See*, south of Lübeck. The seriously wounded stay here in a hospital; where they will receive treatment. I walk down to the lake and enjoy the fresh air after spending so long in the sticky compartments of the train. Since the hospitals here are too crowded, we have to move. The medical staff renew our bandages and serve a hot meal before we are once more back in the train, which is taking us south to the city of *Mölln*. Like Ratzeburg, it is nestled between small lakes and forests and has so far been spared from air attacks.

The military hospital here is a safe haven for me for a while. My wounds are properly treated, my head wound is healing well but the cut in my shoulder is deep and full of pus and hurts; lifting something or lying down is quite painful. I sleep on three pillows and my neck and lower back try to take the pressure off my shoulder. During the first weeks, I only sleep a few hours at night. I can walk already to the lake in beautiful spring weather. For a moment, I forget the war and enjoy the display of color and the fragrance from the spring flowers. It is healing not only for my body but also for my soul, after the cruel fighting on the frontlines.

I send a letter to Uncle Gustav in Berlin, whom we had chosen to be our contact person. Several days later, I get a reply from him that he and his family, including Grandma, are well and that he has good news. My sister Magdalena is safe in the West. Her hospital has been transferred from Marienburg to Schwerin, about 60 km East of where I am now. My next letter goes to Schwerin to tell my sister where I am. A few days later I receive a phone call from her; what a joy to hear the voice of my sister again. She tells me that she has already arranged to have me transferred to Schwerin; which is normally not permitted. The chief surgeon has approved her request. In two weeks, I get an official transfer document and a train ticket to Schwerin. I look forward to seeing my sister again. When I arrive in Schwerin, I am already known as the brother of nurse Magdalena. She is very happy to have me in her care. It is almost a year since we have seen each other. So far we do not know where Mother and our other sister Christa are.

The military hospital where my sister works is in a school building. I am assigned to a classroom with six double bunk beds. My condition improves gradually and I look for opportunities to do something. Once a young nurse asks me to help her get some medical supplies from the main hospital, so we walk together, the basket with medicine between us, through town. I think she is beautiful and I fall in love with her, which makes the drab days in hospital a little more interesting.

Every noontime the nurses have to carry a big bucket with soup for twelve into our room, dish it out and then go and have their lunch. When they come back, they wash the dishes. I notice that they often look tired so I suggest to my fellow soldiers, "Why don't we wash the dishes? That would lighten their workload". I know where the bowl, the water and soap are so I start washing the dishes. Hesitantly one comrade comes and dries them; the others make jokes about us doing women's work. When the nurses come back, we are back in our beds again. They are so surprised and happy and thank us for doing this. The next day a few more volunteers come, word spreads around and soon we hear in other rooms the clatter of dishes while the nurses are having their lunch. Food is becoming scarce and unimaginative. Five days a week we are served dried vegetable grub mainly consisting of turnips and cabbage with a piece of carrot or pea sprinkled in. Having a sister here and being known to the staff sometimes has 'food benefits' for me.

The frontline fighting comes closer and all the able soldiers who can walk have to march west to Denmark, I am one of them. My sister is furious, "That is madness, you are staying here". She asks my nurse to put a heavy bandage around my foot and when the inspecting sergeant comes into our room, I show him my foot and he classifies me 'unfit'. I can stay. The next day several of those who left, come back wounded and tell us that American low flying fighter planes had taken aim at them, killed some, wounded several and a few escaped.

The tension grows; who is going to come to Schwerin first, the Americans or the Russians?. We take bets. It is the beginning of May, sunny weather. A rumor goes around that the army has opened their supply depot to the public and anybody can go and help themselves to food, tools and clothing. I go to investigate and stand in a long cue to get in. After about three hours it is my turn, not much is left and what is there is in bad array. Among the stuff lying around I find a dark blue pair of marine trousers, a small bale of air force and army uniform material and lining which I carry out. As I come to the main street, which I have to cross, I get a shock. US tanks have entered the town along the main road; they stand in a long line about one hundred meters apart, blocking the traffic from one side of the city to the other. I am too tired and weak to find an alternative route; I have to pass through there, in order to get back to my hospital on the other side. Not looking left or right I march right through the American line; I, a young man in a German air force uniform, and no one stops me. My sister is relieved when she sees me back again and tells me to go to bed and await the Americans there. It is the 8th of May the official end of the war.

It does not take long until someone pushes the door open and three Amis step in, guns drawn. One goes to each bed and asks "Weapon, camera, watch". Some hand over their possessions; most of us have nothing. When they have collected their loot, they leave. This is our first encounter with the enemy. A little later we have another more thorough inspection. We are ordered to remain inside the buildings. We look out of the window and see the guard on duty has pulled an armchair to the guardhouse, is sitting in it, feet up and sleeping, an unusual sight for us German soldiers. Gradually the atmosphere becomes more relaxed. We do not seem to present a danger to them anymore and they allow us to go into the fenced-in schoolyard. Only on special requests do we get a pass to leave the grounds. Some do not want to bother the guard and jump over the low fence to go to town, the guard does not seem to mind.

Four weeks later the Allies decide to divide occupied Germany into four zones. The area the Russians have occupied is the Russian Zone. The rest is parceled out, the North to the British, to the Americans the middle and southern region and the French get the area west of the Rhine We, in Schwerin, are now under British command. Now British soldiers come through the rooms and ask for weapons, cameras and watches, they are more polite than the Amies were, but have less luck; the Americans have taken them already. If we want to leave the premises, we have to apply for a pass and show it to the guard; he has no armchair anymore. The food we get is more varied and has a few more calories, otherwise not much is changing.

We have the British as our occupation force for four weeks, then we hear that the Russians are coming. Staff and patients become alarmed, for the Russians have a reputation of stealing and molesting people, they do this usually when they are drunk which is frequently.

Many are considering retreating with the British. Young nurses and some physicians have their packed suitcases beside their beds, my sweetheart nurse too and patients who have connections to the west are prepared to leave at short notice. I discuss with Magdalena what we should do. She feels she cannot abandon the seriously ill bed-ridden patients and decides to stay.

In the middle of July 1945, the British leave their position to the Russians and the guards at the entrance to our hospital change for the third time.

The Allied Command is partitioning Berlin into four sections, according to the Yalta agreement. The Russians keep about one third of East Berlin, the British will occupy the northwestern and the Americans and French the southwestern part. For the third time foreign soldiers come through our rooms and ask for weapons, cameras and watches. We tell them that the Amis and Brits have confiscated everything, they are just too late. They do not like this and start to search our beds. We get used to that treatment too. Our daily meals are becoming less varied and not so plentiful. We are more careful about jumping over the fence when we want to go downtown, those who do, bring interesting stories back. A Russian soldier stops a young man and demands his jacket. Reluctantly he complies and the Russian gives him his old one. The young man puts it on and walks away. After he has gone 50m the Russian shouts, "Stoi, Stoi" and runs after him. The young man outruns him. When he arrives home and takes the jacket off, he finds 10 expensive watches in its pockets. Another Russian confiscates a car that is parked on a hill. He releases the brake and lets it roll down. When it stops he does not know how to start it. He sees a man riding his bike down the road without touching the handlebars. He stops him, takes his bike and gives him the car. The fellow turns the key, pulls the choke and drives away from the cursing Russian who has fallen off the bike. A housewife tells of a simple Russian soldier coming into her kitchen. He sees that water is running from the kitchen faucet and wants to unscrew it and send it to Russia so that his family can mount it in their kitchen and have water too. There are more of such stories around.

After a few weeks, the Russians make an agreement with the British to have our hospital moved to Hamburg.

The hospital administration had arranged for nurses to live outside the hospital, my sister has rented a room near the hospital from an elderly lady, whose husband had died, and her only son had been killed in action. She lives now alone in a big house. Magdalena had mentioned to her that I have been transferred to the hospital where she works, so Mrs. Marten asks her to bring me over sometimes.

We wonder why our sister Christa has not arrived yet. She had phoned on April 25 to tell us that her air force unit was going to be dissolved and she would try to join us in Schwerin; it is now two months since that phone call. Another question is of great concern to us. Where is Mother? If she fled before the Russians came and is somewhere in a refugee camp, we would have heard from her via Uncle Gustav. Is she still at home or have the Russians taken her to Siberia? Is she still alive or did she die of starvation or from Russian bullets? We will never find out unless I go there and inquire. We two siblings have to make a crucial decision now. Shall I go with the hospital to the West, be safe, and wait for news which may never come or go and search for my mother. This could mean separation from my sister, insecurity, danger and perhaps death. We agonize about it and pray for discernment. I cannot shake a feeling that my mother is in difficulty and needs me and is waiting for me.

We go over to see Magdalena's landlady who has invited us. She serves a special meal of *'Dampfnudeln und Trockenobst'* (dumplings with dried fruit) for me on fine porcelain dishes - quite a difference from the food we receive in hospital, spooned out into metal bowls. Mrs. Marten tells me, almost in tears, how much I remind her of her son, who was my age and size. The meal she serves me was his favorite dish. We discuss our plans with her. She finds them noble. Before I leave, she offers me her son's almost new blue overalls which I can wear on top of my uniform. She also knows a railroad official who can provide access to the railway station for me. We are grateful for her help and more and more I become convinced that this is the way I have to go.

I try to keep my plans secret, but Georg, a comrade from Berlin, whom I have befriended, notices that I have something going on and asks, "Do you want to skedaddle?" I avoid a direct answer but when we are alone he asks, "If you are taking off, do you mind if I come along?" I make him aware of the dangers of such an undertaking, he assures me he understands and is ready.and willing to accompany me. I tell him of my plans. We start saving imperishable food from our daily meals as much as possible and Magdalena, with the help of good friends in the kitchen, collects bread and remnants from emergency rations.

I pack my few belongings and the 'treasures' I rescued from the army depot in my knapsack. Magdalena will ask her landlady if she can store them for me. I arrange to meet the railway man at the gates to the station. We get ready. It is summer and we can travel light. The day of my departure comes and with a heavy heart I say good-bye to my beloved sister who cared for me so well. We will be gone when she comes to the hospital tomorrow morning.

Chapter Five

A Dangerous Journey Home

The Russian guard on duty at the gate is dozing. Quietly we jump over the fence which encloses the school building and yard. He does not hear us.

For four months the school has been hospital and a kind of home for us ex soldiers. Here I was reunited with my sister, here my head wound healed and my shattered shoulder was treated. It was a temporary haven of rest after the terror of war and the dangers of front combat. Now I am leaving all this.

Walking along the road we have to be on the lookout constantly because the Russians imposed a curfew until 8:00 h and they are known for shooting first and asking questions later. We arrive without incident at the agreed upon place. It is five in the morning. After a few minutes we hear steps on the gravel path. Is it our contact person or a Russian patrol, we wonder? We hide behind a bush and see a single person approach. It must be the railway man who had promised to let us into the station. He greets us briefly pulls out his keys and opens the hidden gate to the freight train compound. He points to the little bridge in the background and says: "Cross that bridge, it leads to the main station. The train will leave in about 20 minutes. Good Luck!" He locks the gate behind us and is gone. We worm our way between the freight cars to the bridge and there we see it in tall letters, *Schwerin Hauptbahnhof.* The station is heavily guarded - only occupation troops and personnel with special passes are allowed inside. We watch what is going on and wait in hiding until two minutes before departure. Then we climb from the back side into an empty compartment. Quietly we sit down on the back bench until the train moves out. The sun has not come up yet, so it is still dark but promises to become a beautiful day. At the next station the conductor comes in, points his flashlight at us and asks politely "Your tickets and permits please". We have neither one. "How did you get into the train?" We tell him, "An 'angel' opened the gate for us and let us in, he had compassion on us". I tell him that I am looking for my sick mother in the occupied territory. He softens a little but replies" Do you know that when the authorities find out about this I will lose my job and could be arrested?"

Not many people are traveling that early. After a while he comes back and tells us that the second station from here, *Ludwigslust*, is the old border between the Russian and British Zones and all passengers have to leave the train; it will be searched and the GPU, the Russian secret police, will nab you. He suggests that we leave a station before, walk across the border and join the train again afterwards.

When the train stops we disembark and start walking. The sun has just come out, it is getting warmer and our bags are light. We wear all the clothing we own. For me it means a pair of air force pants and a somewhat remodeled black tank soldier's uniform jacket. On top I wear blue mechanics overalls which my sister had organized for me in order to hide my uniform. In our bags we have a change of underwear and some food.

After half an hour's march we meet an older woman coming out of her house. We ask her how to get to the border. She looks us over, than takes us to the back of her yard and points at a man in the distance. "You see that man working there, the border runs at the end of his field". She shows us the best way to get to him and adds: "Be careful! the Russians are controlling the border" We sneak up to the farmer and ask if he needs help with the potato harvest. "No thanks," he says, "You better get out of here fast and don't put me in danger". We lie down in the furrows and tell him our real reason. His attitude changes and he gives us good advice. "That dirt road about 150 m down is controlled every 10 min. by Russian patrols. If the first one disappears behind that hill you have about 5 min. before the next one comes up". We observe the procedure from our hiding place for a while and go into action. We crawl along the furrows to the road, then creep over it into the woods on the other side and disappear behind the bushes. The crackling of twigs under our feet must have alerted the coming guards; we hear "Stoi, Stoi", and two shots are fired in our direction. We stop and listen. Nothing happens; carefully we walk on for a while until we come to a building. Is this the Russian guard house we wonder? We observe it from our cover and find nothing unusual. I gather my courage and approach it from the back, Georg stays behind and waits. The farmer, who answers the door, tells us that we are fairly safe here. I wave Georg to come and the startled farmer shows us the road to the next railway station.

After a good hour's walk we see Grabow station. We are lucky; we find out the next train to Berlin leaves in about half an hour, our typical approach to board it would be from the back, avoiding the gate to the platform. We think the little caboose a fairly safe place to ride in, but we are wrong. I have just settled in when someone jerks the door open. I look directly into the face of a Russian secret police officer. "Come out," he yells. I have no choice. Georg, my buddy, slides quietly unnoticed through the back door and hides behind the tracks. The officer drags me to the platform, where another dozen passengers who were pulled out of the train, are standing, mainly young girls and a few older men. "First they will interrogate you and then send you to labor camp" quips one of them.

This cannot be the end of my journey, I reflect. I start to argue with the officer, "I am an invalid, I cannot work" and I pull my arm out of my sling and let it dangle. My shoulder is still bandaged up and sore. He does not budge. I have difficulty lying to him but out of desperation I try everything. Someone said if you tell them the truth, they don't believe you and if you lie, they listen. "I have to go to see the doctor," I say with a whimpering voice. Watching him carefully, I notice a slight change in his features and, when the train gets ready to leave, I dangle my right arm in front of me, talk about doctor, hospital and treatment and move slowly towards the train. My buddy opens the door and I jump in. "You have some nerve" says a voice with a strong Berlin accent in the background, "He could have shot you for escaping custody".

They tell us that the GPU, the secret police, recognizable by their green caps, will do searches at every station. We will have to come up with another solution. The train slows down and rolls into the next station. We open the door and jump onto the platform before it comes to a halt. I look around and see a two foot long strip iron lying on the tracks. It looks like a wrench. I pick it up and show it to Georg. Slowly we walk along the train bending down to the wheels and couplings of the coaches, knocking with our 'wrench' against the axles. In my blue overalls I could be taken for a trainman. We watch out for the GPU and by the time the search is over and the train ready to leave, we have reached the locomotive again, step into the compartment and do the same thing at the next stations. No problems anymore. The closer we come to Berlin the more crowded the train gets and between the last stations we have to travel outside on the running board, holding on to the door handles and rails.

At the Lehrter Bahnhof in Berlin we have to leave the train. I thank my strip iron and lay it down softly on the tracks. Georg is excited. This is his hometown and soon his trip is over. After an hour's walk, mostly through ruins and rubble, we come to the street where the house of his parents is still standing. When we open the gate to his yard, someone from across the fence shouts "We got your father and did away with him and we will get you too." I ask Georg what he means. "I will tell you later, let's go inside". The joy is great when the mother has her son again but something is wrong, I feel, and soon Georg's mother tells us the story. The communist neighbor, who had shouted across the fence, had denounced her husband. He had been an official in the political education department of the NSDAP and the police had picked him up and tortured him. He came home a sick man. Not long ago they picked him up again and she does not know where he is or whether he will ever return.

She gives us something to eat and we add to it from our supplies. Finally she says "Georg you cannot stay here", and with tears in her eyes adds" I do not want to lose you too". The next night we spend at Georg's aunt but she too gets nervous and tells him he cannot stay much longer. We come to the conclusion that George has to leave Berlin until the dust has settled. The best way would be to accompany me to my home in West Prussia.

We buy and scrounge some supplies and get some official papers. I have a document from Schwerin with my picture on it and a stamp below. Georg gets one through friends from a Berlin office. The family gives us money for tickets. Again we have to sneak out in order to avoid the patrols that check the curfew. We reach the Lehrer Bahnhof and buy tickets to Stettin, now a border town in Poland. No more searches east of Berlin. The train stops on the German side of the city. The station looks like a refugee camp. People are milling around or sleeping on, between or beside the tracks, a very unusual sight. The banks beside the tracks are littered with grand pianos, baroque sofas, beds and other furniture, hand carved chests, chandeliers, fancy bookshelves, washing machines, and various other items. Russian officers had removed them from German villas and hope to transport them to Russia. Some of them must have stood here for a long time as they are split, rotten and falling apart.

First we have to get our bearings and sort things out. We find an empty space between the tracks on the outskirts of the station where we can put our bags down. Beside us a German-Lithuanian family has set up camp. Their trek had gotten through to the British Zone and they wanted to stay there with German relatives but, when the British found out where they had come from, they handed them over to the Russians who forced them to return home. They have been here for over a week and do not know how to go on from here. We adopt them as our family and they become the centre for our operations.

From here we want to get a train to Poland. It looks like a difficult task. We try to get some information from Polish train staff but they reply in curses in Polish, or German if they hear us ask in German but we only know two or three words in Polish and try to pick up a few more. The second day is not much better. We check our supplies and find we should look for some food. I spot an apple tree in a side yard and am climbing onto the bottom branch, when I hear someone shouting and firing a few shots. The bullets whistle through the leaves beside me so I know these apples are not for us. Down in the yard beside a storage building, we see a pile of potatoes guarded by a soldier. We watch him; he walks around the building and returns in about five minutes. We have to be quick. All our pockets are full before he comes back. The family receives the potatoes thankfully. They have all their cooking utensils with them and wood from broken furniture, oak and rosewood, is lying around everywhere and soon we have a tasty potato soup together.

Helmut Soldier in WW II

Helmut refugee, 1946

With Alfred in front of parsonage in Handorf

We are getting worried and impatient. The second day has passed and we still have not found out how to move on from here. We observe an older conductor talking in a friendly manner to some passengers, so we approach him and he waves us into an empty building. "A passenger train to Warsaw leaves Stettin at 22:00 h tomorrow from this platform" he tells us in almost perfect German and leaves. On one wall of the building is an old railway map. We study it carefully and memorize all the German and Polish names of the stations en route. We will have to change trains in Krutsch (Kyrgyz) and find a train from there that is going north-east towards Gdansk.

On our return we pass the potato pile again. Nobody is there so we start to fill up. A sudden, "Stoi," startles us. This time they catch us. In a friendly voice I ask the soldier who has pointed his automatic gun at us, "Parlez vous Francais" He is taken aback. I am relieved he does not understand, because that is all the French I know. I joke and ask: "Franzoski Kartoshki? hungri" and gesticulate with my hands in French fashion. He suddenly smiles "ah Franczuz, Kamerad" and shakes my hand. "Come to the front; there are better potatoes".He gives us a bag and we fill it. "Merci, Kamerad," I shake his hand again and we take off waving to him. Well, we managed that one and enticed a soldier to do a good deed for 'a comrade in arms' and that, perhaps, made his day. Later the Lithuanian Oma bakes special potato crepes for the family for supper, which we all enjoy.

Tomorrow is the big day. I am a little nervous about it. We sleep on the tracks again. The first night somebody warned us to tie our bags down because the Poles would steal them. I use mine as a pillow and have fallen asleep, when suddenly it moves, somebody tries to pull it out from under my head. I had fastened it to the tracks. I jump up and chase him and he runs and curses.

The next day we check our bags and add a few boiled potatoes to our supplies. We say good-bye to our Lithuanian friends and wish them luck. We are sorry that we cannot do more for them.

It is getting dark. We go to the platform from which the train to Warsaw is going to leave and wait until everybody else has boarded, and then we squeeze into the crowded cargo compartment, find an empty spot in the corner and sit on the floor. The train jerks a few times and leaves the station. After a while a noisy conductor pushes himself

through the aisle and his flashlight shines on us, "Tickets!" he demands
in Polish. We had put our collars up, snore quietly and pretend to sleep.
A gentle looking man had watched us when we came in and we hear
him talk to the conductor. The flashlight turns to somebody else and he
disappears. Now we can sleep undisturbed. The first sunlight is shining
into the compartment when we wake up. I hope we have not missed our
transfer station. It is not easy to identify the names in the twilight. We
try to decipher the next one, K-r-z-y-z. This is it. We take our bags and
leave the train. Our Polish guardian angel must have left before us.

We are standing on the platform again, seeing the train to Warsaw
leave and have no idea how to move on from here. Our questions to
find a connecting train are met with the same reaction as before; the
trainmen either ignore us or they curse us. Finally we meet a station
official who listens to us. No passenger trains are leaving in the next days
but a freight train is leaving for Gdansk. This is all we need to know.
We have two more hours to spend, so we hide in empty luggage rooms
or walk briskly from one platform to the other. All of a sudden we hear
some clamor, shouting and cursing. A big blind drunk Russian Officer
staggers up the stairs to the next platform urinates down on the tracks
and molests other passengers. A Polish conductor asks him to leave. He
stares at him takes one swing and knocks him to the floor. The poor
guy picks himself up and fetches the station police. Five burly men
approach the Russian with the same request to leave. When he does not
follow and they touch him he swings again, "You Polish swine don't
dare to touch a Soviet officer". They retreat trying to avoid a shoot out.
They enlist a Russian soldier. He walks towards the drunk, puts his arm
around him, talks quietly and leads him out of the station. Poles and
Russians are often not on good terms. The Poles have a hurt national
pride and the Russians have the power and bad manners. Sometimes
Poles fare better with the Germans, their former enemies, than with
their *liberators*.

The freight train rolls into the station and we take advantage of the
brawl on the other platform to board it from the backside, crawl into
the caboose and then swing ourselves onto the roof of the box car. We
have learned the caboose is not a safe place to travel in. We lie flat on our
backs and hope nobody has seen us or can notice us up here. It seems

like an eternity until the train finally leaves the station. It is not bad up here, the sun is shining, we have a good view, we are going in the right direction and do not have to walk. After a few hours it is becoming dark and cool. We cannot spend the night here, what if we fall asleep and roll off the roof. The train slows down and moves into a switching yard. This gives us an opportunity to slide down from the roof of the boxcar and go inside. We force the door open and see one corner sectioned off with a bench and some straw on the floor. Someone must have slept here we figure. When we come close, two boys about ten and twelve years old crawl out of the straw. They were separated from their parents when they were sent to the *Kinderlandverschickung* (families from cities sent their children into the country for safety from bombing attacks) and are trying to find their way home. Everything is quiet, nothing is moving, so we decide to lie down and sleep. To morrow we have a long day ahead of us.

The jerking and swinging of the cars awakens us. We are moving again and from the light shining through the ventilation holes it must be close to morning. We share some of our food with the boys and when we are finished with breakfast a Polish trainman comes in. "What are you doing here?" he asks, first in Polish and then in broken German. "It is illegal for you to ride in freight cars", he tells us. "Do you have any identification?" We show him our papers; he takes them and moves on. A few hours later he comes back and tells us he is not allowed to let us stay here, we have to move. We know the legality of the situation is not his concern, he wants a bribe, but we have no money and no valuables. We try to explain, but he leaves again with our papers, mumbling something about police. After a while he comes back again and tells us in a few minutes we will be in Tczew (Dirschau) which is the end of the line. We explain our situation to him again and ask him for our papers and the boys beg him too. He finally realizes he cannot get anything out of us. Reluctantly and angrily he returns them to us and mentions, "The Germans have blown up the bridge across the Wisla if you want to go to Malbork you will have to take the ferry". We leave the train and walk down to an old military pontoon boat. A rope is strung from front to back to avoid uneven loading. A big trailer truck, a military jeep, a farmer with horse and buggy, many bicycles and pedestrians are on it when we arrive. The ferry operator maneuvers the strange boat across the wide and shallow river. A Soviet soldier comes with him and is now talking to the truck driver in the back. They discuss something and the soldier goes to the next person. He is collecting money for the crossing we figure. How do we get around that? We separate, walk slowly to the front, enjoy the view, duck under the rope, marvel at the river and get back behind the truck, whose driver has already paid his fare.

We ask the driver of the truck, a young fellow, where he is going. "To Malbork", he answers; that is where the two boys want to go. They had been evacuated from the town and are now going back to look for their parents, could he take them along? "50 zlotys", he says. They have no money, we tell him, so he goes down to ten and finally agrees to take them along. We, as their guardians, would have to accompany them. "No way" he protests. When he drives off the ferry we help the boys onto the trailer and climb in with them. He does not have much of a choice as there are four of us and he is alone. It is only a 20 minute ride and he drives fast. He slows down when we come to the narrow floating bridge across the Nogat. Here he has to drive very slowly and, just before he reaches land on the Malbork side, we say goodbye to the boys and jump off the vehicle.

This is familiar territory. For three years I went to boarding school here. Often we walked the promenade along the Nogat River, looking up to the Marienburg, the proud castle of the German Knights and seat of their Grand Master. Over there was the boathouse of our high school, where we lowered our boats down to the Nogat River with a crane. It is a different sight now. The whole castle, as we see it from the water side is destroyed. We enter the city through the narrow medieval *Marientor;* right behind it is the once famous pedestrian shopping area, *Unter den Lauben* (under the Arches) which consisted of a long row of stores, their lower floors recessed to form an arcade.on both sides of the market place, on the higher side the "Hohe Lauben" on the lower side the "Niedere Lauben" We used to walk along there when I was a student here, looking at the interesting layouts of clothes and sportswear in the windows. All the arches are now collapsed and the stores are a heap of rubble, only the ruin of the tower of the Gothic town hall sticks out like a sore thumb.

We walk through the debris of former stores past the upper part of the castle. A few remnants of the walls of the Grand Master's palace are still standing; the chapel has no roof and the huge mosaic statue of St.Mary, which adorned its gable façade, lies in pieces in the moat. We leave the old city and go down to the railway station. It is destroyed, too, only one wing is haphazardly repaired. We walk in. Two women are cleaning the empty waiting room. They speak German to each other. We ask them about trains to Elbing (Elblag); they are perplexed to see us "Why do you ask and what are you doing here at this time?

The next train is going in two days". We tell them our story and they offer to keep us over-night; we can continue our journey tomorrow. We meet them again after their shift. They take us home, share their supper with us and let us sleep on the kitchen floor. We are up early and leave with them. At the Sandhof Bridge we approach the Polish checkpoint and policemen questioning people that cross it. The girls help us to get through the bottleneck on the bridge by entertaining the policemen so that we can sneak through the barrier.

We are free, marching along the main road which is lined with tall elm trees. There are 28 km to cover before I reach home. Soon we smell some trouble. An army truck with noisy Soviet soldiers is approaching. We had better give them the right of way so we hide behind some bushes in the ditch until they are gone. In Altfelde we leave the main road and use some back roads to reach my uncle Richard's farm.

Perhaps we can share supper with them and rest for the night. A lone Russian soldier stops us and wants to see our papers. He looks at them upside down which tells us that he cannot read. We tell him we are coming from work and are on our way home. He smiles and lets us go. I know the dirt road to Uncle Richard's farm well; I usually spent a few weeks of my summer holidays there with my cousins. It is getting dark. We carefully scout around. The main residence has been destroyed. A Polish flag hangs on the service building and we feel it is too risky at this time of the day to go inside, so we continue on our way home. I want to take the short cut over the small wooden footbridge, but that is gone. We have to take the long way around on the dam of the meandering Thiene River. On the left was the pump house where we used to chat with miller Natkowski. It is smashed now and the low lying meadows, including our property in the Aue, are all under water. Farther on the path splits, the left fork leads across the meadows to Uncle Cornelius' estate. We take the right one along the top of the river dam. The moon has come up and in the background we see the silhouette of Giesebrecht's windmill. The wings are sticking into the sky like huge fingers. We are not far from the road and the bridge. Fifty meters down from the road are the former changing rooms of the fenced- in swimming area where I learned to swim and across from the river is the house of my first 'girlfriend'. We cross the bridge over the Thiene and follow the main road. It is easier walking now. We are in Alt-Rosengart, my home village. On the right is the largest newly rebuilt farm in the village. Our former mayor Peters, a nominal Mennonite lived there. Across from his entrance gates starts the long drive way that leads to our farm. After the first thirty meters down we step into water. It is dark now and the moon gives a faint light. I tell Georg to stay in the middle of the path, between the rows of willows on each side. If he walks past the trees the water will go over his head. Hip deep in the water we grope our way more than we see it. The dark spot on the right must be our house and soon we step out of the water onto dry land again. "Georg, we have arrived", I whisper. It is midnight, August first 1945. I walk around the house where my parent's bedroom used to be and knock on the window. I hear someone snore. I knock again, "Wer ist da?" (who is there) a scared female voice asks. "Don't be afraid," I calm her "I am the son of Mrs. Lemke". Silence for a while, and then she shouts upstairs. "Frau Lemke, ihr Sohn ist da". (Mrs.Lemke your son is here). My eyes fill with tears, Mother is here. Our operation to find her has been successful. Thank you, God.

Home Again

Slowly I walk back to the front door. I wait a few minutes until Mother comes downstairs, still in her nightgown, and opens the door. I am home again. Mother looks at me, "Is it really you? I felt you would come; *Wenn die Not am größten, ist Gottes Hilfe am nächsten* "(when the need is greatest, God's help is nearest), she says. I put my arm around my frail mother. We stand there quietly in the moonlight and tears run down her hollow cheeks."

The power lines are destroyed, there is no electricity and it is dark in the front room when we go inside. Mother lights a candle and sees Georg; I introduce him to her. "I am so glad, that you have come, thank you", she says. "This journey must have been hard for you two, and very dangerous. You must be exhausted". She takes us upstairs and makes beds for us with the bedding that the Russians have left. I sleep in my old room again and Georg in the room next door. We are dead tired from the long trip and the exertion of the day and fall asleep immediately.

It is almost noon when we wake up. Mother has made something to eat for us, a potato dish and fruit, the only staples she has.

We learn to know her companions, Frau Lange, who answered my knock at the window, and her two blind, grown up daughters. They have eaten already and Mother sits with us. I see her now in daylight; she has aged a lot and is still recovering from a severe typhoid fever. Her long black hair has fallen out and is now slowly growing again. With that grey 'crew cut' she looks somewhat strange to me.

I want to know, what she had gone through after I left for the army. She hesitates at first and after a while begins to tell.

"After the harvest uncle Heinrich was drafted to the Volkssturm. (Army of unfit men and older boys) Shortly before Christmas, Anton, our farm hand, took his holiday and never came back afterwards. I had to feed and milk the cows myself. When the Russian front came close, Frau Gehrman, our long time house guest, and the retired couple from Berlin, whom I had taken in when they were bombed out, left with the last train. I packed everything, food, clothing and valuables on the wagon and was ready to leave but the army used the roads to get supplies to the front and we were not allowed to move out until they gave the order to evacuate. That order never came. In the night of the 25th of January, Russian soldiers came to our farm before I could get out. They searched the house, the stables and the barn for German soldiers and took what they found useful. The following days other soldiers came, searched the whole house more thoroughly and took everything that was packed with them; then they rounded the cattle up and herded it away. They needed people to care for it and one day they picked me up and took me to a farm where they had gathered the cattle that was still alive. For three months I had to feed and milk the cows there. Some younger women whom the Russians had taken to work there were often abused and raped by the soldiers. With me was a woman who had two blind daughters. I befriended her and helped to guide one blind daughter. We worked and slept together. When the Russians got ready to take the cattle farther east towards Russia and ordered us to help to drive it, I approached one of the older guards and told him that we could not go along with the two blind girls. He had pity on us and on the night before they were to depart he told us to leave quietly, and he would try to find someone else. We escaped and I took the three women along to our house. The pump house on the river which pumps the water from the low-lying areas was out of order and the water had flooded most of the land around our farms and the water wells.

A few weeks after my return I got sick, a serious case of typhoid fever and no doctor, nurse or medicine was available to treat Germans. I feared I would not survive. I am not yet quite over it", she concludes.

We go into the living room to meet the Langes. The younger of the girls is seriously sick, "Typhoid Fever", Mother tells us. The next morning she dies. Georg and I arrange for her funeral. The old wheelwright, Mr. Driediger, builds an open box for a coffin; we wrap the body in roofing paper and bury her in the Mennonite cemetery. It seems we arrived at the right time to take care of the sad situation which Mother never could have managed.

After a few days of grieving, Frau Lange suggests to Mother, that they should go home. Since Georg and I had come, there might not be enough to eat for all of us for very long. and I could care for her. Mother tries to persuade her to stay but she is determined to go. She packs together the few belongings, that they still have, takes Frieda, her other daughter, by the hand and leaves early next morning.

Georg is afraid he might catch typhoid fever too and decides to go back to Berlin, before he gets sick. His communist neighbor might have calmed down. A few days later I say good bye to my faithful comrade and wish him a safe trip home. I never see him again. The rumor goes that he arrived in Berlin came down with typhoid fever but recovered, studied dentistry and practiced it in the city's outskirts. However, I could never verify that.

Now Mother and I are alone on our farm. I had saved a loaf of corn bread for Mother but when I take it out of my bag, I discover it is completely moldy; time, heat and moisture has probably caused this. It is especially hard for Mother to throw it out, since she has not eaten bread for months.The Russians and Poles took all the flour and grain we had stored and what they left, Mother had used up. It is now up to me to provide food.

As we walked home a week ago, I noticed that not all grain fields had been harvested. There is one with a good stand of winter wheat which belonged to Adolf Deutschendorf, the father of my aunt Tante Ella. He will never harvest anymore. The Russians shot him and his son because they were *capitalists*. Mother found their bodies lying behind their house

Before sunrise Mother and I get into our makeshift boat, a watertight trough, used to scald pigs, to remove their bristles after they have been slaughtered. It looks like an open coffin with the sideboards elongated to form handles to carry it. For better balance we added some outriggers on the sides.

We row to the street, tie the boat to a tree and walk across to the wheat field which lies above the flood water level. We go a short distance into the field so that we cannot be seen and cut the best ears of wheat, stuff them into our jute sacks, and carry them into the boat. I have to help Mother with hers, because she is too weak to carry anything. Our boat hardly carries us and the heavy sacks. We row home and empty them onto a white sheet on the barn floor. With an old flail I beat the grains out, sift them in the old grain-cleaning machine and shovel the clean kernels into the grist mill, a new one which Father had bought. I screw a handle on the flywheel to change it to hand operation. It is hard work turning that wheel a few thousand times around, especially with my wounded shoulder, but it is worth it. We now have flour for fresh, homemade bread and bran for porridge. Mother even tries to bake a cake and make crepes, a good variation from potato soup and fried or boiled potatoes. Our potato supplies are used up, so we have to get new ones.

Several neighbor women, who could not flee before Russian troops came unexpectedly into our village, had planted potatoes in the spring in a field which was not flooded. It belongs to farmer Grübnau who had quickly harnessed his fiery black horse before the sleigh, taken his wife and some food along and galloped away, barely escaping from the Russians who were already entering his yard. Mother had seen him dash by our window. Our neighbor Reddig's house is flooded and they have moved in with the Heskes to higher ground beside the road. Mother is the only one who lives on an 'island'.

The potatoes are now ready for harvest. Frau Cornelsen, who had helped with the planting, will not eat them anymore. She is dead. A neighbor had invited her to bake bread with her. As she was going home, hiding three small loaves under her apron, a Russian soldier stopped her and demanded the bread. She begged him to leave her at least one loaf. "O.K, keep one and run home," he laughed. She had almost reached her house, when he raised his gun and shot her dead from the back. The life of a German woman is worth nothing to the Russians.

We row to the potato field and meet Christel (19), Dora (16) and one of the Heske's boys. I dig the potatoes and the others gather them into their bags. We are happily working together when we hear noises on the street above us and women crying. We hide in the furrows among the potato plants until it gets quiet. Mother goes up and finds Frau Reddig and Frau Preuss sitting there with bloody faces. She gives first aid and tries to console them. Two drunken Russian soldiers had come by looking for the girls. When the two women did not reveal their whereabouts, they beat them with frying pans and finally left cursing and threatening that they would come back and get them.

The girls have to be constantly on guard and hide when Russians are in sight. Mother told me, when the first Russian soldiers came, they had gang-raped them and both had contemplated suicide, they were so upset. In her desperation Frau Reddig asked Mother over and she talked to the girls about God's love, forgiveness and new beginning and they recovered from their shock and stayed in contact with her. They had tried before to find creative ways to protect the girls from the Russians. They had squeezed them into a baby crib, covered them with a baby blanket, and put a soother in their mouth or they hung a big sign 'Typhoid Fever' on the door.

Mother comes back and we finish our job, divide up the potatoes and then we row home. We again have a supply of our staple food.

Everywhere, at any time, we are exposed to the whims of the Russians.

One day, I am out in the boat searching for some additional food and see a truck with bawling, drunken soldiers on it approaching. I am still about 150m away from the road. The soldiers see me, stop and take aim at my boat. I duck and the bullets hit the water right and left of me. They shout and roar off again.

West Prussia is now officially under Polish administration and the Russians are transferring some power to the Polish authorities, the militia and police. A new order is issued: all Germans living in Polish occupied Germany are to be identified. They have to wear an armband over their right arm. Mother sews a white armlet from an old bed sheet and stitches a black swastika on it, as required. I put it over my arm; only the color is different from what we were wearing before, a red armband with a swastika in a white circle. The Poles must have realized that too and next week mother replaces the swastika with a "**N**" Njiemczye (Deutscher) It reminds me of the Polish workers who worked for german farmers in our village, the NS Government made them wear a yellow triangle as a badge, to identify them as Poles. Workers from different countries had to wear different colors. I wear mine stoically, remembering what we did to them.

One day, the Polish militia signs me up to work for the mayor. Alt-Rosengart has a mayor again, I find out. He has chosen the biggest and newest house in the village, the one that belonged to our former mayor Peters. The Polish 'Starost' does not feel safe enough to move into his new house yet, he is afraid Russian soldiers, who are still roaming around, will steal his belongings and take off with his cows. He feels safer living in Grunau beside the Polish police station.

My job is to care for his four cows, herd them from the stable to the fenced-in meadow and watch for eight hours that they don't break out and that nobody steals them. It is an easy job that gives me time to read and learn Polish. In the evening I take the cows back to the stable and tie them into their stalls. The cow owner does not trust me to milk them, but I get one liter of milk as my day's wages. Now Mother can make milk soup with dumplings. Every morning I trudge the four km to my job site. I have no watch, so I work on 'flexible time'. I arrive early when the sun is shining brightly and on a cloudy day, when it is darker, I start work later, the daylight is my guide. The sun sets now earlier and it is getting darker when I come home.

On one of those evenings, coming home late, I see a woman in a black dress, a dark shawl around her head and shoulders approaching on the street, just before I am going to turn into our driveway. She seems to be afraid of me. After we pass each other, we both look back. She hesitates, turns around and comes slowly towards me. She lifts her shawl, looks at me and asks, *"Bist du nich der Sellche ihr Jung?"* (Are you Selma's boy?) It is Tante Mariechen, Mother's favorite cousin. We embrace each other and tell our stories. They too, had been overrun by the Russians. She has walked over 40 km to see if her sisters family is still alive - a remarkable woman. I mention that Mother would be overjoyed if she would visit her and stay overnight with us, but she wants to go on to Grunau before it gets too dark. What an unusual incident!

One morning as I am going to work, a horse-drawn wagon stops. A Russian soldier waves me over and orders me to get on the wagon. I refuse and tell him I have a job to attend to. He interrupts me points at his gun and tells me," get on"! I have no choice. The faces of the people on the wagon look familiar to me and I recognize them as the children of our Mennonite Prediger Bartel. My sister Magdalena did her household practicum on their farm. The soldier drives us to a big potato field and tells us to dig potatoes, which we do all day. In company with them the work is more entertaining. When it is getting dark, he drives us back to the village. Bartels invite me to stay the night at their place. I meet the rest of the family. They share with me their meager supper and we have a lot to talk about. The Russians had caught up with their trek on the way west, had taken their horses and everything they found useful in their luggage, so that they had to walk home which took them several days.

The Russian guard tells me in no uncertain terms to report again for work in the potato field the next day. but the next morning I thank the Bartels for taking me in and go back to my cows. The Russians can find somebody else to work for them and they are good at that.

One evening when I come home from work, I look for my boat where I usually hide it but find it in another place. I wonder who has used it, and if something happened to Mother. I rush home and find her in the living room. She looks sad. I ask what has happened "Do you notice anything?" she replies. I look around, the piano is gone. She tells me, she was playing some of her favorite piano pieces and hymns, as she often does when she feels sad and lonely. All of a sudden she noticed three Russian soldiers standing under the living room window, listening. She was startled and stopped playing. Then they came in, rummaged through the house, came back to the living room and asked Mother to play again. She played a hymn. They enjoyed it so much, that they carried the heavy piano into the boat and took it away; we never saw it again. We have to learn to let go of earthly treasures.

I have been working for the mayor of Alt-Rosengart for a while and am curious to find out what his future home, our former Mayor Peters' new house, looks like inside. Quietly I walk through the alley that leads to the living quarters. All doors are locked. From a piece of wire I bend a skeleton key and carefully try the front door, it does not open. I go to the back door, try again a few times and finally get into the kitchen. What chaos! Drawers are emptied, dishes on the floor, furniture toppled and broken, nothing useful is left in this jumble. The Peters did not enjoy their beautiful home for very long. I get nervous, sneak out and lock the door. On the way out I take a look into the tool shed and see an animal trap. That can be useful I think and take it along. I notice something moving behind the bushes. I am startled. A small white rabbit looks out from underneath. I manage to catch it, slide it into my pocket and take it home. My old rabbit cage is still around; I put the rabbit in and hide it behind the empty chicken coop. An animal is on the farm again. Some herbs and weeds are still around to feed it and I pick some on my way from work. We hope to have a rabbit roast later in the year, when the food becomes scarcer. But that dream is gone, when a troop of Russian soldiers comes to the house. Searching for food and 'valuables', they find our precious white rabbit, kill it and take it along. I am spared the trauma of doing it myself later.

It is late October and totally unexpectedly we have a visitor. Anni, from Aunt Annchen's children's home in Sorgenfrei, comes walking through the water. She has spent many a holiday with us and knows the area quite well. We wonder why she did not go with the other children when Sorgenfrei was evacuated. It turned out that she did not want to leave and, in the meantime, has stayed at several places until she decided to come and see us. She does not want to tell us much about that time. Shortly after her arrival, I become ill and find it hard to get up in the morning and go to work. I ask Anni, who is now sixteen, if she would like to replace me at my job. I introduce her to my boss and leave again. I barely make it home as my head hurts and my stomach is convulsing. My mother suspects typhoid fever which the symptoms indicate. She is right. For two weeks I have to fight off high fever, diarrhea and headaches. Mother has to change the bedding and since I am sweating during the night, wash my nightgown every morning as they are soaking wet

Anni does my job faithfully and brings home a liter of milk every evening. Milk seems to be the only thing my stomach tolerates. I ask God to keep me alive for my mother's sake; she is still weak and can hardly take care of me in my condition. Doctors, nurses and medicine are not available for Germans. Gradually I begin to feel a little better again.

One late afternoon, I am sitting at the window, looking out when I hear voices below and see three Russian soldiers shaking the last apples from our only apple tree that is left. I know what they are up to. I put my old 'loden' coat over my nightgown and go downstairs to be with Mother. After the three have ransacked the house they leave again. The oldest of them, a drunken officer, sees the basement window and wants to know what is behind it. He does not believe me when I tell him the basement is filled with water and inaccessible. He has to find out for himself and demands that I show it to him. When I open the door to the basement, he pushes me in and I step into the water and splash it around. He sees it, seems satisfied and leaves. The two younger soldiers had left in the boat, while he was searching the basement. Mother tells him the others have left and shows him the way, but he insists going in the opposite direction to the other street. We try to persuade him to follow his comrades, but he is stubborn and gets angry. He demands that I direct him as he goes along the flooded driveway. So I stand there, barely recovered from typhoid fever, in a loden coat over my pajamas and shout, "Keep left" or "right" and wave my hands until he cannot hear or see me anymore. We go back inside the home and are glad that they are gone. All of a sudden we see the two younger soldiers coming back. They want to know where their comrade is. They are suspicious and accuse me of having killed him and done away with him. We try desperately to convince them that their comrade chose the other route, but they don't believe us "You killed him; we are going to shoot you". They load their guns. Mother is pleading with them to believe us, but that does not seem to move them. They order me to stand against the wall and raise my hands, I oblige. I do not feel any fear of death. Standing there with my hands lifted up, I try to console Mother "My life is in God's hand, he can save me and, if I have to die, he will provide for you". A few seconds after I say this, the older of the two soldiers lowers his rifle and pushes the rifle of his comrade aside. They start what seems to be a heated argument. I don't know what has suddenly changed the mind of one soldier. Did he understand what I said about being in God's hands or did Mother's pleading remind him of his own mother and his upbringing.they finally tell me they will check out if we told the truth and if they can't find their comrade, they will come back again and shoot both of us.

At that point we hear someone calling my name, over and over again. The two soldiers listen and then leave in the boat. It is getting dark. After a while Anni comes rushing in. "I called you to bring the boat and suddenly two Russians stepped out of it and they frightened me. 'Your brother puuh' they laughed and pointed to their gun. I am glad you are both alive." We look at her, "It is a miracle. It could have had a very different outcome and it is not over yet," we tell her. Mother prepares supper but neither of us feels like eating, we are still shaken. Again we hear someone shouting, this time from the other road. Are they beating somebody up? We are afraid but then the shouting begins again. It sounds as if they are calling a name; perhaps they are calling the drunken officer. We pray that they may find him, that he did not drown. Next morning we wake up with mixed feelings. Shall I hide, in case the Russians come back again? But that would put Mother in danger. Nothing happens all day. Later neighbor Tiede tells us how the incident with the drunken Russian officer ended. He walked dripping wet into Tiede's kitchen and demanded supper. While Tiede was preparing it; he heard shouting on the street and told him, "They are calling you". He did not respond and continued eating. Tiede wanted to get rid of him, so he snuck out and waved the callers into his house. When they saw their comrade they scolded him and dragged him out.

Our supply of potatoes is dwindling, so we row over to our common potato field to dig out some more. We look for our neighbors to discuss the harvesting procedure and notice they are quite upset. "No more potatoes", they tell us. "A Polish family moved into the Grübnau's place and is claiming the potato field for themselves. They are threatening to shoot anyone who dares to dig more potatoes". Can we survive the winter without that source of calories? we wonder. Discouraged we row home.

Bad news again. A few days after we return home with that bad news, we make another discovery. Five families of our neighbors 'across the water' have left Alt-Rosengart for safer ground. We are shocked, very disappointed that they did not share their plans with us. Mother had shared so much with them and had been a source of strength and encouragement to all of them when they had problems. We are now one of very few German families left in our village.

We are getting visitors again. Two Polish militia men walk through the water to our house and ask for me. They want me to go with them to neighbor Reddig's house to search for his Nazi uniform. They must have found files about Nazi members. Mother suspects this is an excuse for taking me with them but they assure her they will bring me back. We enter Reddig's house, it smells musty, since it has been empty for months. They search the main floor and send me to search the attic. From the hay loft I discover a secret chamber and can see through a hole in the ceiling his SA uniform jacket draped over an old chair, his polished high leather boots beside it and the stiff cap and belt on top, ready to be used again some time. I am not going to tell the militia anything about it. We go back without the uniform and they tell Mother, "Here is your son again; we did not take him away".

Mother tells me that the Polish police had found an SA uniform at neighbor Schönwald's, whose son Waldemar, like I did not join the HJ voluntarily. They interrogated him and beat him up so badly that he came home on crutches. After a while they arrested him again and he never came back anymore

Anni likes the job at the starost's house in Grunau and they are satisfied with her work. They seem to be honest people. It is getting dangerous for Anni to walk home alone in the dark, so they offer her room and board for the week and she comes home on weekends only. She must have told them about us. One morning a man knocks at our door, he has been sent by the starost to ask if we have horse harnesses. He speaks German fairly well, I take him to the stable and show him all our harnesses. He selects one and a few other things. To my amazement he asks if I would sell them for 300 Zloty. I have no idea what the purchasing value of the Zloty is and think he just makes a joke. Normally they just confiscate things. I take a risk and point out that the one he has chosen is valuable, almost new. He thinks for a moment, than pads his offer to 400 Zloty, I accept and throw a pair of reins in. He gives me the money and leaves. I still cannot believe it, he *paid* for it, our first Polish money, I hope it is legal currency.

We have visitors again; two Polish militia officials present us with a document signed and sealed. Since we cannot read it, they explain it to us. The Polish government orders us to report to a labor camp in Bromberg within three days. I have to sign it and receive a copy. We have anticipated that for some time but are still shocked when we now hold this order in our hands. We have to outwit them and leave before they come to arrest us. The next morning I walk to Grunau, buy a ticket with the money I got for our harness and take the train to Malborg, which I still know from my school days. I go to the city hall to the government office and ask for a deportation or expulsion order. They have difficulty understanding me and don't quite know what to do, but, after some consultation, give me a document with a stamp and signature. I cannot read it and do not really know if it is of any value to me. I take the train home and check the train schedule for the next days at the station.

We have the first frost and I have to redesign our boat to act as an icebreaker. I put skids on the front of the elongated outriggers and they push the boat on the ice and the weight of the boat and mine added to it, breaks the ice.

Mother is washing and packing the clean clothes and an extra pair of old shoes in a rucksack, I roll two of the best down covers together around a can of syrup from Aunt Johanna, sew an old patch onto the roll, with feathers sticking out on the sides to make it look old and torn and stuff them into jute bags which I had made. In mine I include Father's Bible and a few photos which I rescued from family albums that the first Russians had thrown out into the snow. I pack two linen bags with my stuff, tie them together so that I can carry them over one shoulder, the other is still quite sore. I sew 300 Zloty into the seam of my old loden coat, in case we need it. From bicycle wheels I make a light two-wheel cart for transporting our bags. We are now ready to leave. We share our plan with Anni and ask her to come along with us. She hesitates; she has a good job and the starost wants her to stay. We cannot persuade her to leave with us; we hug her and with a heavy heart say good-bye. We feel responsible for her but she is an individualist and adventurer and has to make the final decision for herself.

As it has become very cold, our icebreaker is not breaking the ice anymore and we cannot use the boat to get out. We look out of the window and see some Polish boys lingering around the house. They have come across the ice to see if they can steal anything. It proves that the ice is strong enough to walk on. I go outside and tell them to go home. We may see more such visitors in the future coming across the ice. It is time for us to leave. The next morning at dawn we dress in all the clothes we own, pack the few things we have gathered on my cart, go through all the familiar rooms and say good bye to our home. Is it still our home or is it already Polish property? Quietly we push our cart across the ice towards the railway station. We look back once more and what has been my home for twenty years disappears into the distance.

Leaving Home

Nobody is on the street this early and there are only a few people at the station when we enter it from the back. We leave the cart behind an old shack and carry our belongings to the platform. Gradually more people gather when the train arrives. I help Mother into her rucksack which is too heavy for the frail woman and take the rest of our luggage into the train. The conductor comes to check the tickets. I show him what I think is my deportation document. That is no ticket he grumbles. I think I paid for it with a farm and that should be enough for the trip. He moves on. In Malbork we have to change trains. The station has not been renovated after the destruction during the war and we have to cross tracks and stumble over rubble and holes on our way to the other platform. Mother goes ahead of me and suddenly a Polish young man jumps at her from the back and with a knife quickly cuts the two shoulder straps of her rucksack and disappears into the crowd with it. I could not prevent it happening. I help Mother up again and we look at each other. The pack was not worth very much anyway, stuff that marauding Russians and Poles had rejected, which Mother had cleaned and mended. We still have my two linen briefcases and the two jute bags with our bedding.

In Dirschau tickets are checked again, I try the same trick as before and show the conductor the same document but it does not work. He asks for my passport, looks at it and puts both documents in his folder. He demands payment for tickets. I know he wants a bribe but he won't get one from me. They have taken Mother's rucksack already.

Some passengers give in to the pressure and take off their sweater, some their wristwatch or other valuables and give them to him. After a while he comes back again and demands payment (or a bribe). We do not give in yet although Mother and I consider paying him with the Zlotys that I still have in the seam of my old coat. He becomes angry since nobody can give him anything anymore and pulls the beautiful quilt from a baby carriage as payment. The baby now lies only in his diapers and shirt in the hard and cold buggy. We are appalled, I am ready to tear it from him and throw him out of the compartment but Mother warns me. The conductor comes back again and repeats his threats.

In Choinice, north of Bromberg, where we were to report to the labor camp, the military police checks our papers. Since I have none left to show them, they order me out of the train and take me towards the station office. One in front, the other behind me and Mother follows. I tell her to stay in the train, it is easier for me alone to escape, but she says "I don't want to lose you again". We pass the conductor, who took my passport, standing with his document folder open, talking to another traveler. I stop and tell the guard he has my documents, go over to him, leaf through the papers and find my passport. I take it out and show it to the police. While he looks at it, the train starts to roll and I turn to the two officers, "Documenta dobre?" (In order) Not waiting for his answer, I take my documents, open the door, help Mother in and jump into the moving train. Nobody follows. I know Mother has been praying all the time.

Often when the train stops at a station, Poles come into the compartments, look at the luggage racks, grab bags or suitcases and jump out. One of those young Poles comes into our compartment, grabs one of my bags and the other, tied to the first, does not come out that easily. I quickly hold on to it and pull both bags back. He curses and leaves without his prey. At the next station, he comes back with two militia men, points at me and the first of the two gives me a blow with his rifle butt. I fall back against the opposite wall, gasping for breath. My sore shoulder hurts. Then he takes both bags from the rack, opens the jute bags, looks at the pads and feathers sticking out and mumbles "Aah old bed", throws it back and gets off. All we have left now are two good down covers with fake patches, two pounds of homemade syrup, Father's Bible and a few photos - perhaps the most valuable items.

In Schneidemühl (Pila) we all have to get out and are herded into box cars on the other platform. The Polish station officials have come up with a new chicanery. The train stops about 200 meters before it reaches the station platform. All passengers have to disembark and walk into the station, to the next platform. It is very difficult for most of us to step down a two foot drop from the car to the gravel ground, especially for old people, mothers with small children in strollers and handicapped people. We try to help each other to get out. Polish men and women come and mingle with us, offer to help with the luggage, then snatch it and take off with it. An amputee hobbles into the train and hides. "They are going to kill me" he whimpers, "one of those Polish striplings grabbed my rucksack and I hit him hard over the head with my cane and he howled; what have I done? They will come now and kill me." The train leaves and nothing happens.

In Landsberg, the last station before we enter East Germany, the train stops so that we can walk around find a bush to relieve ourselves which some of us find urgent to do. We walk back to the box car not knowing when the train will leave again They don't tell us any thing. Among the rubble at the station I find a piece of strong wire, roll it up and put it in my coat pocket, not knowing for what purpose. The station master orders us back into the train, but it is not leaving yet. We hear some shouting and crying and suspect Poles are after our luggage again. In the cars next to ours we hear cries, 'help, help, please help' and 'don't beat me so hard'. We count the people in our car, everybody is in. We close the door and I tie it shut with the wire that I had picked up. We are just finished, when we hear bangs at our door. We don't respond. They pound again, "Open the door, police" they shout and utter threats. Some of the fearful women urge us to open, "They will kill us if they manage to break in". We hope the wire will hold and with all our strength we keep the doors shut. The knocks become stronger and the threats more severe, but we do not give in Some of the more daring women back me up and assure me they stand behind me, they encourage us to hold out. Finally the cries and shouts from tha other cars stop and the train starts moving and rolls west. We are glad that we held out and relieved that we kept the marauders out, that nobody broke in. Half an hour later we cross the bridge over the Oder River at Küstrin and are now in the Soviet occupation zone, in East Germany. The train rolls through to Berlin.

In the Soviet Zone

This time the train stops at the platform in Berlin and we can get out more easily with the few pieces of luggage which we could save. The Red Cross offers us a piece of bread and tea, the first food after two days. We say good-bye to our fellow-sufferers, some shake my hand and say "Thank you!"

Our ways part; those who have a place to go to, leave. We have none. Uncle Gustav lives not far from Berlin but we don't know if he and his family survived the last bomb attacks and the occupation by the Russians. There is no phone or public transportation to find out. We see the destruction of Berlin and wonder how anybody could survive. Large areas are bare of any buildings, only rubble and more rubble as far as we can see. The refugee representative arranges a transit on a passenger train to Magdeburg for us. We receive a sandwich and a little pocket money from the Red Cross. In Magdeburg we are directed to a large concrete block, a former air raid shelter, which will be our abode for a while. We are registered and have to find an empty space on one of the floors among all the other refugees. Two floors below ground level we settle in. Mother sleeps on a wooden bench, I take a wooden door off its hinges and put it on the moist floor, it serves as a bed for me for the night. At least we have our down covers to keep the cold out, for which we are very thankful. Our bones ache when we get up in the morning. We have to go down two more floors through narrow aisles to the washroom. We get to know other 'inmates' and gather information. They tell us where to apply for food coupons so that we can have something to eat. It is cold outside and Mother stays in the bunker. Magdeburg is not destroyed as much as Berlin. Here the last battles of the war were fought and Germans did not put up much resistance to the Americans anymore. Here at the Elbe River, the Americans and Russians met.

After the third night in the bunker I go to the refugee office and tell them that my mother's health will not tolerate another night in the musty bunker. They inform me that a transport is organized and that they will put us on the list. The next day about 120 of us take the train back a short distance and disembark in the city of Genthin. We refugees are asked to gather on the plaza in front of the station and are met by a small delegation of city councilors. The mayor addresses us as *fellow citizens* and welcomes us with distributing a small piece of dry white bread for each person, a precious welcome gift for us. We are moved, we are human beings again.

Trucks take us to a country inn on the outskirts of Genthin. The big dance hall has been transformed into a dormitory with about sixty bunk beds in blocks of four together. A two foot aisle separates one block from the next. It is more crowded than in a youth hostel. I choose the bunks beside the wood stove; we have more room in front of us. Mother sleeps in the lower bed and I in the upper. Beside her is a fine elderly lady who seems to be embarrassed by the closeness of the beds. Her daughter, a young teacher, sleeps above her, beside me. We keep our luggage under our beds. Among the occupants of our camp are three men, one war amputee with a wooden leg, an eighty year old man and I, all the others are women and children. We have to pitch in helping with cooking and housework. I volunteer to bring potatoes and vegetables from the cellar to the kitchen, get firewood and light and service the small iron stove to keep our hall warm.

In order to entertain the children and keep them out of trouble, a retired teacher starts 'school' for them. I volunteer to help. We assess the children according to their ability to read and write. Among them is Holger, an eight year old boy. He writes his letters backwards in 'mirror script'. I find that unusual. I ask one of the ladies to lend me a mirror, hold it against his writing and show him in the mirror how the normal script should look. It seems to make sense to the bright boy and with some practice he learns to write legibly from left to right.

I watch the war veteran weave handbags out of string. He shows me how he does it. He has brought his tools and some supplies with him but runs out of string. We decide to go out and find some new supplies. Nothing is available in stores, so I suggest we go to farmers and ask if they have some binder twine. After a few tries, we tell a farmer's wife, whose husband was killed in the war, our story. We explain to her what we need and for what purpose we need it. She takes us into the barn and we find two rolls of binder twine which she lets us have. Happily we return to camp with our treasure.

I get busy now making handbags. The first I exchange in a textile store for remnants of colored thread. I weave that decoratively into different designs of handbags, shoulder bags, shopping bags and table runners. Others I trade for proper tools and additional food. At the beginning my weaver's needle was a piece of twisted wire which I finally can replace with a proper one and improve my workmanship .

Living so close together allows sickness to spred more easily. Three children of a young mother who sleep on the stage get the stomach flue and cannot eat anything.. T mother fears that the bread, allotted for her food coupons will mildew. I offer her one of my bags in exchange for the two loafs she has left over. She is happy to do that. I have a purpose for it. The next day is my 20th birthday and Mother has planned a birthday party. For my work in the kitchen I earned a few extra potatoes, these we roast in the hot ashes of the stove. With a farmer I had traded a bag for a small piece of butter and our menu is ready: roasted potatoes with butter for main course and cut bread with our last syrup for dessert. A dozen teenage girls and children sit around our table and we have a birthday party with food, story telling and laughter. After they are gone, Mother and I sit on her bed and we reflect on the past time. Exactly two months ago at dawn we left home. What might it look like there now? Could we have survived the hard winter without food; perhaps we would be slaving in a labor camp now? Looking back we are thankful to be here and together; even if we do not know what the future will bring.

Meals in the refugee camp are very simple and scarce but we always have one warm meal. We are appreciated here. Mother can listen to women who are disheartened, suffering and depressed. She tries to console them or give them hope through the strength of her faith. I help teaching and occupying kids and try to keep our hall warm. We have fun sometimes too, play games and tricks.

A short, middle-aged woman snores very loudly at night and talks a lot during the day which often does not make much sense. We plan to give her a lesson and play a prank a la Wilhelm Busch, the German story teller and caricaturist. One night we tie a string to the end of her bed cover and lead it to the back of the room. As she starts to snore, someone from the back pulls the string and the cover moves down. She wakes up and pulls it back. After a while she snores again, the cover moves again, she grabs it, mumbles in her sleep and wonders why it is moving. The third time her cover disappears down the aisle. She jumps out of bed, disturbed, cussing and searches for her blanket. We hear the insiders giggle, they quickly remove the string from the blanket and she has no idea what happened to her cover. The neighbors complain about the ruckus and tell her to be quiet and go to sleep. The next morning she has a lot to talk about. She is a little more careful now.

A rumor is going around that a transport to the West will be organized. Before this becomes reality, Mother gets sick, she has high fever and her body hurts. The diagnosis is: shingles. She is transferred to the hospital and is quarantined for three weeks. I visit her almost every day. The camp 'inmates' get ready to move out. We cannot go with them as mother is not allowed to leave hospital. With a heavy heart I accompany our friends to the station and see them depart. With one of the good-looking girls the good-bye is a little more intimate.

After three weeks, Mother can leave the hospital and I take her to our new quarters in the city. The refugee settlement office has assigned us to a Genthin family. They accept us refugees politely. They know they have no other choice. I am looking for work and the neighbor next door needs someone to split his firewood. My sore shoulder still hurts a little when I hit the logs but I manage. I have stacked the wood to shoulder height when I see a Russian soldier go into our house. He wears the famous green cap of the GPU, I suspect bad news. After a short while he comes out and heads for my wood stack. I duck behind it and he passes by and goes into the next house. I hide behind the wood pile until he is out of sight. Then I finish the work and go back to our room. Our landlady tells me that the secret police had come to search the house for able-bodied people to work in factories, dismantling machinery. She was the only one at home and they enlisted her for the job, she has to start tomorrow morning. If I had been at home, they would have taken me, not only to disassemble machinery in Genthin but later to install it again in Russia.

According to the Morgenthau-Plan, Germany was to be reduced to an agrarian country, devoid of all industrial production. In the Soviet Zone they put this plan into action. But when the two ideologies Communism and Capitalism clashed, the former Allies split and became cold war enemies. The Americans and French wanted Germany to be a strong buffer zone between Russia and the West and they did not carry this plan out anymore.

Mother and I agree that I should disappear for a few days until the dust settles. I take the train to Schwerin and visit Magdalena's former landlady. She is very surprised to see me again and I tell her my story. I ask how she is and if my rucksack is still there which I left with her when I went to West Prussia. She still has it and I take it with me. I go to the school which had been our hospital. Children are studying there again. Magdalena and the hospital she had worked in are now in Hamburg.

The next day I go back to Genthin with my rucksack filled with the stuff I had left there in Schwerin.

The political climate is unpredictable here in the Soviet Zone and we think it is time to leave. Mother feels better again and can travel, so we plan to go to the West Zone. Like our camp mates a couple of months ago had done. We will go first to the refugee camp in Friedland and hope from there across the border.

Magdalena wrote to us that Mother's brother, Uncle Richard, had escaped with his family from West Prussia, always just ahead of the Russians. They have settled now in Hillerse, which is not far from Friedland, on the other side of the border. It will be our first destination. In Friedland we register as refugees. We are crowded into barracks and have to wait our turn to be considered for a transport to the west. Three small boiled potatoes and a slice of bread is our food ration for the day. We have applied for the next transport to the west but this is not that easy. We have to present a signed and stamped document that we have a place to go to in the west, just telling them about it does not count. For three days we go from one agency to the next; nobody is authorized to give us the proper documents. One of the clerks takes me aside and tells me 'unofficially' "There is a man who takes unsuccessful applicants across the border, for a fee. He will be at the west gate tomorrow morning".

Early in the morning we are at the west gate of the camp and spot a man with a small hand wagon between the trees. We nod at him and he nods back. We pay him twelve Marks which is what he asks for, and put our bags on his wagon. After a while more people join us; we are ten *emigrants* and he thinks that is enough for a troop. He tells us he can not guarantee anything. We don't know the man, can we trust him?

He asks us to follow him in single file on an overgrown trail. He entreats us to make no noise and watch where we are going. After fifteen minutes the trail disappears and the forest gets denser. He stops, turns around and puts his finger to his lips, it is getting dangerous. After about ten minutes, which seem like hours, the woods begin to thin out and we come to a deserted country road. "You are in the British Zone", he tells us, we thank him and he waves and disappears. We are glad, the tension is over, but where do we go from here in this forsaken land? A few hundred meters away we spot a single beech tree and an open truck under it. We aim for it. A friendly Red Cross 'sister' stands beside the old truck, "Welcome to West Germany" she greets us, offering each one of us a cup of hot chocolate and a slice of bread. She answers our questions and shows us the way to the railway station. We know now, we made it and are very happy and relieved.

In West Germany

At the railway station we buy a ticket and wait for the train to Hannover. There is only one train going through this forlorn border area each day. After a few hours, it stops briefly at the lone Leiferde station, in the middle of 'nowhere'. Here we have to get off. But how do we get to Hillerse from here, we wonder? We see a horse and buggy waiting at the station. Mother goes to ask the driver if he can take us there. To her surprise she recognizes her brother, Uncle Richard. He has taken visitors from Hillerse to the station and waits to see if anybody wants a ride back, When he sees his sister, the two embrace each other and tears run down their cheeks. It has been a long time since they have seen each other. He operates a horse and buggy 'Taxi Service' from Hillerse to the station and other villages around. We are his only customers on the way home and have a lot to talk about. There is great surprise as we arrive at their home in Hillerse, in the Ölman vegetable cannery. Mr. Ölman had to clear out part of his warehouse to accommodate a family with eleven children. The Wiehlers have two private rooms and a larger storage area which they have transformed into a dormitory for the children. They sectioned it off with blankets into cubicles for boys and girls. Now they have to move together a little to make room for Aunt Selma and Cousin Helmut. Everyone is very interested to hear what their home looks like now since it is under Russian and Polish rule. They want to know how we lived there and how we got out and they tell us about their escape from West Prussia and their new beginning here in Hillerse.

A farmer allows them to keep three of their horses in his stable. The army took seven of the other ones and two died on the way. The municipality is leasing them land on which they grow vegetables and herbs. A specialty here is asparagus. They grow enough to feed the big family and have some surplus to sell to restaurants and on the market. In the beginning the children helped with the hobby farm and the 'horse taxi'. Gradually the older ones found work in the city or became apprentices in different trades.

Lisel, the second oldest daughter, got a job as house maid with a roofing company owner in Peine, a town an hour's bike ride away. Her boss deals with a building company in Peine, the Hanke Construction Company. I apply for a job and am lucky they have work for me as 'odd jobber'. Now that I have work, I can apply for housing. Mother and I go to the City Hall in Peine and fill out an application form. The manager of the housing department sends us to Handorf, a small village four km west of Peine. The municipal clerk checks the application form and takes us to the Rindfleisch's residence. They have been told, they have to give up one room in their house for refugees. Mr. Rindfleisch is a mason. He built his brick house himself and is very particular and protective of it. We can tell he is not very happy to share it with strangers. Somewhat reserved, almost grumpy, he shows us the room.

Handorf

It is May 1946 and we move into our first rental place. Bare white walls and furnished with one old bed for Mother, one chair, an old table and the bottom of a big old dresser with a hinged lid. This serves as a bed for me at night; during the day I slip the mattress, a large jute bag filled with straw, behind it and we use it as a sofa. It is cupboard and closet in one. If we open the lid, we can store all our belongings in it, actually a very versatile but not sightly piece of furniture. The room has two windows facing the street which makes it fairly bright. We have no kitchen and share the bathroom with the Rindfleischs. Our dishes consist of one cup and one plate each and a few pieces of cutlery. The owner puts a tiny wood and coal stove in our room, but we have no pots and pans and cannot buy any in the store yet; there are none available, at least not for refugees..

I still remember how we walked from door to door, asking if somebody could spare or sell us some pots and pans. Some told us they needed the ones they have themselves, others shut the door in our faces. Finally we come home with a rusty black iron pot and a pitted enamel one. We scrub them and they are usable. To start from scratch at this time is very difficult.

We are out of potatoes and the store does not have any either. It is hard to go begging again. The big farmer Nordmeyer does not give anything to refugees. We find out later that a large amount of potatoes had rotted in his mound.

An elderly widow invites us into her entrance hall, asks where we come from and where we are staying. She tells us that she had a good crop of potatoes from her big garden last year and gladly shares some with us, her new neighbors. She does not charge us for them. We go home, our dignity somewhat restored.

On the south side of the village is a small forest and the village council resolves to make a piece, which had been logged, available for refugees for garden land. We take advantage of this offer and for weeks we try to remove the stumps and cultivate our garden plot, plant a few rows of potatoes and sow some vegetables and even wheat. For the first year the harvest is not very promising. On our way to the 'garden' we walk through the woods and look to the top of the old fir trees to see if they have any dry branches left. With a wire hook on the top of a long pole I then pull them down. Higher up are usually a few which other people cannot reach that easily. We use them as firewood for heating and cooking. The forest floor below has been 'swept clear' of all burnable material. We carry the branches home, borrow a saw and cut them to the right length for our tiny stove. While we are cutting, Mother and I sing folk songs and hymns and harmonize. The neighbors stand behind the hedge and listen. They have not heard anybody singing at work.

Slowly we get accustomed to life in Handorf. Farmer Brandes asks Mother occasionally if she could help in the harvest; he values her work ethics and knowledge in farming. Sometimes he has work for me too.

We attend the local Lutheran Church, go to Bible studies and prayer meetings in the parsonage and learn to know more people. Pastor Brandes appreciates Mother's participation and strength of faith and involves her in home visitations and counseling; she is a good listener. He invites me to the weekly young people's meetings and asks me to lead the meeting if he is not available. We study the Bible, church history and dogma, play games, and go to camps. In one of those camps I learn to know Walter Schönbrunn, a refugee from Silesia. He has started a bike repair shop and from scrap bike parts he builds me a sturdy bicycle. New bikes are not available yet and not affordable The bike saves me a lot of walking and bus fare.

The congregation has an impressive church choir and its director, Dr Rohr, welcomes me as a badly needed tenor. Before the war he was a government official but lost his position because of his membership in the NS party. He is a bachelor, lanky, and does not pay much attention to his appearance. Sometimes his tie is partly over and partly under his collar, one trouser leg inside his boot the other over it. We see him occasionally walking along the street, humming a tune and beating the rhythm with his hand, but it is remarkable what he achieves with this group of oedinary people. We sing Bach Cantatas, pieces by Bruckner and Schütz. He opens a door to Bach for me. I learn to love his music and Baroque and Renaissance music in general. Members of the choir are simple farmers, trades people, housewives, no trained voices.

A pretty, blond girl in the soprano section draws my attention. Her father 'leans on me' in the tenor section. Erika is a bright, lively girl. She works in the parsonage helping the pastor's wife with the children and in the household. We seem to respond to each other.

Shortly before Easter we practice a Bach chorale with our choir and Dr Rohr mentions that we can hear this chorale next Sunday during the performance of the St.John's passion in the Jacobi church in Peine; he has tickets for it. On his recommendation I buy one. Mother does not want to come with me, so I walk alone on a sunny Sunday afternoon the four km to Peine. I go with great anticipation to this performance, the first one I attend after the war. Soloists and choir present the passion of Jesus convincingly, a good accomplishment for a small town performance. During the first intermission I discover Erika among the listeners. We talk about the choir and the conductor and decide to listen to the rest of the passion together. After the second hour the wooden benches on which we sit beside each other, make our bones ache. We try to soften the pain by sitting on our hands, when they touch each other accidentally we pull them back. The second time we let them rest beside each other and towards the end our eyes and hands meet. The performance lasts three and a half hours and when we come out it is dark already. We take the train to Ilsede and walk home together. We go through the bog between Ilsede and Handorf. White fog rises from the Fuhse creek as we cross the bridge. We stop and enjoy the somewhat eerie landscape in the moonlight, listen to the chirps of the crickets and the occasional croaking of the bullfrogs. As we go on hand in hand, suddenly the fog lifts and dark forms appear like apparitions. We hold on to each other and laugh about these silly bushes. Arm in arm we go up the village road to her house. I take her into my arms and she snuggles up to me when we say good-bye. We have grown very fond of each other. We 'happen' to meet more often, go swimming in the canal nearby or take a bike ride together. Sometimes I wait for Erika, when she gets milk for the Brandes family in the dairy outlet next door. I arrange it so that I get milk for us at the same time just to see her We meet in choir practice and youth group. Once in an evangelistic meeting we both give testimony of our Christian faith.

Pastor Brandes has a Sunday morning ritual: he plays a chorale on his trumpet from the front steps of the parsonage that can be heard in the village, a kind of wake up call and invitation to attend the church service. He also plays in the brass orchestra. He tells me that they have a few instruments that need a player and asks if I would be interested in trying one out. I agree and walk home with a trumpet. He gives me a fingering chart and I practice if nobody is at home. Soon I join the brass ensemble and we play on special occasions in church. Our leader, Mr.Henke, teaches me how to play the trombone and if there is no tenor player, I exchange the trumpet with the trombone which I like.

My job with the building contractor Hanke is temporary and after the work at the swimming pool is finished, I am unemployed. I don't like this insecurity and think of learning a proper trade. University seems out of the question since we don't have any finances to pay for it. I love to work with wood. With my pocket knife I have carved a writing tray from a piece of beach firewood. I flattened the front making a tray for pens and pencils and from the higher back I carved a big-horn sheep climbing up to a rock from one side and a landing eagle from the other side. I hollowed the rock out to hold an ink bottle. I am quite proud of my achievement and would like to continue working with wood.

I am looking for an apprenticeship as a cabinet maker. The guild master gives me a list of all cabinet makers in the area and I hop on my bike and visit all of them. They either don't have enough work or I am too old to be an apprentice. They like younger boys whom they can boss around and don't have to pay much. Pastor Brandes suggests trying furniture factories in the Solling, a wooded, hilly area 120 km south of us. For two days I travel from one place to the next, none needs workers. Back home I consult with the cabinet guild master again. He asks me what I did before I was drafted. I tell him I went to high school and left with the 'Notabitur', the emergency high school diploma. He suggests that I pick up the lost years of my high school instruction and get the proper *Abitur* which will enable me to go to university. With a university degree I have a wider scope and better chances for a career.

"By the way did you get a discharge from the army?" he asks me. "If you want to visit someone in the American Zone you could get arrested and be put in a prisoner of war camp and from there you might end up in French coal mines doing penance for German war crimes." Right after the war was over, Americans, under the command of Eisenhower, renamed the German prisoners of war '*enemy combatants*', thinking this meant that they did not have to treat them according to the Geneva Convention. They crowded them into big camps, meadows, fenced in with barbed wire, with no shelter, no food for days, and no proper medical care. Guards were instructed to keep family members and friends away from the prisoners; they were not allowed to hand food or medication through the fence to their starving and sick fathers and brothers. One guard even shot a woman who handed her husband a piece of bread through the fence. Imprisoned German soldiers died by the hundred thousands during the first six months after the war. The International Red Cross and reporters were not allowed to inspect those camps during that time.

"I would advise you to get a discharge certificate from an English military post, to avoid that situation," he finishes. I thank him for his advice. It is hard to believe that this was still happening in our civilized society, done by members of a 'Christian, democratic nation'. Later my cousin and my brother-in-law, who were prisoners of war in these camps, confirmed the truth of these stories.

A week later I am on my way to *Munster Lager* the closest English military post. Before I enter the camp, I ask people who come out, what life is like in there and what the procedures are. They tell me it is quite informal and quick. So I go in. The sergeant at the entrance records my personal data, takes my finger prints and asks where I had served. I don't mention my special military unit, the *Hermann Göring Fallschirm-Panzer Division* (parachute-tank) just plain 'soldier in the army'. He doesn't care much about it and assigns me to a barrack. The next morning I have to report to a large assembly room. A commissioner takes my personal data again and asks where I had been posted in the war. I tell him at the eastern front and he seem to be satisfied. A German military physician examines me, looks at my war wounds and classifies me as 'Fit'. The next official has my discharge papers ready, enters 'Fit' into the proper category, hands it to me and sends me to the commanding officer. Captain Brady asks me if I has been a member of the Nazi party and a few other questions about my family. When he is satisfied with my answers, he signs the paper, puts a stamp on it and dismisses me. At the mess hall I get 40 Marks discharge money and a small travel ration and I am on my way home again. I am home just in time for supper. Mother is glad that everything went so well. As of October 8th 1946, I am an ordinary civilian again. I am glad this happened in the British Zone. The British officers are fairer and treat prisoners of war in accordance with the Geneva Convention.

Chapter Six

Das Abitur

I follow the advice of the guild master and inquire at the *Peiner Oberschule* about what I have to do to receive a proper high school diploma. Returning to high school seems to me to be a logical solution to my unemployment situation.. Oberstudiendirektor Unterhorst listens to my story, empathizes with me and allows me to attend one of the graduating classes. Next week I am in school again, in a class with 25 much younger students. I have been out of school for three years, have experienced combat in war, expulsion from our home, living in refugee camps and am now trying to make ends meet. There was not much opportunity for cultural events or studying for school during that time. Now I want to cram one and a half years of instruction that were needed to finish school in Marienburg, into one half year here in Peine. It is difficult to catch up and I try hard, but my first report card lists several *unsatisfactory* marks, which I have never received before. Some teachers write encouraging remarks like 'he has improved considerably and should be able to reach the standard of the class next term'. It was a devastating report for me.

Studienrat Grotefeld, my homeroom teacher and mathematics instructor, does not acknowledge my ardent endeavor to catch up with the class, especially in his subject in which I had done fairly well. In a teacher's conference he claims 'according to regulation, Lemke has not enough credits to be admitted to the Abitur; he has to attend school for six months prior to final examinations'. I was short only one or two weeks; which resulted in my having to leave school for this term. It is hard for me to take that.

Fortunately contractor Hanke has work for me again, maintenance work at the *Peiner Walzwerk* (rolling mill)

After Easter the new school year starts and I am back in school, enrolled in Mr. Grotefeld's homeroom again. I am disappointed. He was the one who did not let me continue my studies last year and students say he does not like people who fought in the war. Dr Sundermeyer, my German teacher, and homeroom teacher of the other graduating class, knows that too. The next day he takes me aside in the hall and tells me "Mr. Lemke, come to my class tomorrow; Mr. Grotefeld has only 28 students in his class and I have 33, but I will arrange this." I am dumbfounded. He hardly knows me and makes me such a generous offer, which means more work for him. I am very grateful and cannot find words to thank him.

Dr. Sundermeyer is portly, bald and has freckles. He is kind, considerate, respectful - one could even say loving. He has good people skills and is a born teacher who can command attention through his personality, knowledge of his subject and the way he presents it to us. He has a good sense of humor. He does arouse in us an appreciation for literature and poetry and through it implants in us values by which we can live day by day. Our generation is thirsting for these. We have been disillusioned by the erosion and final loss of our ideals through propaganda, demands and examples of NS party officials and also through the cruelties of the final war years. We want to rekindle our ideals and be equipped to rebuild a better country. Dr.Sundermeyer, or 'SU', as we refer to him in private, told us later that he had never before or later taught such a mature, cooperative and active class as ours, his first post-war class.

My fellow students elect me to be class president, perhaps because I am the oldest one in the class. Later, one of the girls tells me it is because I am such a solid, dependable and trustworthy person.

School equipment and materials are scarce and often primitive. In art, a subject in which I am good, I have to borrow a pencil and draw on bleached newspaper, which I can buy as wrapping paper in a store. Some of the girls in the class are not very talented in drawing and, when they see that I have finished my assignment, call me over and I quietly complete their work which earns me a pencil but gets me a reprimand from Mr. Gerigk, our art teacher. Uwe, his son, is in our class.

Helmut (middle) in boarding school

Homeroom teacher Dr. Sundermeyer

School play, Helmut guard in drama Antigone

The winter of 1947/48 is especially cold and by the end of January we have no fuel for the central heating system. The principal decides to have instruction in the classroom only once a week. It is too cold to sit there for hours, even the ink in our inkbottles freezes. So every Wednesday we sit in our coats, toques and gloves and wait for our teachers to come and give us homework for a week and collect the work from last week. The second Wednesday, Inge comes to class with a wreath which she will take to the cemetery afterwards. She puts it on the teacher's desk. She also brings a bottle of cognac and small glasses. We exchange the ink containers from the indentations in our student desks with the cognac glasses and eagerly await the appearance of our teacher. Finally the door opens and SU comes in. He senses the tenseness in the class and asks "What is going on here?" He walks to his desk and sees the wreath and the bottle in it. He smiles "You kids are crazy." Klaus mutters, "It is so cold here *Herr Doctor,* and we need some warmth from the inside." SU turns to Irene, who sits beside the door, "Watch that nobody comes in". He shakes his head as he opens the bottle, fills his glass and passes the bottle on. We all raise our glasses and *prost* (celebrate) our favorite teacher. "But don't tell anybody about this or I can get into trouble." We get our assignments and go home with a chuckle.

A highlight in my school year here is a cooperative work between our literature class and the art class. In Literature we have discussed Sophocles' drama *Antigone* and SU wants to put it on stage with us being the actors. Mr. Gerigk, our art teacher, agrees to help with the stage design. Since I take both subjects, I put my creative ideas to work helping to design the sets and playing the guard in the drama. We have to provide costumes ourselves. Since we cannot buy any, we have to improvise. Bed covers and blankets do for Greek togas. I come up with a design for footwear for the soldiers. The performance in the *Peiner Festsäle*, is a hit. We enjoy it and it builds up our class spirit.

The commission, requisitioning space for refugees, is going through the village again. A new transport of Germans, who were forced from their homes in Silesia, Pomerania and along the Czech border have arrived in West Germany and have to be placed with local families. Our host family has to give up another room; the one, they use only once a year, on Mr.Rindfleisch's birthday, the rest of the year it is locked and the curtains are drawn. Mrs. Rindfleisch asks us into her kitchen and tells us that they have to give up one room. They want to offer it to me to sleep there during the night; she will put a bed against the wall beside the door. "But only for the night" she emphasizes. I am not to use the rest of the room nor open the curtains. I notice, she has laid a colored thread on the sofa to be able to find out if I have sat on it. We cannot understand this narrow-mindedness. We have lived with them for over a year and they should know by now that we are responsible tenants. Do they not know that we had a war and millions of people lost their homes and everything in it, that they are now 'homeless' and need a place to live..

We thank them for their 'gracious' offer and accept it but I do not promise I will stay out of the rest of the room. Sometimes I study there and sit on the sofa. I take the wool thread off and, before I leave the room, put it back again. Having another upstairs room gives us some privacy at least for the night. During examination time I do my preparations there, in order not to disturb Mother if I have to work late. It is often after midnight when I write my final essays and, as usual, I am pressed for time. It is cold outside and the temperature in my unheated room is below zero. I have to scrape the ice from the tip of my fountain pen with a strip of cardboard so that the ink can flow again and I can finish writing my work.

Shortly before Christmas 1947 Pastor Brandes' wife pays us a visit. The commission has come again and requisitioned two rooms in the parsonage. She asks us if we would consider moving into these rooms in the parsonage. I am all for it but Mother hesitates. "The Rindfleischs have given us an additional room and we have developed a reasonable relationship with them, should we not be thankful and stay here?" I try to convince Mother with a reality check. Rindfleischs have treated us miserably in the beginning. They would not have given us the extra room if they were not forced to do so and they would tell us to leave as soon as they could. I mention that we often go to the parsonage during the week, for Bible study, choir practice, and young peoples group; it will save us a lot of time and walking. The Brandes like and trust us and the parsonage is in a beautiful quiet mini park setting. I finally persuade Mother and the next day we borrow a wagon, load our few things on it and move to the parsonage. We get two rooms upstairs, a smaller bedroom with a kitchen nook, where Mother sleeps and a larger one where I sleep. During the day my small bed is changed into a sofa and it becomes our living room. We can heat that room separately with a nice tile stove. We have the luxury of a table with chairs and an extra writing desk to do my school work. We are allowed to decorate our suite the way we like it and can hammer nails into the walls to hang pictures and curtains.

The Benders, an elderly Pentecostal couple, refugees from Silesia live on the other side of the staircase. He is an itinerant barber. With Frau Krüger and her six year old daughter Dagmar, who have arranged their quarters in the attic, we can celebrate the unexpected return of her husband from a Russian prison camp. We are a considerate, kind and cooperative house-community.

The Rindfleischs get new tenants, a family from the industrial area of Upper Silesia. They don't tolerate any restrictions or criticism from the house owners and often get involved in shouting matches with them. "It was so nice and peaceful when you were with us", Mrs. Rindfleisch confesses to Mother later.

The school year comes to an end and before we get into the final examinations for the Abitur some unusual events occur in our class. Dr Keitel, our chemistry teacher, is concerned with our mental and physical health. He suggests to some of us to add a little yeast, which may add some necessary vitamins and minerals to our meager meals. In the next chemistry period, he has just introduced a new topic someone knocks at the door Irene opens it and Gerd, pale and shaky, comes swaying into the classroom. Klaus, our 'class clown', is leading him by the arm trying to steady him. He looks bloated, because he put a big pillow on his stomach and wears his dad's old frock over it. They stop in front of Dr.Keitel, who looks at them piercingly. "Sssir, Gegegerd hahas eaeaten tttoo mmuch yeyeyeast, as yuyou susuguesteted" Klaus whines. (Dr. Keitel stutters a little.) The class explodes into laughter. "Rrubbish, ssit down," he says in a stern voice, but he cannot hide a quick smile. It takes Gerd a while to squeeze his big belly behind the narrow desk.

Classes change and Gerd gets relief by doing a handstand on the teacher's desk. At this moment our history teacher enters. She has a sense of humor and starts laughing, when Gerd jumps down and explains the situation.

The next day we are in the music room, Gerd comes late and is alone in the empty classroom. He does not like music and decides to turn all the desks around to get our English teacher, whom we have the next period, confused. While he is doing this, the principal comes in and asks him "What are you doing here? Why are you not with your class?" He tells him honestly, "Oh, I am turning the desks around "The principal finds it very virtuous and wonders. "Who turned them the wrong way around? Find out who has done it and I will talk to your homeroom teacher" SU later talks to Gerd and admonishes him to stop this kind of folly.

In a niche at the end of the hall is a display case with a stuffed crocodile. Two fellows from our class get the idea to remove this reptile from the case, knock at the door of the other graduating class and tell the teacher that the biology teacher has requested it. The class bursts into laughter, as they enter, the crocodile over their heads, because they do not have biology and the topic would not be about reptiles either. With profuse apologies the two fellows excuse themselves and mumble they must have chosen the wrong classroom.

The teachers are concerned about our behavior and attribute it to overwork, stress, preparing for the upcoming final examinations and insufficient nutrition. They feel it would be best to give us some rest and let us stay home for the last three days of this week. I suppose Dr.Sundermeyer, our homeroom teacher, has had some influence on this decision.

We write our final examinations for the Abitur in the cold, poorly lit classrooms. It is difficult to concentrate. In three of our main subjects we have to take an oral examination, at the request of the subject teachers. I pass all examinations. When we get the results of our written tests back, I find the math mark unfair. We had to solve three problems, two of these I solved correctly. The third one, in spherical geometry, consisted of two parts. I had solved each of the complicated operations correctly but had connected them with the opposite sign, minus instead of plus, which made the final result incorrect. I blamed the oversight on the bad lighting in the classroom, but Miss Magunna is not moved, though several of my classmates plead for me, because I am a good math student and had several A's (100%) in my class work, she insists on a C+ for my final mark. I am disappointed because I worked hard and could now have proven to my former math teacher, that I can do it. For me it is important to pass the official Abitur which I do and this time without a single *Mangelhaft* (D). Now I can apply for admission to a university.

When I look back I think it was good that I added this year to complete my formal education, not only to receive a better foundation of knowledge but also to become integrated again into the life of a normal society, after having experienced the rough life in the army and in refugee camps.

School is over. Our class has survived the stress of final examinations and the hardships of the first school year after the lost war. These difficult times have taught us tolerance and compassion for each other and created a good class spirit. This is reason to celebrate. Some of the local students have made arrangements for a big graduation party. I feel somewhat uneasy about it. I am not used to such parties, have no decent suit to wear and I cannot dance. I mention this to some of the class, but they don't want to hear of it. As "class father" I have to be with them on this occasion. To make me feel better, two of the girls offer to give me a crash course in dancing.. Jutta and Elisabeth are good teachers. Jutta is an intelligent good looking girl and I like her but I don't dare tell her this. She is about my size and we make good partners.

About forty years later, when I visit her in Munich on a trip from Canada, she confesses to me that she, too, had a crush on me. She and Elisabeth came on the same train to school as I did and when they saw me at the station, waiting for the train, they hoped I would come into their compartment. Too bad she did not tell me that then.

On the day before the class party I get a cold with fever and have to stay in bed. Next morning the doctor comes to the village and visits me – doctors still made house visits at that time. He gives me some medication and assures me I can go to the class party tonight. I trust him and visualize, that I will be all right. In the evening I dress in my blue marine uniform pants and my jacket, made by our village tailor from dyed army uniform material and, still a little wobbly, walk the three kilometers to the Peiner Festsäle. We have reserved their facilities, the most prestigious in town at that time, for our class party

The organizers of the meeting are glad that I have come. All members of the class are there. In the candlelit room one cannot see that the blues from my trousers and jacket do not match exactly. We have some simple snacks on side tables, food is still scarce. Everybody seems to be happy and relaxed. No one has failed the Abitur, although some just scraped by. We are a jolly bunch together, talk about our families and laugh about the pranks we played on our teachers. One mentions the nasty incident with the bowl. Our school did benefit in those lean years after the war from the *American Hoover Program,* the '*Schulspeisung*'. Big containers of soup were delivered during lunch break to the school yard and each student who wanted to participate, brought a bowl to school and received a ladle of soup in it. When we went back to class again, one student had left some water in his bowl and balanced l it over the frame of our classroom door. When the teacher entered the room and closed the door, it fell down beside him.

Uwe remembered the prank with the alarm clock. He had hidden one high up over the blackboard frame set up to ring in the middle of the English lesson. When it did, Mr. Murray was confused walked around the room and could not figure out what made this noise and from where it originated. Uwe must have laughed too loudly and he suspected him to be the culprit but Uwe denied it. I told him after the lesson that I felt it was not right to lie to a teacher. We are both members of the *Krapp Kreis,* a Christian student group. He regretted it, went to Mr. Murray after school and apologized. Mr. Murray was treating us like elementary pupils, which bothered us and we wanted to get back at him.

SU is celebrating with us, not so much as a teacher, more as a colleague or paternal friend. He tells us stories from the time, when he was young, what they did then and about his teacher training. He asks us about our future plans and shares with us, things we might encounter in life. We like him as a person. I tell him how much I appreciate the fact that he accepted me into his class.

The musicians begin to play and we all start to dance. I still remember the dance steps that the girls taught me and enjoy leading some of my classmates across the dance floor, especially my former dance masters. Time goes by fast and we realize this may be the last time we see each other and here and there someone is wiping a tear from her cheek.

Our secondary school education is officially completed. However, when we hear that Dr .Sundermeyer has initiated a public forum for those who are interested in Literature, a number of us, his former students, attend. We participate in reading and discussing works of classical and modern poets and authors. Dr.Sundermeyer is a Rilke expert, he wrote his dissertation about Rilke and he writes poetry himself.

In 1970 I visited him again as a 'colleague' on one of our trips from Canada to Germany. He welcomed me heartily and we had a good conversation. As we parted he went over to his bookshelf, pulled out three booklets of his poetry, and gave them to me as a gift. When I read them now, I am always reminded of him as one of my most influential teachers.

Mr. Herzog, our former music teacher, recruits some of us former music students for his community choir; I join for a while, since tenors are rare. At one of the practices he asks me:" What mark did I give you in music for the Abitur mark, Mr. Lemke?" "A C+ ", I reply. He thinks for a while and then says that I had deserved at least a B and he was sorry. It cannot be changed anymore, but I appreciate his honesty.

During the time I attend secondary school in Peine I join a Christian student group, the "*Krapp Kreis*". Dr.Krapp, a physician in Peine sponsors our group He has a good way of communicating with young people and has a concern for us especially for our spiritual well-being. We meet, usually once a week, in his home and discuss personal questions with him about our faith, difficult Bible passages and the importance of prayer in our life. We can talk openly about our relationship to our parents and teachers; topics like dating and peer pressure, inherited and acquired values and how we can live by them. I am looking forward to these evening meetings.

Once a year we have a retreat together. The year I attend we reserve a youth hostel in the Harz Mountains in the midst of the forest with a beautiful view from the high terrace of the hostel over the countryside and the small villages with their red tile roofs. The trails invite us to hike and we visit places that we know of from Goethe's Faust, the *Hexentanzplatz*. We play games, have discussions and make music on instruments that we have brought along. I have brought my recorder.

One evening we sit in a grotto in a circle and sing. It is getting dark and suddenly we see sparks flying in the air all around us, a beautiful sight that I have never seen before. Dr.Krapp explains to us; these are glow-worms that fly around to attract females. I am fascinated by this interesting phenomenon of nature. The next morning I go back to make a pencil sketch of this scene. Renate, one of my schoolmates, comes out and watches me. She is quite impressed with the outcome of it. I ask her if she likes it and when she nods, I give it to her. She blushes and is delighted. This incident is the beginning of a close friendship. She invites me to her home and introduces me to her mother. I guess mother has to approve of her friends. This is still customary in a more traditional upper class family. Her mother wants to know who I am and we get into a conversation, she is a narrator and reciter. I ask her if she ever gets nervous before speaking to a large audience. She laughs, "Very often, even after ten years of practice;" I always think of that when I have to speak to a larger group of people and it makes me less anxious.

I tell Renate about the MCC *Voluntary Service Camp,* in which I had participated. She is interested and wants to know more about it. She decides to join one and enjoys the international fellowship. A fellow camper, a young man from a prominent family in Hamburg, falls in love with her and pursues her. Our friendship becomes less intense and I withdraw after she tells me about it.

In1970 we visit her again in Ulm, Germany, and stay in our new VW camper on her property. She is married to a physician and is happy to see me again.

Having passed the Abitur; I can now apply for admission to a university. In Handorf, people assume that the son of Mrs.Lemke will become a pastor or a teacher and that prediction becomes true later in my life. Twenty-three members of our graduation class apply for study in a teacher training college. No one is admitted. German universities at this time use the *Numerus Clausus,* to regulate admittance to certain faculties in their university. Many have just opened again often in makeshift or reconstructed buildings that had been destroyed during the war and have only limited space.There is also a lack of professsors. Returning prisoners of war have preference.

Since I cannot get into the teacher training program, I go for my second choice and apply in the faculty of Architecture. I am interested in Art and was good in this subject in High school, so I hope this will give me a better chance to be accepted in that faculty. Stuttgart has one of the best Architecture departments; so I travel to Stuttgart, again hitch-hiking, and apply for a study place at the Technical University there. I have to write an extensive entrance examination. During that time I stay with the Bartels over night. I had worked with them in the potato fields under the Russians. They, too, had been expelled from their home by the Polish authorities and have now rented a farm near Stuttgart.

After my return I wait anxiously for the outcome. After three weeks I receive a letter, they are sorry but they cannot accept me, there had been a large number of applicants at that prestigious university. I am disappointed but, building on my experience in Stuttgart, I apply to Braunschweig Technical University and am accepted into their faculty of Architecture for the winter semester of 1949. This makes me happy. Perhaps it is the better solution anyway. Braunschweig is only half-an-hour by train from Peine and two hours from Handorf by bicycle. I can be closer to Mother if anything should happen to her. It still leaves me a year to prepare for my studies at Braunschweig.

Now I have a goal and in order to reach it I have to save to be able to pay tuition fees and other expenses. Mother is fully in agreement with my decision and wants to support me in any way she can. She takes on a job with a tile factory. It has opened a branch shop in Handorf and Mother can walk to her work place. She is supposed to grind and polish one square foot size tiles on a sanding belt and is paid by the piece. I discourage her from accepting the job but she insists she will try it. The pay is not very good and the work is hard on her hands for a woman of her age. After a few months her hands get numb and cannot handle the tiles anymore and she agrees to quit. She would rather work for farmer Brandes if he needs her and she is used to that kind of work.

Once again Contractor Hanke has work for me and I can earn some money to save for my studies next year. After a few months, work runs out and I am laid off. I am now entitled to unemployment insurance. I apply for it in the unemployment insurance office in Peine but the process is so cumbersome and time consuming, standing in lines and waiting, that I decide to look for something worthwhile to do

I hear about a Mennonite Voluntary Service opportunity in Espelkamp, about 80 km West of Hannover. I write to their office and the camp director, Milton Harder, replies that they would be glad to have me there. It does not take long to pack my rucksack. I go to the unemployment insurance office before I leave and tell them that I don't want to wait idly and ask if they could keep my application on file until I return.

To save money, I hitch-hike to Espelkamp. Milton introduces me to the rest of the gang. The voluntary service workers there come from different countries, Dora from Switzerland, Maryke and Willem from Holland, Robert from France, and several from Germany and USA. they belong to different denominations, Milton is Old Mennonite, Johnny Amish, German Mennonites, Doopsgesinte from Holland and other denominations, quite a mix of people. Some stay for four weeks, others for several months or years, depending on their work situation at home and how long they can extend their holidays. Some do their alternative military service here. We are from a variety of occupations, students and professors, secretaries, businessmen, tradesmen and unemployed people. The camp is organized and maintained by the Mennonite Central Committee (MCC); at this point we are twenty volunteers. We live in an old wooden army barrack and sleep in bunk beds. We try to make our abode as comfortable as possible. Uncle Bill and Mammy Dick are our 'house parents'. She is a liberated woman and tells us men we have to do kitchen duty, wash our own clothes and iron our own shirts and pants. "Your future wives will thank me for training you in housekeeping," she smiles and the girls in the camp agree. If we don't know how to do things, she kindly shows us.

Every morning we go out to work. We rebuild former ammunition bunkers from the last war, into homes for German refugees. I am one of the 'professionals' in the group, since I have already worked in the building trade. We get acquainted with some of the refugees who have just moved into some of the new homes that we helped to build. They cannot believe that we work here voluntarily, without pay, and even pay for our own transportation. We tell them that we do this '*in the name of*

Christ', the Mennonite way. Their happiness is our reward. They cannot fathom that.

In front of our barrack is an open field big enough for volley ball or soccer. We sometimes play in teams, Germans against other countries or volunteers with or against locals. In the evening we have interesting discussions about the war or lifestyles in our different countries. I want to improve my English communication skills, so I talk to Johnny in English and he tells me with a smile," I can understand you better when you speak German". We also have fun improvising and performing short theatre pieces.

Mother writes that the construction firm Hanke, has work for me again. So I have to take leave from this wonderful group of people, who have become my friends. A few years ago our countries were at war but here we respect each other, have fun and can work peacefully together, 'in the Name of Christ'

MCC and the *Evangelische Hilfswerk* (a German relief agency) work together on this project. Before I leave, I go to the director of the Espelkamp project and ask him for a certificate to indicate that I have worked here in the building trade, without pay. I think it might be useful for my practicum in Architecture later and perhaps for the Unemployment Insurance as well.

Hanke has a project outside of Peine. I have to get up at five in the morning fasten my toolbox to the bicycle carrier and ride an hour to my job. We are pouring large under-water foundations, which often require nightshifts. It is hard work but the pay is good and I can save for my first semesters.

At University

In October 1949 I quit my job and start my studies at the Technical University of Braunschweig. I ride my bike to the railway station in Peine and take the train to Braunschweig. Bombs have destroyed the former attractive classicistic station building. The rubble has been removed but the big entrance hall is still without windows and a full roof. I walk over the Oker river bridge and across the Friedrich Wilhelm Platz to the city square, stop at Dankwarderode Castle, built in 1175 as residence for Duke Henry the Lion, with the upright lion sculpture on a pedestal in front of it, one of the earliest 12th century metal figures. It looks small, against the huge *Braunschweiger Dom*, a five nave Gothic Cathedral on the other side of the plaza. Braunschweig still has a medieval character. The beautiful *Altstadtmarkt*, bordered by the Gothic *Rathaus*, with large sculptures of the residing dukes and their spouses, ranks as one of the most aesthetically pleasing medieval civic buildings. The Martini Cathedral, an early gothic hall church with large interior artwork and the *Gewandthaus*,(cloth-makers guild house) known for its famous Renaissance gable, concludes the square around the old market place. Many other churches and medieval half-timbered merchant and guild houses are still in ruins or in the process of being rebuilt. In this city I will spend the next five years.

I cross the Oker again, which surrounds the centre of the old city, and the University is right behind it. One wing of the classical building has been repaired and is used for lecture halls and offices, the other part is still in ruins and in the process of being rebuilt. The *Carolo Wilhelmina* University grew out of the *Collegium Carolinum, the* oldest technical school in Germany, founded in 1745 for the children of the nobility. As in many other universities, students have to spend a year helping to rebuild the campus before they are admitted for studies.

I register and fill out a few questionnaires. The secretary gives me an important document, my *Studienbuch;* it will accompany me through all my years at this university. I have to record in it all the courses that I am going to take for each semester. After I am finished with the registration I ask her what to do next. She tells me to go to the Department of Architecture on the second floor and select my courses for the first semester; they are listed on the big bulletin board in the main hall.

In high school we received a printed time table and study guide and followed the instructions; here I can plan my own future. It sounds good, but I have no idea how to start. Beside me a student is eagerly writing in his Studienbuch. I ask him for help. He explains: "On this board are the courses for the first four semesters, those on the left side are the courses in which you will be tested in the first examination. Divide them into four and select the ones you want to take in each semester, they are the compulsory courses. On the right side are the electives of which you have to take at least four in each semester; that is it." It is difficult for me to choose if I don't know the professors, what and how they teach and in what sequence the courses are arranged. I take a leap of faith and write six prescribed courses and six electives in my Studienbuch. The most interesting ones are: art history, design, building construction and applied geometry and from the electives: drawing, painting, sculpture and calligraphy. I take my book to the office and they calculate the fees for my first semester, they will be 219.50 DM. The treasurer takes the money and gives me a student card. I am now a 'Student of Architecture' at the Technical University and my first lectures will start tomorrow.

My high school buddy, Rolf, is in the same department and we travel together from Peine to Braunschweig. Study at the university is different from school. The professor enters fifteen minutes later than indicated, the famous *'academic quarter'*. We knock on the table to greet him. Some lecturers step behind the desk, open the book which they or somebody else has written, read for 40 minutes, give a few explanations, ask the rhetorical question, "Are there any questions?" close the book and leave.

Technical University Braunschweig

Helmut overlooking the ruins of Braunschweig

Building construction practicum

Usually only a few of us attend these lectures, we know the book and need only to ask those who attend, which chapter he read and can then study it at our leisure. Dr. Flesche, our art history prof., uses notes, embellishes them with humorous stories and illustrates his lecture with pictures on a screen and sketches on the blackboard. The Auditorium *Maximum* is filled to the last seat for his lectures and if we don't get there early, we have to stand in the aisles.

At the beginning of each semester, the lecturer, who accepts us in his course, puts his signature beside the course we have entered in our Studienbuch. We have to do this for all our courses. It is proof to the administration that we are enrolled in these courses and have fulfilled the requirement for the *'Vorexamen'* (first examination). Nobody checks later to see if we attend the lectures. I am usually a conscientious student and attend the courses for which I have paid. The university provides study halls for students who come from out of town. We can do our home and seminar assignments here in our spare time and don't have to take our bulky drafting equipment home. It gives us an opportunity to exchange lecture notes with other students and they can tell us which professor is good and well organized and who is not. That helps us to choose our courses for the next semester.

The first semester passes slowly. The beginning is hard for me. The lecture style and the transposing of notes is new. Getting to the campus by bicycle, train and a half-hour walk is strenuous and time consuming.

One day I check the pin board and see a small note, "Free room and board for a needy student." I write down the address, mention it to my mother and decide to apply the next day. With some trepidation I ring the door bell at the house of our university president who is the one who posted the note. In a short interview he asks me where I come from and why I am applying. I tell him my story and he thinks I am the right person. With a handshake he accepts me as their guest. I am overjoyed and don't know how to thank him. The maid shows me my room. It is spacious and bright, separate from their living quarters. "Breakfast is included," she tells me. "When may I serve it?" I am still dumbfounded. "Any time that is convenient, I am an early riser," I reply.

Two days later I get the keys and pack my belongings into the closets of my new room. I still cannot believe it, so nicely furnished, a full size bed, different from my army cot in Handorf, an easy chair and a full size table at which to do my assignments and it is only two minutes away from the university. When I tell Mother about it, she is very happy for me. I don't have to travel anymore as in the two previous semesters and can spend that time on my studies.

Studentengemeinde

Not far from the university and from where I now live, the Evangelical Synod has rented a house for the activities of the *Evangelische Studentengemeinde.*

The Studentenheim is open for all Protestant students of the university. It is in an area of the city which still shows the scars of the last war. Where, five years ago, one could see elegant patrician homes with pretty front yards and trees there are now empty lots with fragments of walls and foundations between weeds and rubble and we can see the university farther behind them. The Studentenheim is often frequented by students who want to relax or prepare for lectures and eat their lunches there,. I like to meet with them since it is only a short walk from my place. I visit the student pastor and ask him officially if I, a Mennonite, may join the Lutheran student group. Pastor Wielgoss receives me warmly. He too is from East Prussia and we have many things in common. He gladly accepts and welcomes me. Now, as a member, I participate actively in the life of the Studentengemeinde. I attend the weekly Bible studies and join one of the small groups which discuss ethics, art and literature, theology and politics and we try to relate these topics to our life as responsible citizens and Christians. We music lovers get together, form a choir, sing and listen to music. A church has given us several brass instruments and a group had formed a brass octet; at the moment they need a trumpet player. I sang in the church choir in Handorf and played in their brass orchestra, so I join the choir and the brass ensemble and take part in their performances and enjoy it.

The Studentengemeinde has permission to hold Sunday services in the large St. Blasius Cathedral. We start our service earlier in the morning before the main church service begins. Entering the cathedral, the huge Gothic church interior with its slender columns reaching high up into the vaulted ceiling makes me feel small and unimportant and then the light shining through the high Gothic stained glass windows creates an atmosphere that is uplifting and inspires to praise God in the Highest. It is common here at the end of each Sunday service to have communion. For me the way it is served is different from what I am used to in our Mennonite church so I am hesitant to take part in it.

Sometimes, upon invitation, we drive out into the countryside to share Sunday services with congregations who like a change in their worship pattern or want to give their pastor a rest. They then ask us to take over the service for that Sunday. We drive out in the morning, our brass ensemble plays chorales and etudes half an hour before the service starts and wakes the sleepy parishioners and invites them to come to church before the church bells start to ring. During the service our choir sings and the brass ensemble accompanies and adds some pieces to it. Our pastor or one of the students will lead the service. We enjoy such outings, especially the invitation after the service to share dinner with the parishioners.

Once I am invited to the pastor's house. His wife brings a roast beef in horseradish sauce, steaming potatoes and red cabbage to the table. My mouth waters. I have not seen such a meal for a long time. They encourage me to help myself and I do. When I take the first bite of the delicious beef wrapped in strong horseradish, tears run down my cheeks and I have to stop to catch my breath. Wow! this horseradish is hot. I am amazed at how the others can eat that spicy stuff. I scrape the horseradish from the meat and eat lots of potatoes and cabbage. When they offer me more, I decline and they think I am very modest.

Shortly before Christmas we plan a retreat in the Harz Mountains. Pastor Wielgoss leads the Bibelstudy and discussions, we sing, make music and play games. Some bring their skis along. The Harz Mountains are a well known ski area in central Germany. In our free time we go to the slopes skiing or tobogganing. A fellow student lends me his ski outfit and I try to ski for the first time. It is fun to race down the slopes on skis and I enjoy it immensely.

On our way back to Braunschweig we go through the open entrance hall of the station. Still in high spirits from the retreat someone suggests we have a short Christmas concert before we depart. We gather in a corner of the hall and sing Christmas carols accompanied by trumpets and trombones. People stop and listen or sing along. Soon the hall is filled with Christmas music and Christmas spirit. After a while a station policeman comes and asks us politely if we could continue on the plaza in front of the station as we are blocking the traffic. We oblige and continue singing on our way out and then each one goes to his or her own place.

During the Advent season our brass octet sometimes goes into the neighborhood and we play Advent and Christmas music on street corners and plazas to share the Christmas spirit with our neighbors. Some of them wave or even throw a few coins from their windows.

To one of our evening meetings in our Studentenheim we invite Erna Fast, a representative from MCC, to speak to us. She shares her experience with people, especially refugees, in post-war Germany and the relief work that MCC, a Mennonite relief organization, is doing. At the end she asks what we students are lacking mostly. Many say that shoes are difficult to get even on ration cards and she says she will try to provide some for us. After she is gone one of my fellow students, not knowing that I am a Mennonite, mentions "When the Mennonites promise something, they deliver, I know that from our Munich student group". Two weeks later a box of shoes is delivered, which confirms his prediction.

Rejoining the Mennonites

Since I was drafted into the army I have not attended any Mennonite church service and that is now six years ago. I think Erna Fast told me that a small Mennonite congregation meets once a month in Braunschweig. I should contact Walter Wiebe for time and place. Next Sunday I meet him in the Lutheran congregational centre where thirty Mennonites from the area around Braunschweig gather. Dr.Crous, pastor of the Mennonite church in Göttingen, conducts the service. I talk to him after the service how we can best integrate the West Prussian Mennonite refugees into the congregaton. Walter Wiebe has agreed to oversee the MCC relief centre for the area. He will receive and distribute clothing and food which American and Canadian people have donated to those in need. Dr. Crous is also concerned about the social and spiritual wellbeing of the members of the congregation, especially the young people and he asks me if I could help. He has a list of the Mennonites who live in the area.. We gather with some of the young people who attend the service and discuss with them the possibility od forming a Mennonite youth group. Some of them are enthusiastic about it..

Katja, a high school senior, daughter of one of the few local Mennonite families, a very responsible girl and I take a copy of the list and visit the Mennonite families who have young children. We tell them what we visualize for the young Mennonites in our congregation. In one family we ask the two teen-age girls who had just been baptised if they would like to join a youth group. They are not interested, Baptism does not mean much to them they did this only to please their parents. I am surprised at such an attitude.

At the next congregational meeting about a dozen young people stay behind and we plan strategy. We want to meet once every two weeks and they ask me to lead the group. Katja knows the local Protestant Pastor who will allow us to use their board room for our meetings. It is an avid little group most of them high school kids. We have an open program. We talk about our experiences during the week about our faith in action, our interests and problems.

Occasionally parents invite us into their homes. Wolfgang and Eva's parents have a big house and a lovely garden, we play games. Dr.Nickel tells us about his life after the war and how he worked hard to achieve his present position as s bank director and gives us hope for our future. We are quite flexible in our programs and each one contributes to them.

One winter we plan a ski retreat. We invite 'Pax-Boys', Mennonite young men who chose Alternative Service doing social work in Germany instead of serving in the US army. They pick us up with the MCC Land Rover; we pack our ski equipment in the back and drive the fifty km to the Harz Mountains. We enjoy downhill skiing. One day we shoulder our skis and climb up a steep incline, there are no ski lifts yet, and from the top it takes us half a day to ski back down to the Youth hostel where we are staying. We have a lot of fun and for our American friends it is their first ski experience.

For the Easter holidays we plan a retreat for all young Mennonites in the area. The North German Mennonite youth workers offer to help us with the program and financing. Hans-Joachim, a distant relative of mine, has connections to the Mennonite Conference and Bob, a Pax-Boy from Pennsylvania and a charmer, can get us some food and transportation through MCC. We rent the Braunschweig Youth hostel, a former country estate with a park-like garden, well suited for walks and outside games. Young people from the surrounding area of Braunschweig, from Hannover and Hildesheim have registered. They like it so much that they tell us they would like to organize youth groups in their own cities. We encourage them to do that and offer to help. A few weeks later I get an invitation from the Kauenhofens to come to their first young peoples meeting. With three others from our youth group I take the train to Hildesheim to join them. They ask many questions and we try to demonstrate to them what we are doing in Braunschweig. A short while later, Selma from Hannover wants us to come over and organize a group there; We have now three youth groups in the wider area.

The first Mennonite youth magazine, *Die Junge Gemeinde,* is issued. It is quite versatile, a short overview of congregational life and politics and the main section about youth activities, book reviews and letters to the editor, where young people write about their faith experiences and voice their beefs. It is a good way to communicate with other young Mennonites in Germany.

We read about a Mennonite youth retreat in the castle of Ehrenbreitstein. My adventurous cousin Käthe and I decide to attend. We travel the cheap way, hitch-hiking the 450 km to Koblenz; it is still quite safe to do so at that time. Car drivers are generous about taking youngsters along.. If we have to wait too long for a ride, I wll hide behind a bush, a beautiful girl like Käthe, has a better chance at being picked up.and most do not mind taking me along as well..

About 120 young Mennonites gather in castle *Ehrenbreitstein* on the Rhein River, most from North Germany and a few representatives from the South German Mennonites and even some from East Germany. The youth workers prepared a good program and they persuade me to lead the singing. MCC workers are interested in what the German Mennonite youth are doing and they enjoy participating. The Pax-Boys especially. They are usually good singers and we get a men's quartet together, even get a small choir.

As guest speaker we invited *Onkel Wall.* He was pastor and Professor at a Mennonite seminary in the USA and is now retired and works with MCC. We love him for his sense of humor and his 'humanity' and wisdom. He has a wide heart for us who suffered from the terror of the war. He leads the Bible Studies and discussions and participates in our games, but only as a judge, he says.

We have lots of fun. One morning one of the girls, an Old Mennonite from Pennsylvania, comes limping to the breakfast table. In answer to our question as to what has happened, she confesses that she jumped out of the window in the girl's dorm to join a couple of boys in the courtyard at moonlight - a 'no no', according to youth hostel rules.

At this retreat several celebrate a reunion with friends and relatives whom they have not enn since they fled from West Prussia at the end of the war, some discover new relatives and many depart with new friends.

Slowly the standard of living improves in Germany. The rubble of the destroyed houses and factories has been removed and the barren land is now available for people to build new houses. Reconstruction brings new jobs and new home owners have higher expectations in regards to lifestyle. Mennonites, expelled from West Prussia and Russia, Pomerania and Silesia, have found new accommodation and homes in the west. Mennonites from USA and Canada assisted them with donations of food, clothing, books and educational materials. All that is still in short supply in post war Germany.

Teachers, preachers and experts in different fields come over to help in the training of leaders to rebuild the country. MCC and the Mennonite Conference are providing means for congregations to organize retreats and seminars to train youth workers and assist pastors.

One such seminar is set up in an old castle, now youth hostel, in the beautiful Weser mountain area. The organizers, the North German youth workers, invite me together with Mennonite pastors and teachers from South Germany and North America to assist in presenting material for youth leaders and future Sunday and summer Bible school teachers. To begin the day, I play a tune from a chorale or hymn with my trumpet from the tower of the old castle, as a wake up call. After a communal breakfast we gather in groups for lectures and hands-on demonstrations. I use my architectural skills to demonstrate in a sand box, what a Palestinian village may have looked like at the time of Jesus. Building such villages may help children to visualize and remember Bible stories better and it can be fun too.

MCC's headquarters is in Frankfurt and the director draws interesting people to the centre. This spring he has planned a peace workshop. Participants are given topics to research, such as "How do or did Church Fathers, politicians, scientists and government leaders deal with peace and nonresistance issues in their time and how does that affect us?' Afterwards we discuss the results. My topic is Martin Luther's writings. I must have given a good presentation because Paul Peachy, who was MCC director at that time, tells me after the workshop that Mennonite Colleges in USA offer scholarships for suitable German students and if I am interested, he will recommend me for one. I am honored and gladly accept . At a student conference in Krefeld years ago I had heard about this and at that time wished I could get a scholarship for the USA; now it might become a reality for me.

During this semester vacation I cannot get any work. Magdalena tells me MVS (Mennonite Voluntary Service) runs a camp in Kiel, near the Baltic Sea. I hitch-hike 300km north and show up in the picturesque youth hostel. Margaret, whom I know from the MCC centre in Hamburg, welcomes me. The facilities for us 22 volunteers are more comfortable here than in Espelkamp. This time we dismantle wooden military barracks, take them to an empty lot in the outskirts of the city, put the sections together again to construct a temporary church building in which the congregation can hold their services while their destroyed church is being rebuilt.

During our free time, we drive to the sandy beach, relax in the sun, or dive into the big waves of the Baltic Sea. We play beach ball or horse-play on a small, half-sunken cutter. Somebody pushes me over board and I get tangled up in the ropes and almost drown.

My sister Magdalena, who is now a registered nurse in Hamburg, comes to the camp to visit us. Margaret suggests we take the camp jeep to drive to our work site and asks me if I would drive. I agree somewhat hesitantly, because I have never driven a car before. Hans, who drove the jeep in Espelkamp, had shown me how to drive one but having observed how to drive and driving one myself are two different things. When we drive off, Margaret comments that I drive a little shakily but that this might be caused by the loose steering wheel on the old jeep. After we return I confess that this was the first time I have driven a vehicle. "You did quite well, driving for the first time, but to let you drive an American vehicle without a license could have gotten me into trouble" I apologize for not telling her.

Margaret takes some of us to the Hamburg MCC Centre after the camp is closed. She must have noticed that I always wear the same outfit and lets me have a look into the MCC clothes bin. I find a good blue striped suit that fits me perfectly and she says that I can have it. It is the first proper suit that I have owned since I left home.

Ursula, one of the campers, who came with us to Hamburg, had previously been an exchange student in a Mennonite College in USA. During a walk along the Elbe, she tells me all about it. We are so involved in our conversation that we miss the last train back and have to walk for four hours through the night, to get back to the MCC Centre..

After my next semester I find a job in Hamburg. My cousin Kurt has contacted a rubber boot factory and they have part time employment for students. He invites me to stay at his place for the time. I can visit my sister in the hospital and spend some time with my lovely cousin, Ruth, who is a receptionist and lab assistant with a local doctor. After work and on free weekends I explore the city, make excursions into its surroundings and participate in the Mennonite youth group where I learn to know my future brother in law, Gustav.

Vorexamen

Since I now live in a worry free beautiful room at Professor Imhoffens. close to the university, I have more time to study and will be able to complete all the prerequisites for the first examination in four semesters,(the minimum I have to attend). I went to most of my lectures, finished successfully all the prescribed assignments and labs and can now apply for the *Vorexamen.* For our Diploma in architecture we have to verify our qualification and prove our ability to perform required tasks in two examinations, the *Vorexamen,* after a minimum of four semesters and the *Hauptexamen*, after a minimum of eight semesters. Most students add a few semesters before they feel ready to apply for each one of them.

If I win a scholarship to study for a year in a Mennonite College, it would be reasonable to have my Vorexamen behind me, before I go abroad for a year. It is a natural break in my studies

In the middle of my preparations a letter from the MCC office in Frankfurt arrives. I have been accepted at Bluffton College in Ohio for the fall semester and it is now spring 1951. I am very happy, and even more concerned to finish my examination before I go. My ideal schedule is, to study until 8:00pm, have supper and then ride my bike through the park for an hour; it will supply more oxygen to my lungs and brain and will make me tired enough to have a good night's rest. The next day I can start with a clear mind.

In addition to my studies I now have to make preparations for my trip, write an acceptance and thank-you letter and obtain a passport and visa.

Our Vorexamen consists of several written and oral examinations. I don't have much difficulty with the first ones but am a little concerned about the last one with Professor Rehbock. He is feared by many architecture students and is the reason why some postpone applying for their Vorexamen. He teaches 'Applied Geometry', mathematics for architects, and he is known to be tough on 'artists without a mathematical brain'; often two thirds of the architecture students have to repeat his course.

All written tests are scheduled for nine o'clock; only Rehbock holds his three hour test at eight. I did not pay enough attention to his schedule and appear at 8:45. The assistant, who supervises the test, tells me that officially he is not allowed to let me in after half past eight, but he will make an exception. So I sit in my seat and sweat trying to catch up. I get the main problem solved but the bell rings when I am not quite finished with the final one. I hope I can make up for it in the oral examination. The next day I appear in a black suit and tie, the usual attire for oral examinations, in professor Rehbock's office. He offers me a seat and tells me that I didn't do very well in the last part of my written test. I mention to him that I received a scholarship from an American university and it has required some preparation. (It was still unusual so soon after the war for German students to study abroad.) He asks me from which university I have received the scholarship and when I am leaving. We talk briefly about it, then he congratulates me, shakes my hand and says, "I wish you well, you passed the course". I could have embraced him, I cannot believe it; I have jumped over the last hurdle. I can now make arrangements with MCC Frankfurt for the trip to the United States and think about Bluffton.

Contractor Hanke offers me a job again, this time as a *Baupraktikant*; I will have an opportunity to work in different fields of building construction, a practicum for my studies in architecture. My first job is laying sewers. I dig ditches, lay heavy clay pipes in those, fit them together and seal the seams with a tar rope - a dirty job. When Superintendent Richter asks me to do the same on the next job, I tell him doing this work for two weeks makes me an expert already and I would like to learn something else. I think he does not like students and tells me to do as I am told or he will fire me. I register a complaint and am transferred to *Vormann* Maurer, a very efficient and fair older man. He lost one hand in the war but works faster with a hook on the other than people with two hands. He shows us how to mix mortar and transport it to the bricklayer. Then he demonstrates how to start a brick wall. He builds the corners with level and line and we lay the bricks in between along the line. He lets me start the next corner. He is a perfectionist and acknowledges good workmanship. I like him. My next stop is the carpenter's shop. I enjoy working with wood, building furniture and carving sculptures

Soon my time is up. On this job I have gained valuable experience in the building trade, good practical knowledge for my later profession.

Chapter Seven

Bluffton College

In August 1951, I meet nine young German Mennonites at the harbour in Bremerhaven. We come from different parts of Germany and do not know each other but we are going to the same destination the MCC centre in Akron Pensylvania. MCC has selected us, I am not sure by which criteria, and offered us a scholarship in different Mennonite Colleges in the USA.

We board the MS, Nelly, a former freighter, heading for New York. Our first stop is Southampton on the other side of the North Sea to pick up more passengers. From there we enter the open ocean. The ships bell rings and all passengers are asked to assemble on deck. The captain instructs us how to survive a possible disaster on the high seas. The boat starts to roll which gives the whole exercise a kind of reality. After he finishes explaining the value of lifeboats, he turns around looking for able men to help manning the lifeboats. I stand beside him watching carefully his insructions. I must have looked able and trustworthy to him so he appoints me passenger-mate for one boat. I am so overwhelmed by that honor that I rush over to the reeling and empty my stomach. A good start for a seaman, I think. We slowly get used to the rolling of the boat. When the ocean is calm and the sky is clear, we lie on deck, absorb the sun, chat and exchange family information and pictures. I know Gerhard vaguely from Mennonite youth meetings; Ingrid and Hanna are from Berlin and Hanna has a few semesters of art history behind her. Margot from the Pfalz and a few West Prussians make up the rest of the group.

We are feeling a little nervous when we pass the Statue of Liberty. In the harbor of New York Margaret Harms, welcomes us. I know her from her MCC service in Germany. She helps us to proceed through customs and immigration and buys us our train tickets to Akron.

The personnel director in the MCC office welcomes and introduces us to America. We sit in the lounge and he asks where we come from and what we expect from our stay here. We discuss differences between Germany and America and how these may affect our relationship with students and professors at our college. He informs us about what we may encounter and what may be expected of us. The next morning we wish each other luck and everyone travels in a different direction to our Colleges, for me it is Bluffton.

Bluffton is a small town in Northwest Ohio. At the station I ask a man how to get to the college, "Oh, that is not very far, I can drive you there" he replies. The college campus is in a park-like setting on the outskirts of the town. It consists of seven different buildings, which are referred to as *'Halls'*. The registration and other offices are in *College Hall*, recognizable by the tower over the entrance. This makes it look like a church. Registrar Hilty knows that I am coming; he welcomes me kindly and registers me as an exchange student. He tells me a little about Mennonite Colleges and then calls my *big brother*, to take me to my dormitory. Every new student in Bluffton is matched with a student in a higher semester, who takes him under his wing and familiarizes him with college procedures. Arden is a shy, slender third year *Junior* student, in the third semester. We chat while we are going through the park. He points out the different buildings; *Lincoln Hall* in the back is the girls' dorm; the brick building with the white window frames is *Science Hall* and the smaller house that looks like a residence is the *Music Hall*. We cross the wooden bridge that leads over the *Riley*, a little creek that meanders through the park. A little further on we walk up the steps to the open portico of *Ropp Hall,* my new 'home'. With its four Doric columns it looks more like a Greek temple than a boys dormitory. Arden takes me to the end of the hall on the second floor and introduces me to Joe, a senior in theology, a pleasant local fellow who welcomes me as his roommate. I am a little apprehensive but think we might be able to get along together for a year. He shows me my bed, study desk and closet. Our room is bare, painted in mute wine-red. When he finds out in our conversation that I study architecture, he asks me if I would mind painting some pictures on the walls. I tell him to wait a little.

The next day all freshmen and new students have to take an entrance examination. The supervisor allows me to use a little dictionary to make sure I understand the questions. For me it is a strange kind of test. True or false questions can be so ambiguous to me. How do I answer if only one part of the question is true and the other false? What answer do I choose in multiple-choice questions when all of the suggested answers have some truth in them? I am a perfectionist; everything has to fit properly. Besides that, I have to be familiar with the intricacies of the English language in order to distinguish between the good and the better. I do not know much about details of American history and literature. So, understandably, I do not do too well. I pass with 60 % and am classified a sophomore, a second year student. I feel a little overqualified after having studied four semesters in a German university, but I do not mind. For me it is more a *Studium Generale* to widen my horizon in general. I know I cannot transfer any credit from here to my Technical University.

At the beginning of the fall semester freshmen and sophomores have a ritual; the strongest of each class line up on opposite sides of the Riley, throw a rope across it and in a tug-of-war they want to prove who is superior in this semester. The losers are pulled through the water. The sophomores urge me to help them and I give in. I pull as hard as I can and that very likely gives us sophomores the advantage; we drag the freshmen, some of them tall guys, through the creek.

Dr. Shelly, my staff advisor, discusses my plan of studies. with me I have to take the compulsory subjects, English, Natural Science, Human Resources, a combination of New Testament and Psychology and, as electives, Art, including Pottery, which is new for me, Music and Mennonite History. Dr. Berky is our science prof. At the beginning of the semester, he tries an experiment with us, to test the value of true and false questions. He shakes a dime, drops it on the back of his hand and we have to guess if the tail or the head shows He repeats the procedure ten times at the beginning of the class and we record how many times we do guess correctly. After we have done this for a few weeks, we add up our result. I was above average, 56% of the time I guessed right. The highest was 60%, the lowest 38%. The result of this exercise indicates that with luck you could get a passing mark without studying.

I take piano lessons hoping to be able to accompany simple hymns for congregational singing at our church service; this is the reason I give them for enrolling in piano. After one year's training with my good instructor. I still find it difficult to synchronize four parts with two hands into one pleasant melody. Perhaps I expected too much for the little time I spent practicing. There are too many distractions; I would rather do more exciting things than sitting and practicing scales.

With my foreign student friend, Zacchaeus, from Nigeria, I sometimes play duets. He plays the piano and I borrow a trumpet from my big brother and accompany him or harmonize. It is fun and the others applaud.

Joe reminds me of my promise to decorate our room. We buy some silver paint and I design a mural. I draw a bridge crossing the ocean, connecting our two countries, Germany, symbolized by a destroyed church and a castle, arching over to the United States, with the Statue of Liberty and the skyline of New York as background. In the foreground, I draw the Bluffton campus with College Hall opening its doors. The whole picture is simplified, abstract, silver lines on the burgundy color of the wall. It covers the main part of one wall. "Quite impressive", some of our visitors remark. Our room becomes the talk of the college and students sneak in to look at the artwork. The sports coach must have heard about it. He asks me to paint a centerpiece on the gym floor, a beaver in a large circle, the mascot of Bluffton's sports teams. He gives me twelve Dollars for it.

Bluffton College has a number of clubs, cultural, religious, musical and sports clubs. I look at their mission-statement and choose to join two of them, one is the *Public Relations club,* in which we discuss world events and participate in Study Conferences. At the International Relations day, the president of the club asks me to help with decorating the stage for a presentation. At the Sunday service, foreign students are asked to read the Bible text in their mother tongue. I do it in German.

My roommate invites me to join the *Men's Gospel Team.* In our meetings, we share personal events and problems, invite guest speakers to talk about topics of interest to students. The musically inclined members sing as a guest quartet in neighbor congregations and talk to young people's groups.

Carl, a junior whom I have befriended, invites me to his church a Methodist congregation to share my experiences during and after the war in Germany. Joe helps me to formulate and pronounce my presentation correctly. Some of the parishioners have relatives and friends in Germany and they are interested in my report and want to hear more from me. They hold a collection for me which I did not espect but appreciate. I also give a talk to a college audience.

At the end of the year, all the clubs want to see their pictures in the college yearbook. The members of those clubs position themselves in front of a blackboard on which their name and motto is printed to identify their club. Our clubs ask me to do the printing, which I do using calligraphy that I learned from my Swiss graphic instructor at University. Other clubs see it and want me to do the same for their club too.

Every Monday morning students gather in the chapel for a service before they go to their classes. A staff member or a senior student gives a short devotion, liturgical or a brief sermonette. When it is my roommate's turn, he asks me to join him in the presentation. He will talk about the Lord's Prayer and I shall draw a picture to illustrate it. I reluctantly agree and we prepare for it. Monday comes, Joe gives his introduction and when he starts playing a record of the Lord's prayer, sung by a male voice, I walk up to the stage, move the big blackboard to the centre of the stage, get my special colored chalk sticks out and draw, almost life-size, '*Jesus praying in Gethsemane*'. It is quiet while I am drawing and the students wonder what the outcome will be. It works out fairly well. President Ramseyer also attends the chapel service and as he is leaving, he shakes my hand and thanks me for my contribution. Joe tells me later he heard people mention that this was one of the most meaningful chapel services

I spend a lot of time in the art department with Professor Klassen, a distinguished artist and teacher from the German settlements in the Ukraine. I take three art courses with him. In drawing and clay work, I have some experience from my Braunschweig University, but working on the potter's wheel, throwing vases, pots and bowls, is new for me and I enjoy it. Occasionally I assist Professor Klassen, helping students with their drawing skills and centering the clay on the potter's wheel.

Student at Bluffton University   *Hitchhiking through the USA*

Meeting the Schefflers

Bluffton Secondary School gives a musical and the students ask Professor Klassen if he could design a poster for them to advertise it. He asks me if I want to take on this job, otherwise he will tell them he has no time for it. I take the challenge and produce an acceptable design. The school offers me two free tickets for their performance as a thank you. I ask Joe if he wants to come with me, he declines and suggests I should arrange a date and take a girl along. I have no experience in that field but he offers some information and I think, "I came here to learn about customs and people; so I have to try dating too". In the next art class, I ask a beautiful fellow art student for a date and she accepts. Harvella is one of three missionary siblings from India. On the day of the performance, I ring the bell at Lincoln Hall, the girl's dormitory, and ask for Harvella. The dean on duty calls her; the girls in the dormitory have to give notice when they leave the dorm in the evening and when they return. She comes down the steps gracefully and greets me. I am a little nervous and wonder why it feels different now from when I am helping her in class to centre the clay on the potter's wheel. Harvey is somewhat reserved, unlike her sister Betty who is bubbly. I try to converse with her but my English is limited and awkward, and she does not make a great effort to help me either. We have fun at the musical but on the way home, she joins the other girls until one of them reminds her that she has a date. We walk back to Lincoln Hall and I thank her for accompanying me to the show. My first date has been somewhat embarrassing for me but Harvey is as cordial as ever when we meet again in the art room and obviously does not take it as seriously as I do.

Another incident, which I ascribe to my early language difficulties, occurs in my relationship with an elderly woman, an alumnus who has a slight hunchback. She is very friendly and helpful to foreign students and asks me where I come from and how I am; she tries to practice her broken German on me. In a group conversation with her, I mention that she is *curious* (by which I mean 'interested, eager to learn'). When she hears that, she gets up, leaves, and does not talk to me anymore. I ask Joe if there is another meaning to this word. He laughs and tells me it can also mean strange or odd. The next time I meet her I try to apologize and explain my faux pas but I do not exist for her anymore.

Our drama department intends to present the play *Our Little Town* and they offer me a part in it. In our drama production *Antigone,* in high school in Peine, I played the role of the *Guardian* and have some experience on the stage. So I agree to take the role of the *Neighbor,* who has only to say one sentence. It is an interesting experience.

If some of the younger students have not much to do, they get into their cars and drive to the next town. Once they invite me to come along. I get into Stan's old 1940 Ford and off we go. Stan asks me if I can drive. When I tell him of my one time experience, he offers to teach me properly how to shift and operate the clutch and at the end lets me try it. In two weeks, I am sitting in the driver's license office and writing my driver's test. Stan waits as the examiner takes me for a road test. When we get out of the car, the examiner tells me "I will see you again next week" I ask him what I did wrong. "You did not obey the 25mph speed limit". I thought everyone was passing me and I did not want to appear fearful, so I adjusted to the speed of the passing cars. Next week I shall know what to do and I pass, pay five dollars and am now the owner of an American driver's license. I did not think it would be that easy.

The college offers students the opportunity to earn some money by cleaning the college buildings and surroundings or helping in the cafeteria. It helps both the student to have cash for tuition and the college to keep costs down. I take advantage of this offer and apply for a job as a janitor in College Hall. We work on an honour system. I write down the hours I work and am paid at the end of the month, $0.85 per hour. My assigned job is to sweep all the lecture rooms and hallways daily and to scrub and polish them twice a month .At first, I have to learn to operate the electric polisher. It is quite a struggle to operate that big horizontally rotating brush disk on a handle. It has no wheels. It scrubs, polishes and moves forward sideways or backwards, depending on how I tilt the brush disk. The art is to keep it in balance. If I push the handle down too quickly, it jumps ahead and I have to use all my strength to hold onto it. If I lift the handle too fast, it moves backwards and the handle kicks into my stomach and knocks me over. If I tilt it too far to one side it hits the opposite side wall of the hall with a big bang. It takes a few days before I become an expert in handling the monster and then it is even fun working with it. The art department, with which I am quite familiar, is also my responsibility and sometimes, after I finish cleaning it, I work a little in the pottery studio.

In the Advent season, in my free time, I get a piece of wood and carve shepherd figures for our crèche. Zacchaeus, who came from Nigeria to Bluffton just after he got married, is sometimes lonely. He watches me and admires my work. When I have finished polishing my first figure, I give it to him as a Christmas gift; he appreciates it very much.

For the American Thanksgiving, Robert, a fellow student from the Men's Gospel Team, invites me to his home in Chicago, the big Metropolis. His mother welcomes me kindly and is a good hostess. We explore the city, its business and shopping areas with skyscrapers and slums; I get a glimpse into American city and night life which is a new experience for me.

Mennonites from the Bluffton congregation occasionally invite foreign students to their homes. One Sunday after church service, the Mosers ask me if I would like to visit them on their farm. Millard, who is a freshman at Bluffton, has told them about me and he takes me along to his home for a weekend. I am interested in finding out how Americans farm. Mr. Moser shows me around, we go through barns and stables and he explains his machinery to me when he sees that I understand something about farming. He and his two sons do all the work on the big mechanized farm. We compare differences between his and our farm, which was smaller than his. I enjoy the hospitality of Millard's parents. Before I leave, Mrs Moser takes me aside and asks if I would accept Millard's suit. He has worn it only a few times and has grown out of it. I try it on, it fits perfectly and I accept it thankfully. They offer me their old jeep for the journey back, Millard can drive to town with his father tomorrow. It is good that I now have a driver's license.

Foreign trainees have a conference in Bern, Indiana. One student from Bern asks me if I want to attend; he is going home for that weekend so I gladly accept. The Trainee exchange runs parallel to the Student Exchange. The participants are getting some hands-on experience on farms, in hospitals, care homes and other institutions. We drive to farms, which employ different farming methods, visit Mennonite care homes and hospitals and attend the Mennonite church in Bern with over 2000 members, the largest Mennonite church in America. Some of the trainees I still know from the Espelkamp MVS camp.

Most students go home for the Christmas holidays. It is too far for me, but Mother writes that the immigration papers for my sister, Magdalena, and her husband, Gustav have been approved and they will arrive in Winnipeg shortly before Christmas. They will stay with Gustav's mother and sisters until they find a place of their own. I plan to surprise them and make arrangements to go to Winnipeg for Christmas.

On December 22, I board the Bus to Winnipeg. It is snowing. The snowflakes are getting thicker the farther north we go and the snow starts to pile up, which makes driving difficult, especially at night. Since not many people are traveling through the night, the bus is half-empty and I get a good front seat. Gradually it stops snowing, the moon is coming out and is throwing a light glitter over the snow. We are driving quietly through a winter wonderland. I doze off for a while and wake up when a dim yellow light appears on the horizon. The snow reflects the pale yellow and the shadows turn a light blue, it is amazing how the light influences the colors. The sky changes to gold, and then orange and finally bright red as the sun climbs over the horizon. The shadows respond and the light blue becomes an intense violet that fades slowly when the sun rises higher up and begins to reflect the warm colors of the sun. It is breathtaking to watch the orange sun, the pink snow and the deep violet shadows. It is 'surreal'. All these transformations happen in a matter of minutes but these images will stay with me forever.

We arrive in Winnipeg at 2:30 next morning, twenty hours late. It is too early to visit Gustav's mother and sisters, so I stay in the bus station, wash myself and shave with the electric shaver that Robert gave me in Chicago. At seven, I go to a bus stop and wait for the next bus. The temperature is minus forty and I have been told to rub my cheeks to avoid frostbites. When I arrive at the Gauer's place, they are all still asleep and I have to wait a while before I hear steps coming down the staircase. The door is frozen shut and I have to push with all my strength to get it open. Hilde and Frieda, with their curlers still in their hair, pull from the inside. They laugh and welcome me. The two sisters of Gustav had been waiting for me until two o'clock in the morning. Mother Gauer prepares breakfast in the kitchen and we all eat together. I had never met Gustav's mother and sisters. When I arrived in Winnipeg, I had expected that my sister would be here already but they had phoned from the ship that strong winds had delayed the crossing by six days. The day before Christmas Frieda shows me the town and I buy Christmas gifts for Magdalena and Gustav from my janitor wages. Christmas Eve comes and they are not going to be here. I go with the Gauers to a Sunday school Christmas pageant. They usually go to church on Christmas Eve. I miss the contemplative, cozy family atmosphere, sitting around the Christmas tree with music and meditation that I have been used to.

On Christmas day, all the relatives come together and I can learn to know all of them at the same time. They are all nice, friendly and joyful people. We talk, sing, and eat a lot.

On Boxing Day there is great excitement: Gustav and Magdalena are arriving in Winnipeg. Abe rents a truck for the luggage and we take a taxi to the station; it is cheaper for five people than taking the bus. I slip unseen through the barrier, run to the platform and sneak up on Magdalena from behind. I take my sister into my arms. She is surprised to see me here. I welcome both to Winnipeg. While the others are coming to the platform, I walk through the compartments and greet my cousins, the Schowalters, Hermann Cornelsen, Heinz Wiehler, Waltraud and Hans-Peter and the others who are immigrating as a group traveling on to British Columbia.

There is coming and going in the Gauer house. All Gustav's relatives and friends want to welcome them. Finally, things calm down. The house is overcrowded so Gustav and I are sleeping in a neighbor's house. When we get up in the morning, we meet a German master mechanic, who had come to Winnipeg four weeks ago. He had hoped to get work in his trade but had only worked a couple of days at odd jobs. He has no relatives or friends here and does not speak English. He is now saving for a return trip to Germany; we sympathize with him and suggest holding out a little longer, opportunities may come up when his English gets better.

This is not good news for Gustav. We talk at breakfast about his expectations and plans. Later I have an hour with Magdalena alone and she tells me that parting from Mother was not easy and about her and

Gustav's life together, they got married a week before I left for USA. She hopes to get a job as a nurse. In the evening, we celebrate Christmas with the two new immigrants. We exchange gifts; for Magdalena, I bought a woolen housecoat and, for Gustav, a fur-lined parka; they will need these here.

It is now important for them to find suitable accommodation. We walk along the streets in the neighborhood and check the houses that have a sign, *'rooms for rent',* in their window. I am the translator. After several tries, we find a two-room apartment that is clean and not too expensive. Next week, they can move in. I am glad I came to Winnipeg to welcome them and help them to get started. Now I can tell Mother first hand what life is like in Canada. Tomorrow I will take the long trip back to Bluffton.

Bluffton is quiet. Most students are still on holidays. I go downtown to buy some food as the kitchen is closed and does not open before school begins again. I have agreed to cover some janitor jobs for students who come back late, so I have something useful to do waiting for school to reopen.

The over eighty year old widow of former college president Dr.Mosiman lives next door to the college. The Library is named after her husband. She always has open house for students, especially foreign students. She is interested in our lives what we enjoy and what we miss. She usually has some special treats for us when we visit her.

It is now New Year 1952. I am alone in Ropp Hall and am a little lonely. I go over to visit Mrs.Mosiman. She invites me into her living room and while we are talking, I discover a large picture of the Marienburg in her living room. I tell her, this is the castle in my hometown in West Prussia. She wants to hear all about my home and my war experience. She tells me about her past in perfect German. At the end of our conversation she promises that she will deed the Marienburg picture to me when she dies.

Life returns to normal again at Bluffton. Students are back from holidays. Stanley tells me he and Anita got engaged during the holidays. Now he has to observe a ritual at Bluffton, 'the *baptism of trust'.* His friends take him to the Riley creek and dunk him in the ice-cold water. His fiancée, Anita, has to watch the procedure. When the shivering Stan comes out of the icy water, he kneels before her in the snow, promises her eternal faithfulness and asks if she will accept him. She does. Among his friends are some musicians who play suitable musical interludes to give the procedure more status.

In the beginning of March, the snow melts and it rains. The Riley flows over its banks and floods parts of the campus. As a result, the College is closed until the water recedes.

On February 3, I get an invitation from Mrs. Mosiman. When I enter her house, she congratulates me on my birthday, gives me a big box of chocolates and slips a $5 bill inside. I wonder how she knows that this is my birthday. In the evening, the boys of Ropp Hall surprise me with a birthday cake, which Joe has arranged. We eat it in our den and have fun.

Edna Ramseyer, the sister of the president, invites us foreign students to her country home during Easter vacations. She is home economics instructor at the college and serves us excellent meals. We learn to know each other better and discuss our similarities and differences. At night, I sleep for the first time with a black student in a single bed. I did not sleep too well.

Once a year foreign students have a seminar in one of the Mennonite Colleges. This year it is in Hesston College. The president from Eastern Mennonite College where Gerhard studies, comes to Bluffton to take Ruth and me along on his way to Kansas. In Missouri, we have a break. It is lunchtime and we go into a fine restaurant and order a meal. It is busy and we wait our turn but the server overlooks us and serves customers who came much later than we did. We get up, leave, and try a simpler restaurant; the same treatment. Dr Hostetter asks the waiter why he does not serve us. He points at Ruth and shakes his head. Dr.Hostetter tries to explain to him that we are a group of foreign students and belong together; he raises his eyebrows and walks on. Ruth, a self-confident Jamaican with a nice chocolate colored skin gets suspicious. In her country, all people are treated equally and it does not make any difference what color of skin a person has. However, here in Missouri, it matters and she is quite perturbed to find out that she is the reason why the waiter does not serve us. She starts to weep, she will go out and we could order a meal. "No way!" we tell her, we leave the room together and slam the door behind us. In the nearby railway station restaurant, they make an exception and we can all order a meal.

Gerhard and I are quite appalled. It is the first time we have encountered discrimination in USA

.

Professor Lantz, our Dean of Music, asks me one day in the cafeteria if I like to sing and what voice part I sing. I tell him that I sang in school and church choirs as a tenor. "That is just what I am looking for. Two boys from the choir did not come back and I need first tenors for a good balance in our Vesper Choir, would you like to join?" I am honored; I know it is not easy to get into Professor Lantz' Choir, he has high expectations and the auditions are rather strict. I had wanted to sing again and being part of the choir gives me a chance to do that and to participate in the choir's tour through eastern USA and Canada. In order to improve my performance I take *Sight singing and Ear training* in the next semester. I am no match for my fellow students in class, who are voice majors, organists and pianists, but it helps me to become more confident. We have to memorize the music and text of all the motets, cantatas, hymns and Negro spirituals that we sing; no music folders are allowed at the performance. Before the final semester ends, we start our tour through the northeastern states. We present our musical program, give a short meditation and tell about the great life at Bluffton. The purpose of our trip is to stimulate better support for the college and recruit new students from the mainly Mennonite congregations that invite us. At the end of the performance we mingle with the young people, the church members pick their billets from us singers, and take us home. We spend the evening and the night with them.

One evening I am billeted with a young assistant pastor's couple. In the morning at breakfast, I get a dose of modern American child rearing. They have two boys aged two and three; both sit in high chairs beside the breakfast table. Mother puts a bowl of porridge on their little table. The first one throws his spoon on the floor, the other copies him, Mother picks them up, cleans them and puts them in their porridge bowl again and encourages them to eat. They throw their spoons to the other side, mom gets up and puts them back. This game is repeated over and over with mom patiently retrieving the spoons each time. The boys stick their fingers in the bowl put some porridge into their mouth, smear some around their high chairs and on each other and giggle, the rest goes on the floor. Mom takes the bowls to the kitchen, gets a rag and cleans everything up. She gives them a piece of bread of which they eat a small piece, dissect the rest and throw it on the floor. In the end, Mother cleans up the boys, the high chairs and the floor without saying much. I itch to comment but just say compassionately, "It is hard to bring up two such lively boys that way, isn't it. "Yes", she replies wearily. "Dr.Spock, the educational psychologist, suggests that parents refrain from restricting the hunger for exploration and creative activities of young children and let them do what they want, but that is sometimes exhausting". I agree and ask, cautiously, if it would not be easier to accustom our youngsters to the reality of life by setting some protective boundaries, while they are too young to make rational decisions themselves. These boundaries could be extended gradually, when they have learned the basics and can understand the consequences of their actions. She answers with a sigh.

After we have visited several congregations in northwestern America, we plan to go across the border to Canada and bring our program to congregations in Ontario. Professor Lantz asks me to read scripture and say a prayer in German in the German-speaking congregations.

At the Canadian border, the customs officer checks our passports and he tells me that my passport to enter the USA is only valid for six months and is now expired. He would gladly allow me into Canada but his colleague on the US side will not allow me back. We go back to the Americans and their customs officer confirms this. Professor Lantz tells him, he needs me in the choir's Canadian program and tries to persuade him to let me into the USA when we come back from Canada; he will vouch for me. Nothing helps and I have to say good-bye to my choir friends. They buy me a bus ticket and send me back to Bluffton. I am disappointed and angry with these sticklers. I had been looking forward to visiting German-speaking congregations in Canada. It is hard to believe that customs officers can be so inflexible.

We are all back again and ready to prepare for the final examinations. In the first one, Mennonite history, I get a perfect score. Professor Klassen gives me very good marks in my art courses. My marks for the other courses vary.

Professor Moon is retiring. She has taught science for thirty years and the staff wants to honor her with a special program. The organizers of the program ask me to help with the decorations .We decide that I should build a scale model of *Science Hall* where she taught and they will later present it to her as a memento at her retirement party. A picture of it is in the college yearbook.

At the end of the last semester, someone asked Professor Klassen if he could paint a picture of a life-size Christ figure. He wants to dedicate it to his congregation as a 'thank you' for help he had received from them. Professor Klassen asks me if I would like to do it, and he is willing to give me some advice. I have not painted in oil nor in these dimensions. He encourages me and I agree to take it on. The motif of 'Jesus knocking at the door' seems applicable and the sketch of the composition is not bad. The painting, however, is another question. I have to learn to blend the colors properly from the light to the darker tones. It takes much longer than expected and I do not want to spend all my art time and free time on the painting. I cannot finish it before I leave and Professor Klassen has to add the final touches to it after I am gone which he does not like.

At the end of May, the *May Queen* is crowned. She is chosen from the senior girls. The criteria are beauty and scholarship. Students have chosen Anita for their queen and Stan, her fiancé, is *Popular Man*. A great choice, I think. I know both of them and we have had interesting conversations during the year. They give me valuable tips for my planned trip to the west. Anita even invites me to stop at her parent's home if I should travel through Indiana.

For the May Festival the girls may ask boys for a date. I am surprised and self-conscious, when Martha asks me. My English is now much better than on my first date and we have a good conversation, walk in the park, go to a movie and have supper together. We write to each other a few times after that date and she says she wants to come to Germany as an exchange student. I do not know if this will ever happen. We eventually lose contact.

Students celebrate the end of the academic year with the *Graduation Party*. Again, we have to have a partner for the banquet and I am not too eager to find one. Someone else has asked Martha and on the day before the banquet, I ask Arlene if she is still available. I have a few classes with her and we often tease each other. She tells me she would like to accept but she has just got engaged and her fiancé might not approve of it; but nobody has asked her friend Mary yet. We three decide to sit together at the party and have fun together.

This graduation banquet concludes my academic year in Bluffton College. It has been very interesting and definitely worthwhile for me. I have learned a lot about College life, how to live more intimately together with other students, how to arrange a date and about life in America in general. I have met a number of fine people in and outside of the college and received help and kindness from them.

This, however, is not the end of my exchange year. I still have two more months until my return to Germany and I want to find out more about life and customs in other parts of America.

Exploring America

At our spring foreign student conference in Hesston, I had asked Gerhard, a fellow exchange student, if he would be interested traveling across the USA with me after our academic year was over and he was willing to come along.

My staff advisor, Dr. Shelly, helps me to plan our trip. I had previously told him that I had written a paper about MCC Voluntary Service camps in Europe and my participation in them. Now I want to find out, how they operate in the country of their origin. He knows where units are stationed and we select the ones that are on our route. He writes to the camp leaders and asks if we may visit their unit and they replied that they would be delighted to have us. So now, we have a few places where we can stay and participate in MCC work.

Gerhard knows the Schefflers from Mennonite conferences. They emigrated last year from southern Germany to California. I was together with Ruth, their daughter, in the MFD camp in Espelkamp and I would not mind seeing her again. They settled in a place not far from the west coast where we want to go, perhaps we might be able to stay with them. He is going to contact them

Dr. Shelly offers to drive me to Toledo, to the nearest immigration office, so that I can have my visa extended. When we come back, he gives me a blank check on which I can draw up to $50 (210 DM) when I am in need. I accept it hesitantly but return it the next day and tell him that I am very grateful for his generosity but think it is too risky to carry a blank check with me. I would rather earn some money.

I have the opportunity to work for a building contractor from the Bluffton Mennonite church. This has a twofold benefit; I can earn money and learn about American house construction. Mr. Badertscher, my boss, pays me $88 for a week's work. He wishes me well and adds a five Dollar handshake when we say good-bye at church.

My college friends have organized a farewell party for me at Mrs. Mosimans. We reminisce, play games and have a meal together. At the end, they present me with a useful gift, a pair of trousers and a shirt for my trip. I am overwhelmed. My 'college mother' gives me a hug, wishes me well on my trip, and puts an envelope into my pocket. I thank her for her generosity and understanding. I open the envelope – a twenty-dollar bill is inside with a note, wishing me an enjoyable and safe trip...

Gerhard and I had arranged to meet in Kansas City, where an MVS unit is stationed and that is my first destination.

Hitchhiking in the US is not much different from Germany, only here there are more cars on the road. I travel lightly. The few things that I need, I pack in a solid sports bag from the 'lost and found' and put a big 'Bluffton College' sticker on it, underneath a sign 'Foreign Student'. I hope this will interest drivers of passing vehicles enough to stop and pick me up. At first, it is slow going. Some locals take me five or ten miles in their pick-up, until a black Pontiac stops. The sole driver, a Nazarene Pastor, invites me into the front seat. Shortly after I have closed the door, he asks me if I am 'saved', if I have accepted Jesus into my heart, and he continues driving 130km/h, with one hand on the steering wheel and the other leafing through his Bible. I say,' yes,' to everything, in order not to divert his attention from the road and quote a few Bible verses myself to convince him. At this time, seat belts are not com- pulsory. The good thing is that he is going in the direction of my first stop. After several hours of driving, he catches up with his companion, another Nazarene Pastor, whom he had lost in Detroit. The two play 'catch me' traveling at up to 145km/h. We are driving all night with only a short stop for coffee and coke and a half-hour's sleep at the roadside. At that speed, they cannot avoid driving over rabbits that cross the road at night, blinded by the car lights. They are plentiful in Missouri. I count 68 bumps, which means sixty- eight fewer rabbits.

I travel 600 miles with them. The time goes fast and I get used to their style of traveling, but I am thankful and relieved when they let me out. Shortly after this journey, a black businessman in his black Mercedes stops. He is very kind and takes me the last stretch to the MVS camp building. I have a somewhat uneasy feeling, sitting alone in a car with a strange Afro-American man, who hardly says a word.

Gerhard has not yet arrived, so I have time to talk to the volunteers and visit them at their workplace in a home for mentally handicapped people. They work there during the day and have instruction in psychology, psychiatry and medicine in the evening. Gerhard comes two days later and tells me about his adventurous trip. He had stayed overnight in a haystack at a farm where a cop spotted him and interrogated him thoroughly but let him go.. Later someone shot at the car in which he got a ride.

We give him one day's rest. In the evening, the volunteers ask us to lead the devotion. The next day we are on the road heading in the direction of Los Angeles. Most drivers that take us along are very helpful. Some stop at gas stations and ask if someone would give us a ride before they let us out. Another suggests asking a car dealer if he needs a driver to take a car or truck to the west, (it is cheaper for them than having it transported). No luck for us, so we tramp on. We must look a funny pair; Gerhard, short, with a French beret and a *Foreign Student* sign in front of him and I, with flying hair, the Bluffton College and the Arizona sign on my travel bag. It is the end of June and terribly hot, thirty-eight degrees in Kansas.

We have to stretch our thumbs out from a shady place, to avoid suffering a heat stroke. Finally our ideal driver comes along in the person of David Levi, a haughty young executive. He has missed his plane from Chicago to Los Angeles and would have had to wait six hours for the next one. The service apparently was so bad that he decided to buy an expensive Chrysler car and drive. When he sees us, he thinks we might be good company, stops and invites us in. We travel with him for 1500km. We have good, often heated discussions about religion and politics with him, a Jew, which makes the time pass quickly. He invites us for lunch and we share the cost for a motel room with him. In order to save time, he drives very fast. Once we reach the top of a hill, which has been obstructing the view and see a car just below us, stopped in the middle of the road before a crossing. David slams on the brakes and slides sideways into a ditch and up against a fence. We could easily have ploughed into the other car or rolled over several times. Still trembling, we meet the other driver, who had been looking at his map for direction. The drivers bicker about who was at fault and exchange data for an insurance claim. We inspect our car and only the tires, which have almost come off their rims, are damaged. We are thankful that we are still alive. David drives slowly to the next service station, gets a new set of tires and we drive on. We could have gone another 1000 km with him to Los Angeles but Dr.Shelly had arranged a short stay for us at a mission station in an Indian Reservation not far from the Grand Canyon and we do not want to miss that. So David lets us out at a Winslow motel. We phone the mission and they say they will pick us up. We want to use the opportunity to get in contact with real Indians. The only things I know about them are the stories I read in the Karl May books. We spend the night in the motel and late next morning an old truck stops at the motel and the short, lively missionary, Goossen, greets us. He has picked up supplies for the mission and is on his way home. In order to avoid the heat at noon he left at four in the morning, is now tired and asks us to drive his truck to Flagstaff. We have never driven a truck and certainly not an antique like this one, where we have to double clutch. Our driving is rather jerky and he does not get much rest. From Flagstaff, we drive north for miles on a sand road until we reach the Kliewers in Tuba City. They speak German and are happy to practice it with us. We have lunch together and they ask us to speak in their church. We are unprepared and do not know what Dr Shelly has told them about us. In the evening, we hear announced to the whole village over the loudspeaker system that two guest speakers from Germany will share in the Sunday service. We are shocked. The next morning Gerhard shares his faith as an evangelist would do it and I talk about life and conditions in Germany six years after World War II and about the new orientation and awakening in our Mennonite congregations.

The Kliewers accompany us to the next mission station in Hotvilla, There is not enough room in the cab for all of us, so brother Goossen and I volunteer to sit in the back of the open truck. It is windy in this desert-like part of the country and the wind whips the sand into our faces and penetrates our clothes. My lips are dry, crack open and start to bleed.

I ask him about his work and he tells me that it is very hard for a native Indian to become a Christian. His life is so entwined with his native religious tradition that he will be rejected and shut out from his clan if he converts to Christianity; it is especially hard for the Hopis, who live in close settlements, different from the nomadic Navajos.

The old heavy-laden truck plods along the lonely sandy road and suddenly the engine stutters and gives up. I wonder what happens now. Brother Goossen sighs; "The gas tank is empty," he says. "Sometimes we make it with one tankful to Hotvilla". He pulls out a one-quart glass, fills it with gas from the reserve canister in the back and passes it on to brother Kliewer in front who empties it through a funnel into the gas tank. We repeat this several times. A hose, connected from the canister to the gas tank would make the operation much easier, I muse, but I don't say anything. It is getting dark when we reach Hotvilla and Mrs. Goossen has been waiting with supper for us. I am not very hungry, wash sand and sweat off and go to bed early. It has been a strenuous day.

Tomorrow is Mission Outing. Four mission families, school inspector, Jantzen, and some voluntary service workers, known as the VSers. cram into five cars and drive to the Canyon de Cheley. They invite us to come along. On the way, we watch an Indian Pow-Wow. We drive close to the canyon, walk along the crest and look down to the now dried-out-riverbed. The Navajos have planted patches of vegetables in the wet ground and goats and cows are tethered beside small grass fields. Centuries ago, they lived in the rock caverns on the cliff walls. Now, all that is left, are the ruins of their caves on the *White House Rocks*. We walk a little closer and admire the bizarre forms of the *Speaking Rock* and the *Spider Rock*. According to Indian legend, the Speaking rock watches the children playing below and if they are bad, it tells the Spider on the other rock, which will then crawl down and take the bad children to the top of its rock. The white spots up there, their bleached bones, are the proof. The *Grain Rock* is a monument for the natives; a sad reminder to the Navajo tribe of the time when, after a long draught, they were starving and the Spanish conquerors gave them grain to survive but in exchange took their children into slavery.

We stop at an interesting historical monument. We read, 'On Sept. 8, 1906 two hostile Navajo parties solved their dispute over accepting the ways of the white man or remaining true to their native tradition, through a tug-of-war. The losers had to leave the settlement.' It shows that a controversy can be solved without bloodshed.

On the way back we visit the Presbyterian Mission. A Belgian sister shows us the imposing layout of residences, church, hospital and school - much more elaborate than the Mennonite mission. They invite us for supper. On the way back, Gerhard and I take leave from the group and stay in the Old Oribi mission station. The next morning when we get to work, we are surprised to be greeted by a native Indian with "Guten Morgen, kommt ihr uns hier helfen?" He tells us, he was raised in a German missionary family and German was his mother tongue. I borrow some work clothes and help to dig a cistern. It will become a water supply for the new school.

We stay for a few days and help with maintenance work and in the church service. We visit the villagers. The Hopis live in settlements and build their houses, some two stories high, with clay bricks at the edge of the dried out riverbed. We watch a woman grind corn between two stones and notice meat strips air-drying under her roof. A Christian Hopi woman lets us enter her house and we are surprised to see an almost modern interior. She has ten children among whom are some very beautiful girls, who are rather shy. She shows us artifacts, which she creates from natural materials. I buy a well-designed plate that she has woven from rabbit weed and dyed, for a special price of one dollar. The natives are very friendly and curious; they respect us as visitors and when they hear we are Germans they want us to sing German songs which we do.

We learn a lot about Indian culture, We can talk and work with them and observe how they live in the different tribes. By talking with the missionaries and helping them in their work, we gain a better understanding of their struggles. I admire their ingenuity and the courage with which they meet the challenges that this work poses for them. Each of the three missionary families has their own method of relating to the people of the Hopi and Navajo tribes. There seems to be trust and appreciation of the work the missionaries are doing among them and of the operation of the school, but I have the feeling that most native adults want to keep a distance from the white people.

The time comes to move on. We join the 'VSers' who have organized a children's retreat near a Navajo reservation. We pack the old truck with food and the belongings of the teachers and I get an opportunity to drive for part of the way. A few Navajo women in lively colored dresses working near their Hogan (clay roundhouse), catch our attention. We get set to take a picture of them but when they see us, they run inside and close the door. In camp, under the care of the VSers, the children are not as shy and gather around us as we tell them stories about our experiences during the last war and how the children in Germany lived during that time and how things have changed. Gerhard and I sing a few German songs and harmonize for effect. They like the lullaby: *Heitschi Bumbeitschi* best; they like to join us in the chorus ...*bum bum, bum bum* at the end.

The VSers take us to the main road and our thumbs point towards Los Angeles. It is extremely hot again, forty-five degrees, and we can endure it only in the shade. The roads are almost empty; nobody drives in this heat except some local people who make deliveries. We get two short rides and, by the evening, we have only traveled forty miles from where we started in the morning. Most people drive very early or at night, when it is cooler. The last driver, who took us the last ten miles along, has pity on us and takes us to a motel. For $3.50, we get a reasonable room. The next morning, very early, we are on the road again. After two hours waiting, we decide to separate and see if it is easier to get a ride on our own. I walk two hundred meters ahead and wait. Soon after our separation, Gerhard, with his 'Foreign Student' sign, is successful. A Buick cabriolet stops and Gerhard gets in. It stops in front of me and I am able to join him again. A very nice couple who are actors are driving with their son to Los Angeles and want our company. We soon get into an animated conversation. They ask about our impressions of America, about politics and if Hitler is dead or if he escaped. We talk about religion and Gerhard tries to evangelize. The driver gives us some background about the history of the native Indians in this area.

The Hopis lived in rock caves until the eleventh century; we saw one in the Canyon de Chely. Later, they dug underground huts, with only the roof above ground. In the thirteenth century, the Apaches attacked them and drove them out. In their new settlements, they started to build houses with rocks or air-dried clay bricks. We went into one of those in the Hotvilla Mission. He tells us about one custom, which we find very interesting and unusual. When a young native man builds a house and gets married, he gives the house to his wife as a wedding gift and to prove that he can support a family, he has to feed his parents in-law for a year. If the wife does not like him anymore for any reason, she puts his saddle in front of the house and he has to leave.

The Navajos build their Hogan, a mud roundhouse different from the houses of the Hopis. They ram poles into the ground in a circle and wind branches in-between. They cover the outside with mud, which the sun dries hard, to keep the wind, rain and cold out. The opening is to the east. Some have a second hut, a summer residence that is not mudded. In the morning, the head of the clan walks out first and greets the sun, before any other of the clan may leave the hut.

Such conversations with our 'hosts' make the time pass fast and soon we are crossing the bridge over the Colorado River which has its origin in the Rocky Mountains and flows south west through the Grand Canyon into the Pacific Ocean. We are now in California, about two hundred miles east of where they picked us up. Twice our ride took us past the sign: 'to Grand Canyon' and we were very tempted to take the side road and add it to our vacation experience, but we did not want to leave our ride.

In Needles on the other side of the river, our driver decides to stop and rest, stay for the night in a motel and continue early next morning at 3:30am, when it is not so hot. It is now noon and we do not want to wait so long. We find a shady place on the lawn beside the railway station and have a short snooze. It is again +forty-five degrees. We cannot walk with our bags in this heat. We take a taxi to the outskirts of the town, and wait. Finally, at 8:00 pm, a social worker takes us to the other side of the desert. It is midnight. He invites us to spend the night with him. He puts two cots on an open trailer in his back yard and we sleep there. At 7:00am in the morning we are on the street again, our Foreign Student sign in front of us. A green Ford stops and a big, middle-aged man gets out, approaches us and flashes his Sherriff badge. "Who is the foreign student?" he demands. I show him my passport and visa and he seems to be satisfied. Then he asks for Gerhard's papers. He has none. He had applied for a visa to the Mennonite world Conference in Basel, Switzerland, which he wants to attend when he gets back. His passport had not come back from the consulate in time for the trip. He has only a letter from his college. The officer orders him into his car. Gerhard tries to explain but the officer cuts him off. "If you don't come voluntarily, I will have to handcuff you. Hitch-hiking is illegal in California." I ask the sheriff if he will take me along too because I have correct papers and can confirm Gerhard's identity. He lets us out in the next town, takes our personal data and tells us he is on an official assignment and cannot take us any farther. He requests that we report to the police and immigration department in San Bernardino. We take the bus to town, look for the police station, but phone first, and ask if there is a jail connected with it. The secretary tells us there is an immigration office, which will take care of us. We tell the immigration officer our story and what the sheriff has told us. He laughs and muses, "We know, he is quite particular; we are not that bad, I can give you a temporary identity card". We are relieved, thank him and take the Greyhound Bus to Los Angeles.

In the Mennonite Yearbook, we look for the address of a Mennonite church and try to locate it. When we find one and walk up to it, we see in front of the church a sign saying that the congregation has moved and does not meet here anymore. We knock at the door of the house next to the church, which we assume was the former parsonage. We explain to the woman who greets us, who we are and what the purpose of our visit is. She invites us in and tells us the story of the Mennonite church. When more and more black people moved into the area, Mennonites moved out and the church followed. The pastor, her husband, felt that this was wrong and they stayed. He is now working part time as a mechanic, in addition to his duties as pastor. He wants to earn extra money to study to become a missionary to Africa. A little later the pastor comes home from work, greets us, talks to his wife and they invite us to have supper with their family. We admire the harmony in the family. After the meal, we talk for a while and he asks us if we know LA. When we tell him this is the first time we have been here, he offers to show us the city and drives us around in his car. It is getting dark and we have a glimpse into the nightlife of Los Angeles. He takes us up to Mount Lee, the highest point in the city, and we have a magnificent view of the whole city, a sea of lights. We are overwhelmed by its enormous size.

We return from our sightseeing tour after midnight and Brother Dirks invites us to stay overnight. The next morning he takes off from work and shows us LA. from Long Beach to Hollywood. At noon, we stop at a restaurant and he invites us for lunch. While we are waiting to be served, he tells us about the history of LA and its people and his work as a MB pastor in a big city. He then drives us to the main road that goes north towards San Francisco. When we say good-bye and thank him for his kindness, he gives each of us five dollars and wishes us a safe trip. He is one of the finest people we have met during our trip through the USA. He lives his Christianity in his family and with neighbors and 'Brethren', as he calls us. He waits until we get a ride and we wave to him until he is out of sight.

We change cars in Bakersfield and the next driver takes us close to our next destination, Reedley. Dr Shelly had made reservations for us to visit the MCC voluntary service unit there. We are courageous enough to hitch-hike again. Gerhard is not feeling well and when the driver lets us out of his car, he has to throw up on the roadside. I phone Reedley and ask if someone could pick us up from the Freeway. Mr.Friesen comes with his pick-up truck and takes us to the Dettweilers, who will host us for a few days. The VSers have planned a program for us. First, they show us their workplace, the *Kings View Home,* a mental hospital managed by Mennonites. Then they drive us through a fruit plantation and for the first time in my life I pick oranges, grapefruit and peaches from a tree. They are delicious; we 'taste' a lot of them. I visit Mrs. Lichti, Magdalena's American pen pal and bring her greetings from my sister. She is very happy to receive them and hear from her long-time German friend. On Sunday, we attend the service in the Reedley MB Church. The young people plan an outing to the Sequoia National park in the afternoon and invite us to come along. We walk through those magnificent tall Redwoods, the biggest tree, the General Grant, is about three hundred years old, one- hundred meters high and nine meters in diameter.

In the evening meeting Pastor Bartel asks us to share what we and Germans in general have endured during and after the war, especially Mennonite refugees from West Prussia and Danzig. They want to know what life in post war Germany is like now and how Mennonite congregations are coping. I am surprised at how open and uninhibited

I can be when speaking to the large congregation. We talk to the people afterwards and answer their special questions. Several had worked in Germany after the war and inquire as to what has changed since they left. We are given the collection at the end of the evening, fifty-five dollar for our travel fund. In the audience is Mrs. Schmidt, who had been a missionary in China. Her two sons, Günter and Hans, are students in Berkeley and she thinks they could perhaps show us the university and arrange for us to stay in the University dormitory, since most students are on holidays. She gives us ten dollars and sends greetings to her sons.

Mr.Friesen brings us to the Highway and we hitch-hike again, in spite of the sheriff's warning. It is cheaper; probably the only way we can afford to travel and it is more interesting. We see more of the country side and learn to know a variety of American people. It does not take long to get rides to San Francisco. In the afternoon, we meet Günter on the Berkeley campus and he arranges an overnight stay for us in Westminster House. He shows us the campus and in the evening, we eat together in a Chinese restaurant. He demonstrates how they eat with chopsticks in China. We try it, too, but with less elegance.

We spend the next day exploring San Francisco, one of the most interesting and beautiful cities in the USA. We try the cog-wheel-streetcar and travel to the largest Chinatown outside China. I am interested in the architecture, the modern office buildings, shopping centers and churches. There is even a German Lutheran church having services in German.

The next morning the manager from the dormitory wants to drive us to the ferry but we desperately want to see the Golden Gate Bridge and take the bus that is going across. The one thousend-fourhundred meter long, bridge is in thick fog, as is often the case at this time of the year. Once in a while we get a glimpse of the city and the boats on the bay, seventy meters below us. We can barely see the thick steel ropes that support the span of the bridge and curve up to the twohundredfifty meter high towers, whose tops are completely hidden in the fog. On the other side of the bay is bright sunshine and we have a last look at the bridge and the wide spread out city.

Our Foreign Student sign attracts the attention of two engineers, who stop and ask us from where we come. They take us along and we answer many questions about Hitler and Germany; how people cope now and how the reconstruction is progressing. They tell us about work opportunities in America. They are very friendly and even take a side road to show us a part of the Redwood Forest and take a picture of us driving through the hollow trunk of a huge redwood tree. Occasionally we come close to the ocean and see the water glittering in the sun. It is getting dark and they take turns driving all night. We sleep for a while in the back seat. In the morning, we are in Portland, Oregon. They treat us to a lavish breakfast and take us to the main road leading east, along the Columbia River. An angler takes us to the historic Bonneville Lock and Dam and we admire the huge lock, the spillways and electric power-producing facilities.

We are looking for a strategic place to continue our trip, when a police officer comes over, checks our papers and gives us a warning ticket. This dampens our admiration of the Columbia Valley and canyon with its bizarre rock formations and hoodoos, its gorges, the wild, high Multnomah Waterfall and the white top of the 3425m high cone-shaped Mount Hood.

We stand on the road discouraged, not knowing what to do next, when a car stops and takes us along. We squeeze into the back with the somewhat noisy kids and play a little with the two small boys. The father, on his way home from a vacation, tells us about his experiences and gives us information about the area and its history. It is noon and they invite us for lunch and drive us to the bus station afterwards. They suggest we take the bus to Ritzville. There is not much traffic on those small roads. Again and again, we find nice people who help us. Maybe the other ones do not stop for us.

For more than an hour, we drive over rolling hills and through wide golden wheat fields, until we reach the little town of Ritzville. We ask a woman at the bus station how to get to the Schefflers. "Are they the new immigrants from Germany?" she asks. We confirm it "They live on Broadway on the other side of town, I am going in that direction, I take you there. They are nice people" she lets us out on the other side of the boullevard. "I think the house with the white and red hollyhocks in front is the house where they live" We knock at the door of the well-kept older house on the hill but nobody answers. We leave our luggage on the patio, go to the other side of the boulevard and wait. I ask Gerhard if he is sure that he had told the Schefflers that we are coming. We watch a man going to the house and unlocking the door. He sees our luggage and puts it inside. We walk over, introduce ourselves and he invites us into the house. "They should be here any moment, make yourselves comfortable; by the way, I am Herbert, the nephew of Tante Susa" he says and leaves again. Shortly after he leaves, a black Buick stops in front of the house. A stately woman with her daughter steps out and they come into the house. Tante Susa welcomes us and Hilde, a handsome teenager, greets us the German way, with a hearty handshake. Onkel Hugo, as Gerhard calls him, comes in after he has parked the car. His West-Prussian accent sounds homey to me. I remember the Schefflers vaguely. They lived in the neighbor village in West Prussia and were friends of my parents. I was only four years old when they moved to southern Germany. With Ruth, the second of the four girls, I had served in the MVS camp in Espelkamp and I was looking forward to see her again. Eva, the oldest, I had met briefly at a youth retreat. It does not take long to get familiar with them. They tell us about their experience as immigrants in this secluded country village, the different customs and the way of life in America. They are homesick for their green Palatinate hills and the historic city of Kaiserslautern, where Onkel Hugo had been pastor of several small Mennonite congregations. Because he does not speak English, he now works in a Safeway store in the vegetable department. The reason for their emigration was Tante Susa's fear of the Russians. She was born in a Mennonite village in the Ukraine and had lived there during the horrors of the Revolution. She has a half-brother here, who sponsored them.

All of them work, to pay off the debt for their journey, the mortgage and the car. Three of the girls work on wheat farms and Hildegard, the third one, and the only one living at home, is teller in a bank. The next morning, Tante Susa shows us the town and, after the others are finished with work, we visit Eva, who is working on a wheat farm and cares for the farmer's wife who suffers from cancer. She calls her employers "Daddy" and "Mammy". Ruth is helping in the harvest on another farm. She, like Hilde, had started out as waitresses in a local restaurant, when they first arrived in Ritzville. The manager of the Safeway store saw Hilde working there and asked if she wants to work for him as cashier and a little later the bank manager offered her a job in his bank where she works now. Gertraud, the youngest, is living with an older farmer's couple and helps in the household while finishing her high school. On the way back in the car, Hilde tells me about her interest in art, which nobody here understands and values. The girls here are only interested in boys. Tomorrow she will show me her art collection. When we arrive home, we continue our conversation about our impressions of America, the differences between young people here and in Germany until late at night. The next morning I drive Onkel Hugo and Hilde to work. For lunch all come home and we have an opportunity to take a photo of the family and I ask Hilde if I may take a picture of her alone. She does not mind and poses for me. After she is finished with work, we pick her up and go swimming. It is very hot. On the way back from the swimming pool, we visit Onkel Hugo at work in the Safeway store. She parks the car very close to the fire hydrant and when she tries to move out, she scratches the door. She stops and goes to tell her father about the accident and asks me to drive the car home. I admire her honesty and trust in her father and notice the good relationship between children and parents and between siblings.

In the evening, Hilde invites me to her room, we sit on the carpet and she spreads out her art collection. She has cut out from Life magazines full page reproductions of Giotto's frescos, Michelangelo's paintings of the Sistine Chapel, Grünewald's Isenheim Altar, Rembrandt's biblical scenes, Rouault's Christ figures and from other sources many pictures of paintings and sculptures of different artists, all nicely gathered in folders and arranged according to art periods. I am amazed about her interest and knowledge of art. We discuss the life and work of these artists, how they have influenced the world and what they mean to us. My heart beats faster when I look with respect at this natural, inspired and inspiring beautiful young woman beside me. I love her honesty and openness.

Time flies by and I would like to stay longer with the Schefflers, over the weekend if possible but Gerhard is determined to leave. He has promised his aunts he will visit them in Pennsylvania and fears time is running out. The last evening we are happily together washing the dishes and singing an old German hit, "Zum Abschied reich ich dir die Hände und sag' ganz leis Auf Wiedersehn, ein schönes Märchen geht zu Ende..." (in parting I stretch out my hands to you and say softly good-bye, a delightful fairy tale is ending …)

The next morning we thank the Schefflers heartily for their hospitality. Hilde takes us to the bus station. When I hold her hand saying good-bye, I ask her if she minds if I write to her when I am back in Germany. "Not at all," she says quite naturally. I wonder if she feels how much she means to me.

In the bus, Gerhard and I talk about our memorable visit in Ritzville. We could speak German again in meaningful conversations and have healthy meals and clean clothes. I had been looking forward to meeting Ruth again and, instead, learned to know her younger sister, Hildegard, more intimately, I wonder if this was destined.

Deep in thought, I suddenly remember that I wanted to visit my sister in Vancouver, threehundredfifty miles north of here, but the immigration office did not send an extension of my visa to Ritzville and, without it, I do not dare to cross the border to Canada again. When we stop in Spokane, I get out and send a telegram to Magdalena, explaining why I cannot come.

There is not much traffic on the roads in this sparsely populated part of the USA. Sometimes we have to wait for two hours for the next short ride. It is getting dark and we have to look for a place to stay overnight. The first hotel we find, charges ten dollars a night, too much for us just to sleep there. The next one looks decent, we can sleep there for only thee dollars and it has a bathroom with shower. The next morning we check the parking lot and see two men getting into their car. We ask them politely if they are going east and they invite us to join them. They take us along to Montana and let us out in Yellowstone Park. It is still early in the morning and we decide to spend the day in the park. We do a lot of walking. We observe the Old Faithful Geyser belching out a high jet of steam and enjoy the varied fauna and flora in the different parts of the park. An old Buick stops and a fellow asks us in German, "Do you want a ride?" and we gladly accept. He moves his blankets and food supplies on the back seat aside before we can get in. He is also a foreign student and is exploring the United States in his own vehicle; unfortunately, he is traveling in the opposite direction to ours. He bought his car from a friend for hundred fifty dollars and spent hundred sixty to have repairs done. He takes us to the other side of the park and we wish each other luck. It is getting late and cold. We are at an altitude of 2500m. We ask a warden if there is any place where we can stay over-night but he tells us not at this time of the year, everything is booked far in advance. In desperation, we stop an old pick-up truck that is heading south and the driver allows us to climb on the open back. The couple inside look like lumberjacks. They drive out of the park to a little store to buy some supplies. It seems hopeless to get a ride to the next village at this time of the day, so they offer to take us back to their camp. Since some of the loggers that work there have gone home for the weekend, there will be room in their tent. We drive twenty miles back into the park, the last stretch on a very rough logging road; it is so bad that we are thrown from one end of the open truck to the other. It is dark now and we have to feel our way to the tent. They light a kerosene lamp inside and in the dim light; everything looks spooky and smells musty. In the back of the tent is a double bed, beside it an old wooden shelf and a red Coca-Cola icebox. Gerhard finds an empty spot and spreads his sleeping bag out. I don't have one and the woman offers me a cover from the absent loggers. She stays out for a while and we fear she will bring in some buddies and they will help us to "undress". She comes back alone and throws a bunch of smelly blankets to me. I button my shirt up and keep my socks on so as to have as little contact with them as possible when I crawl in. It is cold at night and I need them to keep warm

The two whisper in the back and turn their flashlight on briefly to find the next can of beer. Shortly after midnight we hear voices, it sounds like a heated argument. We act as if we are sleeping but observe as much as we can in the dark. Then the man crawls out of the tent, accidentally grabbing Gerhard's feet; he is scared, sits up and asks if it is time to get up. "Shut up" he tells Gerhard. He needs to empty his bladder we think. After a while, we hear the dog from the neighbor tent barking, loud noises as though garbage cans are being tipped over and people swearing, A few minutes later, it happens again. Now they are going to get us, we fear and are ready to get into action. We hear someone running and then it is quiet. We finally fall into a restless sleep.

Morning dawns, the man gets up and lights a fire. It is rather cold at this altitude of almost 3000m. We awake and are glad to be still alive.

We get up and wash in the little creek that flows near the tent. In the sunshine, everything looks more peaceful and normal. When we come back, the two have made breakfast and invite us to share with them. They tell us that last night bears were rummaging through the garbage cans and made all that racket.

The woman and her friend plan to go shopping this morning and ask us if we want to come along. While they are getting ready we go out to the loggers and watch them cutting trees they even let us try their chain saws, which we have never seen before. We say good-bye to the fellows and climb on the truck with our bags. The two women and the dog sit in the cab. In the little village at the south exit of the park, we thank them for the ride and their hospitality. The traffic in this desolate corner of Wyoming is minimal. No cars means no rides. After waiting for a few hours, we see a big sign hundred meters down the road: horses for rent, one dollar an hour. We take turns, each one half an hour. It has been a long time since I have been in a saddle and it feels good to gallop along the sand road. We think both the horses and we need some exercise. I am still paying my fare, when I see Gerhard waving; a car has stopped and takes us along. It is not going exactly in our direction but takes us to the next more traveled highway. We drive through a wonderful landscape; behind us the grandiose and interesting Yellowstone Park and beside us the majestic Great Teton National Park with its 4400m high Teton mountain range and its turquoise-blue lakes. We do not have to wait long for the ideal ride. A car with a high-loaded trailer stops and a young man rolls down his window and asks where we want to go. I tell him Ohio. "Well, come in that is where I am going." He had been discharged from the air force and is going home with all his belongings on his trailer. He seems to enjoy our company and we have interesting conversations about the army, politics and his family. He drives too slowly for Gerhard and we consider looking for a faster ride. But our friendly ex-soldier is driving during the night as well, with only short stops, that adds miles and saves us hotel costs. We decide to stay with him and keep him company for the next two thousand five hundred kilometers.

In Fort Wayne Gerhard leaves us and goes south to Virginia. We have had lots of fun together and complemented each other well. He was good company and I will miss him. About an hour later, at the cross road to Bluffton, the driver stops and lets me out. I thank him for the long ride and he says he was happy to have us to keep him awake. While I am waving him good-bye, a car stops and takes me to the doors of Bluffton College. This closes the circle. I have visited twenty-nine sates of the USA, more than many Native American citizens have done. I have learned to know a good cross section of people, their life styles and their customs. I saw a great variety of landscapes, prairie grasslands with a variety of animals, large herds of cattle, fertile farmland with lush vegetation, bare deserts and dense forests, high mountains and the wide ocean. I will have good memories of this journey.

Farewell to Bluffton

I arrive in time for lunch. I still can take a shower and change, for we did not get out of our clothes for three days. I can stay on campus for a few days before I go back to Germany. To pay for board and room I help clean Lincoln Hall for the next set of students. Carl keeps me company. He had invited me during semester break to speak in his Methodist congregation and we have become friends. He teaches me how to play tennis properly and we play and talk about all topics of interest. He also drives me to Lima and I buy a suitcase, underwear and a white nylon shirt, made of a fiber that is new on the market.

Vice President Dr. Schulz invites me for a farewell dinner. We talk about my impressions of Bluffton College and America in general. I tell him about my travel experiences and my family. Dr. Schulz and his wife speak German quite well. She asks me to speak at their Sunday school picnic for the college class. I am not as nervous anymore as I was when I first came here. I take the opportunity to thank them for their friendship in accepting me so generously and for all the help they have given me. I will give a good report about Bluffton College when I return to Germany. They take a collection for my travel expenses. Mr. Soldner, my boss, for whom I worked for a short time in construction before I went on my trip comes over to me and we have a friendly talk together; he gives me a ten dollar bonus for my work, when he says good-bye to me.(which is almost a day's wages)

I ask the Mosers if I might spend a workday on their farm. Having grown up on a farm, I am interested to see how they farm in America. John picks me up with the jeep. They are harvesting. Machines, operated by family members do most of the work. They need little outside help. Mr. Moser takes me along on the combine and explains the procedure of harvesting. It is quite different from harvest at home. We did a lot by hand and with horses, but that was ten years ago during the war.

Tomorrow is my last day at Bluffton and I start packing. I have added quite a few things to my possessions and my suitcases do not hold all of them. I have to put what is left into a cardboard box. My last visit is to my motherly friend, Mrs. Mosiman. We sit on the swing-bench and reminisce about the events of the last year. I thank her for her friendship and she gives me a beautiful pen as a remembrance gift and promises me the picture of the Marienburg over her sofa when I come back to Bluffton.

The next morning at eight o'clock, Dr. Shelly takes me to the railroad station in Lima; Carl, Mary-Ellen, Agnes and Leona join us. They help me with my luggage and wave good-bye as the train moves slowly from the station.

I have completed an academic year at Bluffton College. I have met a number of people, mostly friendly, well-meaning and helpful ones, people of different backgrounds, different skin color and different interests. I have gained some insight into their lives, their attitudes and aspirations, which helps me to widen my horizon and understand this world a little better.

The next morning I arrive at the MCC headquarters in Akron again. Since there were few people in my train compartment, I was able to sleep for a while. I pick up my mail from home and the photos from Ritzville, which I had been expecting and about which I am very happy.

Neufelds, distant relatives from West Prussia had emigrated a few years ago from Germany to Ephrata, twelve miles from Akron. They pick me up in their own car and I spend an enjoyable evening with them in their recently purchased home. All of them are employed and active in a Mennonite Congregation, are happy and feel quite at home here. They bring me back the next morning. Gerhard and the other exchange students have arrived and we all get our papers, only Gerhard's passport has not been sent back. A few frantic calls to the immigration office help. They promise to send it to the ship.

We pack our entire luggage in the MCC's Land Rover. The next morning at four o'clock, Kenneth drives it to New York and, as he has two empty seats and likes company, I drive with him.

At the pier, we arrange our luggage registration and walk over to the *Friendly Relations to Foreign Students* bureau. They want to hear our response to the exchange year, wish us good sailing and give each one of us a thirty-five dollar coupon. I quickly write a card to Carl in Bluffton and a letter to Hildegard in Ritzville, which is the beginning of a long-lasting intimate correspondence.

We are boarding the *SS America,* a much more luxurious steamer than the refitted freighter, *Nelly,* which brought us to America. Four of us share one spacious cabin in the tourist class. We take a tour of the boat, looking at the gorgeous lounges, the swimming pool, sun deck and the comfortable dining room with a variety of food offerings. Five of us exchange students and a young economist from Hamburg sit at one table. We have much to discuss, Germany's evolving economy and life styles in Germany and in the United States as we have observed them. The food on the ship is delicious and we can eat as much as we want. We take advantage of this while we think of the frugal meals awaiting us in post war Germany. The ocean is calm like a mirror, when we leave New York harbor and glide again past the famous Statue of Liberty.

It is quite hot and we spend time in the swimming pool for first class passengers and exercise on our sport deck. On Sunday, we attend the ship's Sunday service. We have plenty to share with our fellow students about experiences in our different colleges last year. We also have good discussions with other passengers on the boat. The time passes quickly and soon we see land. On August 9, 1952, we are back again in Bremerhaven and have to leave our comfortable steamer.

Chapter Eight

Back in Europe

My thoughts are still in Bluffton and Washington when we land in Bremerhaven. I board the train to Peine and take the bus to Handorf. It has been a long time since I opened that rusty gate that opens to the bridge over the Opfergraben and walked along the path to the parsonage. Some flowers are still blooming beside the walkway and the old chestnut tree is spreading its branches over our kitchen window. Mother is happy to have me back again and for the next days, we have much to share. She always takes great interest in my encounters and adventures. I know she has accompanied me on all my trips in her thoughts and prayers.

I have a wonderful mother. I appreciate her trust, her positive outlook on life, her thoughtfulness and understanding.

The 'parsonage community' celebrates my return and I share with them my experiences in America and show my slides which we took of our trip with a borrowed camera.

While still in the USA, Gerhard and I had arranged to attend the Mennonite World Conference in Switzerland, which would start a week after our return. I just have time to get things in order, buy a small camera from the money I have left over from my work in the USA and pack a travel bag.

I am on the road again, hitchhiking to Basel for the big conference in the homeland of the Mennonites. I am excited to meet Mennonites from all over the world, to find out about their faith and what it means to them to be a Mennonite, how they relate to people of other denominations and their church.

There are the friendly, pious Old Mennonites in their special garb, the men in their jackets closed with hooks and eyes and a stand up collar, the women in their long, plain dresses and white head coverings, the Amish with beards and black hats and the women in plain long dark dresses. We have an open, intimate conversation with two Amish brothers. I like their generosity and simplicity of faith, which influences their life style and image of the world.

Gerhard and I attended an Amish service in Kansas. Members of that group still speak an old south German dialect, which Gerhard could easily imitate in conversation with them. We sang hymns with them from their *Ausbund* songbook, dating back to the seventeenth century. Some of the hymns had over twenty verses and they sing them slowly, often five or more notes to one vowel. The people were surprised that we strangers knew their songs and asked us if we, too, were Amish.

Two messages were given that Sunday. The first preacher spoke about a Bible text and a second lay preacher embellished one part and gave a different interpretation to the rest of it. The service lasted about three hours. The children could not of course sit that long, so they ran in and out and young mothers nursed their babies while listening.

The Amish in that area have no separate church buildings. We sat in a barn on simple wooden benches without backs. After the service, they invited us to a fellowship meal with the other parishioners and we had a lively conversation with them.

Besides these conservative Amish Mennonites, there are a number of other branches of Mennonites at the world conference, the more liberal Doops- gezinde from Holland, the 'pious' South Germans, the West Prussian and North German Mennonites and some from Indonesia, Africa and other continents. Some women come in long dark dresses, others in pants and shorts and sleeveless blouses, since it is quite hot. We meet a number of friends and relatives. I greet Onkel Wall and some young people with whom I had been in youth retreats and Voluntary Service Camps.

A number of conference departments give reports about their activities which are followed by discussions and suggestions for actions to be taken. For me it is interesting to find out how multifaceted the work is in whiich the Mennonite Conference is involved.

After the official closing of the conference we attend a memorial service in honor of two Swiss founders of the Anabaptist movement, Felix Manz and Konrad Grebel. A large number of people gather at the Felix Manz' House where a memorial plaque is attached to commemorate the two Anabaptist martyrs and the house where the first adult baptism was performed. It is an impressive event. Afterwards we go to the Cathedral where Zwingli had preached and had disputed church reform with the Anabaptist leaders.

At a restaurant on the banks of Zürich Lake, we have lunch and go on to Luzern. We take a walk around the beautiful Vierwaldstätter Lake, admire the picturesque Swiss houses with their painted walls, and flower boxes around their balconies. Here and there, a few houses are built high on the slopes of the mountains that surround the lake.

Our next stop is the Swiss capital Bern. From the high bridge over the Aare, we have a good view of the city. and the river down below. One of the main attractions for me is Rodin's *Bourgeois of Calais* on one side of the market place He portrayed a group of city council members surrendering the key of the city to their enemies. The figures are over life-size and express the agony, shame and courage of the individuals.

Switzerland we find expensive. Soon we run out of money and leave this interesting country via Basel. We climb up the *Bienenberg* to the campus of the European Mennonite Bible School. The principal shows us around and explains the program to us. We try to imagine being students there. (Later, my future father-in-law would be teaching there for three years.) We stay overnight in Bienenberg. The next morning we go down the hill to the city and hitchhike to the Rhine falls outside of Schaffhausen. We go as close as possible to the actual falls and get some good pictures.

Gerhard goes home from there to Karlsruhe and I go on to Nürnberg. I visit the Voluntary Service Camp and help for a few days pouring foundations and raising brick walls for the construction of refugee houses. I am familiar with this kind of work which I had done in my practicum with contractor Hanke.

The inner city of Nürnberg has preserved its medieval character. The old castle has kept its outside appearance with walls, moat and tower but the interior has been renovated and serves now as a youth hostel. Across from the market place with its Baroque Fountain, the *Schöne Brunnen* is the *Dürer Haus,* now museum for Germany's famous painter and printmaker. The *St.Lorenz* Church displays the famous *Renaissance Tabernacle*, a filigree stone structure carried by human figures, created by Adam Kraft, and the Annunciation, *(Englischer Gruß,)* by the German woodcarver and sculptor Veit Stoß.

Many people are perhaps more familiar with Nürnberg through Hitler's political activities there and the Nürnberg Second World War Trials.

The final Years

I have to find my way around again in Braunschweig. It has changed since I saw it last a year ago. Rubble from the destroyed buildings has been removed. Where empty lots and broken walls had been before, the former owners have built new houses again.

Our University has changed too. Its north wing at the Schleinitzstrasse that had been started when I left is now reconstructed and this has added new lecture halls and labs to the existing buildings. Our architecture department is planning a further extension, a new high-rise tower on the open west side with additional Institutes, offices and further lecture halls. The plans for it are displayed in the foyer.

I go to the registrar's office and enroll for my fifth semester, select my courses and have them authorized by my professors.

With some hesitation, I go to Professor Imhofen and ask if the room in his house that he let me use before I went to America would still be available. Unfortunately, he is not renting it out anymore and I have to look for another accommodation. Since many of the former homes in the city were destroyed during the war, there is a housing shortage and it is not easy to find a room. After looking for four weeks, I finally find a small room on the third floor of a formerly upper class building facing a narrow back yard. It is part of the residence of a ninety-two-year-old retired colonel. I assume he needs the money to supplement his meager army pension. His wife, who takes care of him, is quite talkative and overpowering. Like a sergeant, she tells me clearly what I can and cannot do in her house. The furniture is a conglomeration of different period pieces but the room is reasonable and clean. I think I can get along with the landlady and so I sign a one-year contract with her. It takes me about ten minutes on my bike to get from my new place to the university.

In Ohio, I had gotten a driver's license. I wonder if this is acceptable in Germany. It is I find out. The examiner in the motor vehicle branch tells me I only have to write a theory exam about traffic signs and regulations. He asks me if I want to apply for a second or third class license. I tell him a second class, not knowing that it is for driving cars and trucks. One of the questions is 'how air brakes work' I have no idea and another 'how to hitch a trailer to a truck'. I try to guess but it is not good enough, so he tells me to come back again for a second chance. and gives me a pamphlet to inform myself. The second time I have no problem passing. I pay twelve DM and am the owner of a German driver's license good for a lifetime. For German applicants it is very expensive to get a license.

The members of the Studentengemeinde come and go, some old friends have got married or engaged and moved away but Pastor Wielgoss is still here. He has planned a retreat for new students at the beginning of the new winter semester in the *Haus der Helfenden Hände,* (house of the helping hands) an estate that belonged to the *Protestant Confessing Church of East Prussia.* That group had opposed Hitler's politics and paid heavily for it. Many of its members, pastors, such as Bonhoeffer, and large estate owners from the nobility, like Graf von Stauffenberg and Helmuth von Moltke, were killed after the failed assassination attempt on Hitler on July 20, 1944

During these retreats, we learn to know each other better. I join the choir again, brush up on playing the trumpet, play in the brass ensemble and participate in other activities.

A former member of the Studentengemeinde, now president of a well-known coffee roasting plant, offers free lunch tickets for us students in his worker's cafeteria. I am often the recipient of these. I had noticed in America that people give compliments for something they appreciate. After a tasty lunch, I tell the cook "The meal was very good today; thank you". She looks at me and replies, "Was it not good before?" In America, she would have said, "thank you, I am glad you liked it" but Germans are not used to compliments. I noticed another difference. While riding my bike across a busy intersection I stop for a pedestrian and a woman drives into the back of my bike and scolds me, "Keep going, dummy."

In our university student drafting room, I manage to get a good window seat where I can do my architectural designs. In my small, dark rented room, I have only a tiny writing desk with a foldout table, far too small for my drawings. On top of this antique rococo piece now stands a picture of Hildegard, which I have enlarged to postcard size, flanked by two small Indian sculptures – mementos of my exchange year.

We are now writing more often to each other. From once in three months, the interval of letters crossing the ocean has shrunk to once a week. They have become more intimate since she once included in her letter a picture of herself reading a poem about love by Shakespeare. She included the poem and signed it, from *your* Hildegard. Now I sometimes sit late at night and write to *my* Hildegard and my thoughts accompany her from Ritzville to Bethel College where she is now studying. We exchange thoughts about our daily work, about art, politics and our faith, about what we both understand by love and how we visualize our future. With each of her letters, for which I can hardly wait, a picture for our future becomes clearer to me. Hers is still somewhat blurred.

Mennonite Youth Activities

The summer after my return from Bluffton I get two letters from MCC headquarters in Frankfurt. In the first one, the director asks me if I could assist Hugo in leading a Voluntary Service Camp in Leutesdorf. Hugo is a new MCC worker for Germany and unfamiliar with how things are done here. In the second letter, they invite me to help teach summer Bible school in the new Mennonite refugee settlement in Neuwied. Since both places are not far from each other on the banks of the Rhine, I respond positively to both requests.

In Neuwied, I am teaching a group of ten to twelve year old boys and girls, lovely children who believe everything I tell them. I introduce them to the life and teaching of Jesus and explain how he influenced people in his time and how he can shape our lives and guide us today. They are sharp little kids and I have to come up with new ideas to have their attention and keep discipline. They like the Bible stories from the Old and the New Testament and are eager to illustrate them, building a Palestinian village with temple and synagogue and houses with flat roofs, where Peter had his vision about Cornelius and where friends of the sick man open the roof to lower him down to Jesus' feet. Here I can apply my architectural skills about city planning.

From Neuwied I go down the Rhine to Leutesdorf. Hugo is there already. He is an amiable fellow, a little shy at first; we work together quite well in planning and managing the camp. Our task is to restore the trails along the Rhine River. Seniors from the Mennonite old folk's home use it to enjoy the Rhine land-scape, get their exercise and walk to the cemetery where their beloved ones are buried. With wheelbarrow and shovel, we bring rocks and sand to fill the holes that last year's high flood had washed out. We have to make the trail smooth and safe enough for disabled and wheelchair patients. Some of the old people watch us working and we benefit from each other; we bring laughter and variety into their lives and they share their life-stories and experiences with us. I have the opportunity to meet my aunt Martha there. She attends to the senior's medical problems. We have a lot to share since I visited her in her Guesthouse in Silesia, which is now under 'Polish management.'

Next summer I am on the road again, this time to Austria. MCC has a voluntary service camp in *Ebensee* on the picturesque *Traunsee,* east of Salzburg. Volunteers from many countries help to build a church for a Protestant Diaspora congregation, Most Austrians are Catholics. We befriend members of the congregation who join us in the evening after work on the building site. Some invite us to their homes and village activities. In our free time, we hike around the lake or climb up to the *Feuerkogel* a 1544m mountaintop and take the cable car for a free ride down. On one sunny weekend morning, a group of us hikes up to the crest of the *Höllengebirge,* about 1800m high. We have a breathtaking view of the other mountain ranges and the little villages with their red roofs and pointed church steeples nestled in the valleys. On the way back we have to walk around a rugged mountain to get to the rescue hut on the other side. A narrow path leads up and across the mountain, a shortcut, I figure. I leave the group and hike up that path.. After a while, the path changes to a steep mountain goat trail and I have to grab on to the rocks so as not to slide down. It would be difficult to go back now and my pride does not allow me to consider this option. The view from the top is magnificent and I rest for a while and enjoy it. But the descent is even more treacherous, often there is no trail at all, and I have to find my way through thick intertwined underbrush or swing over crevices. I have to use my wristwatch as a compass so that I will not lose my bearing. Finally, I see a dark spot through the thicket; it is the cabin of the mountain search and rescue team, where we have agreed to meet. When I enter the cabin, it feels good to have solid level ground under my feet again. The rescue guide is not pleased to hear my story. "You could have slid down the mountain and killed yourself and we would have had to get the rescue team out to search for you, don't do that again" he tells me. I apologize and promise to be more careful the next time.

Our work at the camp comes to an end. We have become friends with some of the parishioners. Jörg, one of the youngsters, loves to be with us volunteers on the site. He seems to like me. We often work together, I show him how to use some of our tools, and he is eager to learn. He is sorry to see us leave and tells me once after work that his parents have said that if I want to stay a few days longer, I could stay with them.

Since I have no urgency to get home, I tell him I will consider it, and go home with him to find out if that is all right with his parents. They tell me Jörg has told them about me and I am welcome to stay.

We celebrate *Richtfest*. When the most risky work is done, the walls are up and the roof rafters are nailed in, it is customary to celebrate this event with a speech, a prayer and a meal. We volunteers participate in hanging an arched wreath of flowers in the framed church steeple and share the soup that members of the congregation have made for the workers and some drink beer with them. For most of us Mennonites, it is juice. We all sing and are happy and get the rest of the afternoon off.

The congregation arranges a farewell party for us volunteers and after that is over everyone travels home. I take my bag and walk over with Jörg to his home. His parents welcome me heartily; they are simple people and are not quite sure how to relate to me as a stranger. Jörg asks me if I want to join him and his two friends on a bike trip tomorrow. His father lets me have his bike. Early next morning the two boys are waiting for us and we travel through the lovely village along the Austrian Romantic Road. Beside us, we hear the rippling of the Traun River. We move away from it and take a smaller road through the foothills of the Höllengebirge. Two weeks ago, I looked down from the top of it onto this road. We bike around the mountain range down to the south end of the Attersee. The deep blue surface of the water reflects the white mountain tops on both sides of the lake. The reflection of the trees on its banks gives the water a turquoise shade. With its variety of landscapes, high mountains, surrounding a number of lakes, and valleys with picturesque villages, the *Salzkammergut* is one of Austria's most beautiful areas.

We cross a creek that connects the *Attersee* with the *Mondsee* and ride a few kilometers alongside the quiet lake. The panorama changes; the mountains are a little farther back and through the trees, we see little villages and color dots, tents of campgrounds along the beach. Another six kilometers and we enter St.Gilgen on the *St.Wolfgangsee*. We sit on a bench beside the lake, unpack our Sandwiches and eat lunch. The tall white tower of the ancient Pilgrimage church of St.Wolfgang on the opposite side of the lake greets us. I cannot wait to get there. It is an interesting historical town. The old Romanesque church, its interior now decorated in the baroque style, houses the famous Renaissance wing altar by Michael Pacher, altar paintings by other Baroque artists and the relics of Bishop St.Wolfgang, which draw many pilgrims and tourists to the little town. It has gained reputation through the operetta *"Im Weißen Rössl am Wolfgangsee"* (White Horse Inn). We leave the picturesque town with its frescoed old buildings and flower decorated balconies and head home. In Bad Ischl we make our last stop. Its spa draws people from many parts of the country who seek treatment and healing. It is getting dark when we return to Ebensee and we are tired from our almost hundred km long bike trip. It was a high point of my Austria visit.

When I say good-bye to my friendly hosts, they invite me to come back for a holiday again. I thank them for their hospitality and hitch-hike home.

Handorf has had some changes in the last year. Pastor Brandes received a transfer to a small town congregation in Dassel and moved out. It gets somewhat lonesome here since his lively family is gone. Shortly after their departure, the Brandes have an addition to their family, a little boy, the sixth child. Pastor Brandes asks me if I would consider being a godfather to him. For me this is something new. We Mennonites do not have this custom. We do not baptize babies. Before I respond, I inquire first what my obligations will be. When I find out what they are, I gladly accept this position and consider it an honor that they name their son Helmut and give me a place in their family. On October 10, 1952, I become godfather to Helmut Brandes.

Directing singing in youth camp

Student brass octet in Braunschweig

Laying bricks in a Voluntary service camp

A fresh wind blows into the empty parsonage when the Lohmann family joins us. Frau Lohmann is a young widow, friendly, outgoing and communicative. She is very spontaneous and affirming and tries to bring out the best in any person she befriends. She must have been a good partner and co-worker with her husband, who was a pastor.

Now, being a single parent, it is not so easy for her to take full responsibility for her young family. For our house group in the parsonage the arrival of the Lohmanns seems to be a good complement to the childless young teachers couple, the elderly barber Bender and his wife and Mother and me. The three young boys are the missing generation in our house family and they bring life into the place. Frau Lohmann has a very positive attitude towards life and wants to live it fully. She talks to the young wife of the teacher whom she feels is not very happy. So she suggests to her husband that he should bring his wife flowers occasionally and take her out for a meal. Her advice is well meant but has unintended consequences. He finds Frau Lohmann attractive and his wife becomes jealous, which strains their relationship.

We converse openly with Frau Lohmann about our faith and Christian living and notice a tension arising between the sincere more literal Bible-believing Pentecostal Benders and the more joyful, socially active and tolerant protestant pastor's widow. We peace-loving Mennonites try to help them understand each other's position and background.

After Frau Lohmann becomes reasonably acquainted with life in our village, she sees Karl, the oldest boy of the Hundt family, running around in rags, playing alone in the dirt. She feels sorry for him and invites him to come over to the parsonage and play with her boys, which he does. She asks him about his family and finds out that his mother is an alcoholic. He is one of several children and looks quite neglected and dirty. She wants to bring a change into his life, offers him a bath, and selects some clothes from her ten-year-old son, Christoph, who is about his age and size. She gives these to him and sends him into the bedroom to rest. After an hour, she quietly opens the bedroom door to see if he is still sleeping and finds Karl gone. She looks around and sees the window open. This is very likely the way he left, she thinks. She walks over to the night table and cannot find her wristwatch that was lying there. Karl must have taken it with him. She is sad that her well-meant help is so little appreciated. Her enthusiasm for social justice and bringing people out of their misery has been dampened. A few days later, she sees Karl again in old torn clothes. She is incensed and asks him, "Where are the pants and shirt I gave you last week?" He does not look at her, "Mother sold them for booze". Frau Lohmann is disappointed and angry with the whole situation.

The three Lohmann boys are fond of me; they greet me heartily when I come back to Handorf after my year in Bluffton. I think I am a kind of father figure for them. I like them too and enjoy talking and playing with them when I am home. The seven-year-old Hans tells me that I am his friend and he would like to be my friend. Once I show my slides to the house-group: he moves his chair close to mine."Friends should sit together," he whispers.

The youngest, a cute fair-haired boy, is a little dreamer. He likes to play. His mother is worried about him. "Volker is not telling me the truth and I don't know how to teach him to be honest" she confides in me anxiously. 'Shall I punish him if I find out he is lying?" I have no convincing answer. I tell her I notice he is very involved in his play. For him toys are alive, he talks to them and they talk back to him. He is quite creative and imaginative. At age five, he still lives in a different reality. Fantasy and reality may be interchangeable for him. I think teaching him the difference between the two and helping him understand the possible consequences, is better than punishing him. He might not understand why he is being punished. I am sure he will soon grow out of this stage. Frau Lohman wants to try this.

It is a Sunday in April, the fruit trees beside the path to the parsonage are in full bloom and the spring flowers display their colors. The half-timbered building under the big chestnut tree looks inviting. I have invited Alfred, an intelligent, sensible fellow architectural student, to come to Handorf. He tends at times to be depressed and sad. He seems to see in me a more solid, stable person. We sometimes walk home together from university after a busy day, talk and go to a concert or a movie. He is a refugee, as I am. We have some things in common; he lost his father and served in the army in Africa.

We sit in the garden and he shares with me his war experience at the end of the combat in Africa. Field Marshal Rommel's army had been cut off from supplies and was in some disarray. He watched remnants from one company, who had run out of ammunition and food, surrender to American and Canadian troops. Though they approached them with raised arms and a white flag the Americans and Canadians opened fire killing them all. It was easier and faster to do away with them that way than go through the trouble of taking them prisoners. Shortly after that massaker he saw an American Tank rolling toward his own dugout in the desert, turning around on top of them and burying him and his comrade. When the infantry followed, they shot into the dust-covered hole, killing his comrade and wounding him. Later a medic found him and took him prisoner. He still has nightmares, severe headaches and bouts of depression as a result of these experiences.

While we are talking we hear music from the house, Frau Lohmann is playing Mozart on the piano and has her living room window open. Alfred plays piano well but has not played for a long time and would like to try it again. I introduce him to Frau Lohmann and she lets him play for a while. Later on we sing folksongs and popular hymns harmonizing together and Frau Lohmann accompanies on the piano. We like making music and talking together. I think Alfred enjoys this sunny day in the country.

At Christmas, the youth group presents a Nativity play and Frau Lohmann, knowing that I like to sing, asks me to stand on the balcony and sing "Vom Himmel hoch" (From heaven on high) as a part of the play. I think she is a little disappointed at the result, because I do not have a carrying solo voice.

The Braunschweig Mennonite young people are glad that I am back again, I feel somewhat responsible for them. One day coming home from University, I see Renate and Katja, the most active girls from our youth group, in front of my door waiting for me. "Joachim died," they greet me with tears in their eyes. We go into my room and they tell me what happened. Joachim, the treasurer of our youth group, a strong and healthy young man, had been admitted to hospital a few days ago. I had not had a chance to see him yet. They visited him and talked to him. He told them he was weak but hoped to be out soon and start his training as an electrical engineer. Two days later, he was dead, his kidneys stopped working and he died of blood poisoning,. This news affects us deeply. We talk for a while about death the readiness to die and about mourning. Joachim's father was killed in the war and we wonder how his mother might deal with this shock and think of ways to assist her. We pray together before the girls leave.

The *Junge Gemeinde*, the new youth magazine of the Mennonite young people in Northern Germany, asks for contributions. I enter an article about *Mennonites and Nonresistance* based on biblical and historical principles. This topic drew my attention while I studied at Bluffton College. It starts a lively discussion and a fair number respond to it, some defend their position as former soldiers, others would accept alternatives.

The post-war generation slowly gains more hope in life after their disillusion-ment at the traumatic ending of the war. They take a more critical look at their former values and select what is still applicable for their present situation. They become more involved in advocating changes and building a new future for themselves and their environment.

The two German youth workers plan an international youth leaders' retreat, supported by German and American Mennonite conferences. In our training sessions, we discuss critically our inherited Mennonite principles of faith, to find out if they are still meaningful to us to day and if we can apply them to our practical daily life. We North-German young people, mostly West Prussian refugees, went through many difficult personal struggles during and after the war, we lost our homes and the sanctuary of our congregations. Life had formed us and put our faith to the test, perhaps somewhat different from the South-German Mennonites. Most of them still had their home environment and congregations. For personal and spiritual support.

The main thrust of the Swiss Mennonites is on personal salvation, while the Dutch put more emphasis on social issues, organization and congregational care. These differing priorities bring some tension into our dialogue. We finally agree to a general resolution and statement of faith. For the southern Mennonites it is perhaps too interlectual and not spiritual enough they would rather distance themselves from it when they come back to their congregations.

The youth-leader workshop, sponsored by MCC, is a little more harmonious. We work on Bible study patterns and how to lead a discussion. We are able to record our work and play it back again. Onkel Wall, our spiritual advisor, helps us to analyze this critically and improve our performances.

Shortly before we go home again, I take the opportunity to share a personal concern with him. I feel responsible for our Mennonite youth work and congre- gational affairs and like to take part in special events of the Studentengemeinde in Braunschweig. These activities consume much of my time and energy, which I need to study and prepare for my final Examination. It is getting to be too much for me and I don't quite know how to deal with the pressure. I would appreciate his advice. He takes me aside and tells me, "Helmut, I think your priority at this time is to finish your studies successfully and come up with the best results you can achieve. After that you can pick up the other activities again" I am relieved and thank him. I had feared, as pastor of a Mennonite Brethren Church and professor emeritus from a Bible college, he might tell me, 'The kingdom of God comes first.'

The Last Semesters

At the end of the semester, a fellow student tells me that she is moving out of her room and it will become available. If I am interested in relocating I should have a look at it. I had recently had an encounter with my landlady. My room is furnished with an antique hunting chair of her husband's with leather seat and leather straps for armrests. Ron, a Pax-Boy, whom I had befriended in a MVS camp, pays me a visit and, before I can warn him, he sits down in this chair, leans on the leather strap and tears one. He apologizes for it, but it is done. The next day, when I come home from the University, 'Frau Oberstleutnant' stands in the doorway and scolds me about how recklessly I have treated her furniture. This chair is an heirloom of her husband's grandfather. I humbly mention three generations is a good age for a leather stool and it should perhaps have been retired, in a museum. I offer to pay for the repair of the chair.

My rental contract has expired and I think it is time for a change. I decide to have a look at the room which my classmate vacated. It is on a quiet street on the first floor, bigger and much brighter than my present one. The landlady, a seamstress, is friendly and very accommodating. She lost her husband in the war and does not use the room very often and needs the extra rent income. It is an older house without running water and has a toilet in outhouse style. The rent is therefore quite reasonable. Everything is clean and friendly. On a table beside the door stands a large jug with water in a porcelain washbasin and a towel beside it, as it was at home in West Prussia when I was a child. I do not miss the bathroom that much, since I go swimming in the public swimming pool twice a week. It is free for students before seven a.m. I like the room and the landlady too and I tell her that I will take it. When I inform Frau 'Oberstleutnant' that I will move out at the end of the semester, she is not very happy and even offers to lower my rent.

In Professor Thulesius' drawing and painting classes, we often go to the Museum to sketch vases, sculptures and other objects. In summer, we sit in front of the ruins of the Gothic *St Magnus Kirche* and sketch the church steeple and parts of remaining cross vaults and side chapels. Two of these sketches are still hanging in my study.

To complete one of our semester assignments for him, I drive with a fellow student to Hillerse, where my life in West Germany began. Onkel Richard's family has moved to Holstein in the meantime. Hillerse has a unique old Romanesque church. Our task is to draw up accurate plans, side views and sections of it, so that the building could be reconstructed from our plans. We make detailed sketches from the carved wooden pews and the wing altar withsimplw carved sculpture.

I have applied for a special government study subsidy for refugees in Peine. To qualify and prove that I deserve it I have to take examinations in three main subjects and they have to be evaluated with at least a B average. I still attend the interesting lectures with Dr Flesche, in art history and history of architecture. I ask him if he would evaluate me in these two courses and sign the application. He is generous and gives me an A in both of them. The amount of the subsidy is increased for each additional semester. If I live frugally, I do not have to work the full time during semester vacations any more in order to pay for my tuition. I can now use the time to prepare for final examinations.

In our study room, we finish our assignments, exchange lecture notes and discuss design problems. Occasionally we play table tennis for relaxation. Coming close to the end of our training we feel we should practice our signatures that we may use as architects later to sign contracts and we have fun comparing them. Alfred pushes a sheet over and asks me to set my signature at the bottom of the sheet. I sign it for him, wondering why he wants me to sign at the bottom of an empty sheet. Later he tells some of us in a smaller circle that he met a girl at a friend's house in Wolfenbüttel; he fell head over heels in love with her, and feels she would be a good life partner for him. He can sometimes be facetious and we don't know if he is serious about it.

A week later, I get a postcard in the mail with a postal stamp from Wolfenbüttel. A girl by the name of Melanie wants to see me, in a very urgent matter. She will tell me more when we meet. I do not know a person by that name and wonder if anybody wants to pull my leg. But it sounds rather serious and perhaps I should respond and I agree to meet her.

I walk slowly through the entrance hall of the Braunschweig station when the train from Wolfenbüttel arrives. At the place, we had agreed to meet I see a young, good-looking, almost delicate woman. Her well-proportioned profile is framed with straight blond hair, held together at the back of her neck and falling over her shoulders. It gives her a solemn appearance. I go over to her, introduce myself and ask, if she would feel comfortable discussing her concern in my room. She would prefer a more neutral place. We go to the Lessingplatz nearby. The small restaurant is almost empty. We sit down in one corner and I order a cup of coffee and a piece of cake for each of us. "Is he still alive?" she starts the conversation. "I don't know what you mean, to whom do you refer?" I ask. "Alfred, you wrote me about him, didn't you?" "I do not remember ever having written to you" I reply. She pulls a letter from her purse and hands it to me. I glance over it briefly. "...he loves you with all his heart and often talks about you. He cannot live without you and would take his life, if..." I do not read any further and give the letter back to her. I am dumbfounded and finally tell her, "only the signature is mine, the rest he must have written himself." She feels betrayed; a mixture of sadness and anger is in her eyes as she takes the letter from me and slowly rips it up, piece by piece.- After a while I pick up the conversation again "Alfred has told me about you. He likes you very much and could see you as his life partner, but I do not know any more than this about his relationship to you. He is an intelligent and caring friend to me. He told me that he often suffers from periods of depression and severe headaches, dating back to his traumatic experiences during the war."

We walk slowly back to the railway station. "I told him at our last date, when he asked me if I would consider marrying him, that I was not ready to make a decision - and now I am sure, a marriage under pressure or out of pity cannot be fulfilling for either one of us and will not endure." She more or less talks to herself with some sadness and compassion in her voice. When I say good-bye to her, I assure her that I can understand her feelings about him.

On my way back to the university, I try to reconstruct the whole event again. I feel used and am sad and in a way angry about it. Did Alfred have this in mind already, when he asked for my signature? Is he serious about taking his life?

Alfred is not in our study room when I come to the university. I am ill at ease and go over to the Studentenheim. Robert, an older Student whom I know well is there and we talk about the incident. He assures me that Alfred would not take his life; I need not worry about it. We pray together and I go home, somewhat comforted.

The next morning I have doubts again. Will he be at the university or will someone tell us he has found him dead in his room.

When I enter our study room, I see Alfred at his desk and am relieved. I observe him for a while and decide not to say anything, at least not yet, about the meeting with Melanie. At an opportune time, I mention the letter and he is embarrassed and does not know what to say. After that, the topic is closed for me and our relationship becomes more relaxed again. We go to a concert, Elly Nay, the famous Beethoven interpreter, gives a performance in Braunschweig and we can persuade her to play for us students in the big hall of the Mensa. I am fascinated to see her playing almost beside me and enjoy her performance immensely, especially when she plays my favorite *Sonata # 8, the Pathetique.*

I had been one of the first students from our semester to finish the basic course in architecture and conclude it with the passing of the Vorexamen. It was a natural break before my year in the United States, Now most of my fellow students have caught up with me and so has my school friend Rolf with whom I worked together for contractor Hanke..I am glad that Hanke has work for me again. I need the money to pay for tuition and rent for the next semester. I don't want to go into debt. Once in our lunch break an older laborer asks me, "I observed you, how come you are so different from the other young workers, they swear and brag about how they conquered girls and you do your work as assigned without much fuss." "It is my Christian upbringing," I tell him and I am pleased that he noticed it.

In the last semester break, I do a practicum in an architect's office.

Some of our professors conduct research for the industry besides giving lectures. Professor Kristen teaches the science and application of building materials. His institute tests chemicals and substances that are used as ingredience for different building materials and how effective the are. At the end of the last semester, he plans an excursion for his students to see how these different materials are produced and we visit several factories that make them.

On our trip to one of these we drive to the Ruhr district. We notice that the *Autobahn* is often rerouted. The heavy truck traffic from German and foreign vehicles crossing Germany, makes frequent repair of its surface necessary. While this is done, the traffic on the divided four lane autobahn has to be temporarily rerouted from the side where the repair is done to the other, which reduces it to two undivided lanes.

Our bus approaches one of these route changeovers when we see a speeding truck with trailer coming towards us and switching over from one side to the other just in front of us. The trailer of the truck is packed high with heavy tarpaper rolls. Through the centrifugal force, it loses its balance, tilts over, rams our bus and slices one side open. Our driver dies in hospital, the tour guide is critically wounded and so are the students in the front rows. Police arrive quickly and ambulances drive up. I was sitting in the second row behind the driver and my head hit a metal rail; I have a concussion and many bumps all over my body. Fortunately, the *Miner's Hospital Gelsenkirchen* is close by and doctors of the hospital examine our injuries. Most of the students from the back seats get a thorough examination and are sent home by another bus. Six of us remain in the hospital. After a few days, my head feels better. All my bruises, however, leave big blue spots everywhere and hurt; my comrades tell the nurses I am blue-blooded, meaning coming from nobility. The nurses are very friendly, pamper us young students and treat us with preference over their often grumpy miners and other patients. We try to entertain them through jokes and compliments. I think they come more often into our room than our injuries require. One of my comrades has a short mustache and when he drops his hair into his forehead, he looks like Hitler. The nurses have to laugh when he greets them with Hitler speeches. After two weeks, the two fellow students from my room are discharged. The doctor keeps me a week longer for observation.

The building supply factory, which had invited our student group, provides a lawyer for us to settle the injury claims with the insurance company. I am allotted the sum of 2100DM for my injuries, just enough to pay my fare for the passage to Canada and to buy a few personal belongings and gifts.

After I have recovered from the accident and am back at university again, I hear that Professor Flesche is offering an excursion to southern Germany, the region of the Renaissance and Baroque. He wants to show his students some of the buildings and paintings he discussed in his lectures in art history. I join; I want to see as much of Germany as I can before I leave.

In *Würzburg,* we have an example of three building epochs in one cathedral. The construction of the *St Kalians' Kirche* was started in the Romanesque style, an addition was built to it in the Gothic period and it was finished in the Baroque period.

In the Wurzburg castle, we see a good example of high baroque architecture in the grandiose central stairway designed by the famous architect, Balthasar Neumann. Because of its good acoustic, chamber orchestras like to use it to play Baroque music on its landing for selected guests. Tiepolo's large ceiling paintings of that period above it complement the Baroque experience.

The Bamberg Dom, built in the thirteenth century takes us into the Gothic period. The *Bamberger Reiter* (horseman) is one of the oldest large Gothic sculptures. The biblical group, including Elisabeth and Maria in the side chapel and the portal flanked by sculptures of the Bavarian princes and the female sculpture, the *Synagogue,* all positioned in the typical slight 'S-curve', conclude the cycle of huge gothic sculptures in the Dom.

It is much more meaningful to see and admire these structures, sculptures and paintings in their original size and environment than to look at them on the screen in the lecture room. Professor Flesche explains the development and distinctive features of different styles and epochs while we are looking at real examples whichs makes the experience so much more valuable

My student years have come to an end and I gather the courage to go to the Dean of Architecture and apply for admission to the final examination; I hope I am ready for it.. We are free to choose the time when we want to sign up. I have fulfilled the minimum requirements, have attended eight of the required semesters in the faculty of architecture (one of my fellow students needed 19 semesters before he had the courage to to take the finals) and have done all the prescribed assignments. The first hurdle, a prerequisite for admission, is a public display of my work which I have done in all semesters. The faculty will   evaluate it, the criteria being creativity, accuracy and ingenuity. The outcome of this evaluation will determine whether or not I am admitted for the *Diplomprüfung*.

The date for the exhibition has been set and we are all busy giving final touches to our different designs and construction drawings covering the areas of residential, industrial, educational and sacral buildings, also city planning, garden architecture, interior design and, in addition, we display our sketches, paintings, sculptures and calligraphic samples. We also have to demonstrate our proficiency in structural and mechanical calculations and geodesy

The great day has come and everyone is somewhat nervous. The evening before, I have prepared everything and feel this is the best I can do. Now I sit in my cubicle in the big hallway of the university, separated from my fellow students by a few partitions. On the sides of these, I have pinned my drawings, paintings and sketches. On a side table, I put folders with additional drawings and pictures and my best sculptures

Students come and look at our displays. They want to measure their own work against ours and pick up some good ideas for their own exhibition. Most of our professors visit us, look at our work, ask questions or make suggestions. From their evaluation and conversation with them, I get an idea of where I stand. After eight hours of talking and waiting, I find out that the overall evaluation of my display is assessed as 'good' work and I can go on to the next step.

I now have two weeks to prepare for my written examinations. Perhaps the most challenging one is in building design, because we have no idea what topic Professor Kraemer will choose for our examination assignment and I can therefore not prepare much for it. We wait in our examination room for Professor Kraemer's assistant to bring our assignment. He offers us two themes to choose from. I take a 'Restaurant in a Bus Depot'. I have nine hours to do several design sketches and to complete proper final scale drawings with construction details. I am exhausted by the time I am finished.

Most of the other written examinations are shorter.

After I have completed all written examinations successfully, I have a few days to concentrate on the oral examinations. Thirteen times, I have to appear in my new black suit, white shirt and tie in the offices of different professors and answer their probing questions. Some of them offer us a chair and we chat, for others we have to make sketches and explain them. Professor Flesche asks me to draw a plan of the Cathedral in Strasburg and Il Gesu in Italy and sketch a typical section of their vaulting systems. After this is done, I have to explain to what period they belong, what their basic differences are and what the reason for this is, based on the political and spiritual climate of that time. In art history, he shows me different pictures and wants me to identify them according to period and painter and talk about different artists, typical themes and techniques of that period; again he wants me to relate the artist's work to social and political problems of that time.

I am glad when this most stressful part of the Diplomprüfung is over. The last hurdle is the *Diplomarbeit* (similar to a dissertation); we have a choice of three topics. I choose *'Omnibus Bahnhof for Braunschweig'* It is a very timely topic.

The city of Braunschweig is planning a new central bus station. We can count on cooperation and information from them for our project and they are anxious to find out about our solutions to their problems. We have to research the traffic pattern and density of different feeder lines within the city limits to find a suitable location for the bus station, taking into account future growth. From bus companies and bus drivers we learn about frequency and occupancy of buses as well as size and turning circle of their vehicles. From this information, we can calculate the proper size and number of platforms, which will guarantee a quick and easy flow of traffic.

We drive to different cities and look at their solutions. We have to decide which amenities we have to provide and which are already available close to the different locations. It takes time to gather all the necessary information.

I want to get my design done as well and as quickly as possible. A strong pull draws me to the other side of the ocean. My correspondence with Hildegard in Seattle becomes more intense and intimate in the three years we have been writing to each other and the wish to be together for a lifetime becomes more evident in our letters, at least in mine. We are quite open with each other and do not want to create an image of ourselves that is not true to reality. I try to express my feelings as honestly as I can; men usually have difficulty doing this and I am no exception but I do not hide my shortcomings- we want to know what the other thinks and does. To answer Hildegard's question as to what I am involved in, I write her in a letter from July 5, 1955 about my daily routine:

"…there is a soft knock at my door, my landlady opens it just a crack and slides a thermos bottle of tea through it onto the table beside the door. Shortly afterwards I hear her going down the steps to work. I pull my arm from under the cover and look at my watch; it is shortly before six o'clock. I had been daydreaming for a little while, thinking that you must be getting ready to go to bed now.

Sometimes I plan my work for the day at university or I think about a topic for devotion or Bible study for the young people's meeting next day in the early hour.

It is now 6:15am. and I get up. Morning gymnastics help me to wake up and the cold water running over my face, arms and chest drives the rest of tiredness away. It is Tuesday and I usually go swimming in the morning, but the swimming pool is being repaired and is closed for a few weeks. Swimming between 6:45 and 7:45 falls under "Physical Education" for students and is free of charge and I take advantage of that, since I have no bathroom of my own.

Before breakfast, I have my quiet time. The *Losungen* (watchword*s*, a meaningful verse from the New Testament) which I try to memorize and the corresponding poems, give me the basis for my meditation and prayer.

Breakfast would be much more enjoyable in your company perhaps prepared by a loving hand.

I would fit in quite well with the *silence in the morning*; I am not a very talkative person anyway. I am thankful that I have enough to eat. A quick look into the morning paper helps the digestion. At 7:45, fellow students of our student congregation have a *morning devotion*. I have not yet joined them regularly. I do not want to be rushed in my personal quiet time. In general, I do not like to run my day exactly by the clock, if I do not have to.

Around eight o'clock I am in our study room at the university and work on my Diplomarbeit. It takes longer than I expected. Sometimes, my fellow student, Alfred, puts his hand on my shoulder, "Don't dream so long, it does not get your work done; I assume you are in Canada again." As nice as it is to dream about you and to plan with you, I have to get back to reality.

I have my hot meal at lunch in the Mensa, the student cafeteria. Today we had hash browns with a piece of headcheese and a small bowl of soup. The food is nourishing, often not very tasty and not enough to fill an empty stomach but it is served in tastefully designed dishes and with nice cutlery. That is one positive side.

The afternoon activities are similar to those in the morning. I sit at my drawing board and plan my central bus station. I have finished the general layout and am at the stage of designing the details, the entrance hall with ticket office, travel agency, fast food outlet, restaurant and a number of different kiosks. I am not satisfied with my sketches and have to try different solutions.

Supper, I prepare myself and eat at no specified time. If I have the opportunity to listen to a special lecture or get a free student ticket to a concert, then I eat earlier. Normally I quit at 10 pm, ride my bike home, eat and go to bed. Before I fall asleep, I sometimes take your picture from my night desk, touch the cold paper with my hot forehead and think of you...."

I have three months to finish my Diplomarbeit and at the same time there are a number of things I have to attend to. The Canadian

Consulate wants to see me in person, they request a physical examination before they start to work on my immigration and I have to explain to them my reason for wanting to go to Canada. Magdalena and Gustav have agreed to sponsor me. A few weeks after my interview, after I have handed in all my documents, I get the confirmation that I am accepted for immigration. Now I can apply for a visa. The travel agency works out the best affordable passage for me. I have to think about what to take along to my new country.

I am still active in Mennonite young peoples' work, although perhaps not quite as involved as before. The two north German youth workers draw me into their planning and organization of summer Bible school and youth retreats. We have to look for proper facilities and have to find suitable staff and helpers. We think of ways to make it possible for young Mennonites from East Germany to participate in youth activities. They are not allowed to organize any religious youth group meetings there; it is the same as it was under Hitler.

At a retreat in Berlin, I learn to know Doris, an interested High school student who joined the FDJ, the communist youth organization, in order to be allowed to go to High school and study. She would like to have contact with young Mennonites. I tell our youth group her wishes and they spontaneously agree to sponsor her. We write the required letter of invitation and pay for her train ticket. We pick her up from the railway station and Katja's parents agree to have her stay with them. Our girls like her and she fits in quite well with our youth group and enjoys taking part in our activities and retreats.

The girls are busy one day, shortly before she has to return. I have a little time and show her the university and Braunschweig; she is overwhelmed seeing the outlay of goods in the shop windows. "We have nothing like this at home, we have to line up and often the last ones in line don't get anything." I notice her eyes are on a pair of sandals. We go into the store, she tries them on and they fit perfectly. She puts them back again. I ask her if she likes them and she nods. I count my money, it is enough and I pay for them; she is very happy. It is hard for her to go back into the East Zone again.

After the summer, one of our official youth workers plans to terminate his job and the young people want me to take the position.

After some arm-twisting he can be persuaded to continue for a while which spares me the need to make a decision.

Some time ago, the Mennonites purchased the *Menno Kate,* the cottage where Menno Simons had lived his last years around 1550 and the small print shop, in which many of his writings had been printed. Many proposals are made for its practical use; the most common one is, to transform it into a youth centre and I am asked to make plans for it. I drive out to Bad Oldeslohe in Holstein and assess the situation. The building is rather small and the outside appearance cannot be changed since it has been declared a heritage building. I make a number of design sketches but the committee cannot make up its mind.

Some of these activities coincide with my work on the Diplomarbeit and I have to ask for an extension which, fortunately, is granted.

On August 8, 1955, I hand in my Diplomarbeit. This is the conclusion of six years' study at the Technical University of Braunschweig. I am relieved that everything is over. Now I have to wait for the evaluation of my written and oral examinations and my Diplomarbeit. The results are issued together and if I get a passing grade, I can call myself 'Diplom Ingeneur' Helmut Lemke, the official degree for an Architect.

Farewell to Germany

A new epoch of my life begins; I wonder how it will unfold. My decision to emigrate is final and I look forward to seeing my sister again and my beloved Hildegard.

Gradually I plan my departure from my home country. My first leave- taking is from my landlady who had offered me her best room, kept it clean, occasionally shared her kitchen with me and once in a while had a friendly chat with me. Now I have to give up my comfortable place, where I felt at home for two years, and say good-bye to her. She tells me I have been a very pleasant tenant and she wishes me the best for the future.

It is a little harder to depart from my good friends in the Studentengemeinde where I spent a lot of time and my fellow students in the common study room at the university. Alfred promises to send me the results from the evaluation of my Diplomprüfung to Canada as soon as they come out.

When I come home to Handorf, the 'house-community' have decorated my room in the parsonage with flowers. I count six bouquets. I am overwhelmed. I think it was done on Frau Lohmann's initiative

On one weekend, I get a pleasant surprise; several from our Mennonite Youth group from Braunschweig and Hannover come to visit me in Handorf. They want to say good-bye and wish me well. They present me with a beautiful book about Germany, a thank-you gift for my concern for them. I shall remember them when I turn its pages and not forget 'Old Germany'. I am moved.

Now I have to find time to pack my big antique sailor's trunk wondering what to take along and what to leave here.

On my bookshelf are a number of books from the 'Bertelsmann Book Club' to which I belong, so my favorite books have to go in and a few musical instruments, my trumpet and recorders and a violin, which I purchased in a Braunschweig music store. Perhaps I can revive my violin playing again. Some architectural drawings might come in handy when I apply for a job as an architect, so do certificates and photos. I do not have much in the way of clothing but I can buy some in Canada.

Mother and I go to Braunschweig to do some last preparations. In a jewelry store we see a beautiful lady's wristwatch, we buy it. Hildegard has none and I would like to give it to her as an engagement gift..

I already have my boat ticket. Last week the shipping agency picked up my big trunk; only my carry-on luggage has to be packed. I quickly write a few fare- well letters to those to whom I could not say it personally.

It is not easy to leave Germany where my roots are. For me it is almost like a tug of war between Germany and Canada - and Canada is winning this time. It was hard for me to leave my home place in West Prussia, the house I was born in and in which I had been raised; but there I had no choice, the decision was made for me, I was forced to leave. Handorf and Braunschweig are my second home.

I have learned to know many fine people here and made friends in youth groups, at university and in Handorf. My mother, whom I love very much, is here. We have experienced much joy and much pain together and learned to support and appreciate each other.

In Canada is my only sister. She would love to have me over there and give me accommodation. And most important for me, I would like to be close to Hildegard, hoping we can start a life together soon after I arrive there.

The last farewell is from the people in the parsonage, Frau Lohmann and her three lovely boys, the Benders with whom we lived on the same floor for nine years and, of course, from Mother. My sister and I tried hard to convince her to come with me but she is not ready yet. She has three siblings living here and a number of nephews and nieces for some of whom she is a mother substitute. She is financially stable and in good company in the parsonage. She is involved in church work, where she feels a responsibility to help. I think she does not want to be a burden to us when we start out in the new country where she would be dependent on us, not knowing the language and customs, but she leaves the possibility open to come later, when we are established.

We go together to the railway station. A last long hug, she wishes me God's protection and blessing as I board the train and I wave to her as long as I can see her as the train leaves Peine.

My big trunk is already in Bremerhaven when I arrive there. I spend one night in the *Überseeheim* (home for emigrants) and have time to check all my papers carefully. In the evening I go alone through the town to take leave from my home country

I sit down on a park bench and look over the water, lost in thought. How would my life turn out if I were to ask Hildegard if she had ever contemplated coming back to Germany - I would not have to emigrate. I actually have never made that suggestion to her. Why have I not done that?

The next morning I go to the dock, walk up the gangway on to the boat, shove my carry-on luggage into my cabin and go back on deck. I take a last view over the harbor- over Germany, the country where I learned my first prayers and sang my first songs, where I received the foundation for my profession in the one room country school, in the boarding school in Marienburg and the Technical University in Braunschweig, where I found friendship and love..

As the *Seven Seas* leaves the dock, I take leave from all of that and my thoughts are directed to the future

God, how condensed seem the years
of my life in my memory,
I feel as if I have experienced all that
which Is worthwhile for a human being;
what remains when I look back at life
is thankfulness for everything.
                                    Sabine Naegeli

Addendum

1. Site and floor plan of my home place in Alt-Rosengart. A typical 'East German farm house lay out.

2. A map of former West Prussia with Danzig, Marienburg and Elbing. After 1945 it has become a part of Poland.

3. A map of my home village Alt Rosengart (Rosany) and part of Pr.Rosengart (Rozgart), with the location of the "Grüne Aue", the Mennonite church, the Thiene River and our land on the other side of it., the location of our farm (Hof) and that of neighbors, the school (Schule) and the pub (Gastwirtschaft) as they are mentioned in the book.

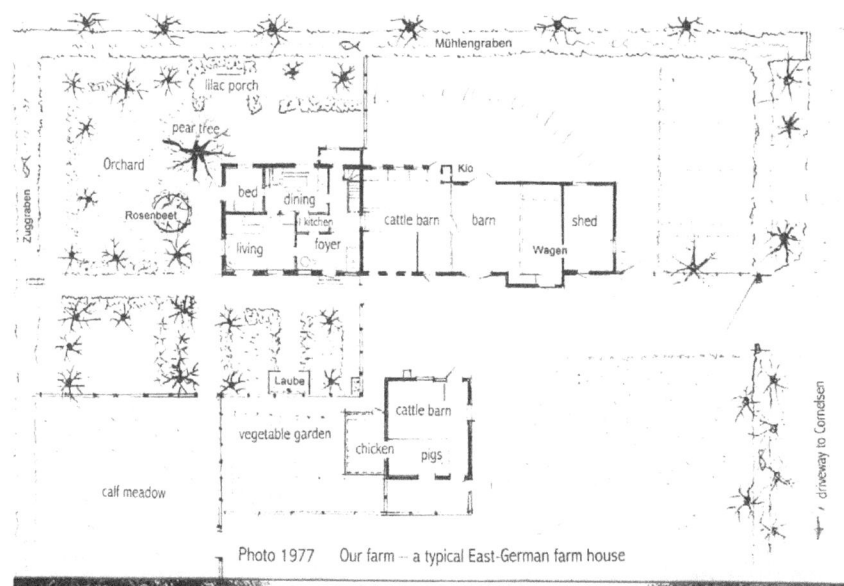

Mühlengraben

lilac porch

pear tree

Orchard

Rosenbeet

bed

dining

kitchen

living

foyer

Kio

cattle barn

barn

shed

Wagen

Zuggraben

Laube

vegetable garden

cattle barn

chicken

pigs

calf meadow

driveway to Corndsen

Photo 1977   Our farm — a typical East-German farm house

262

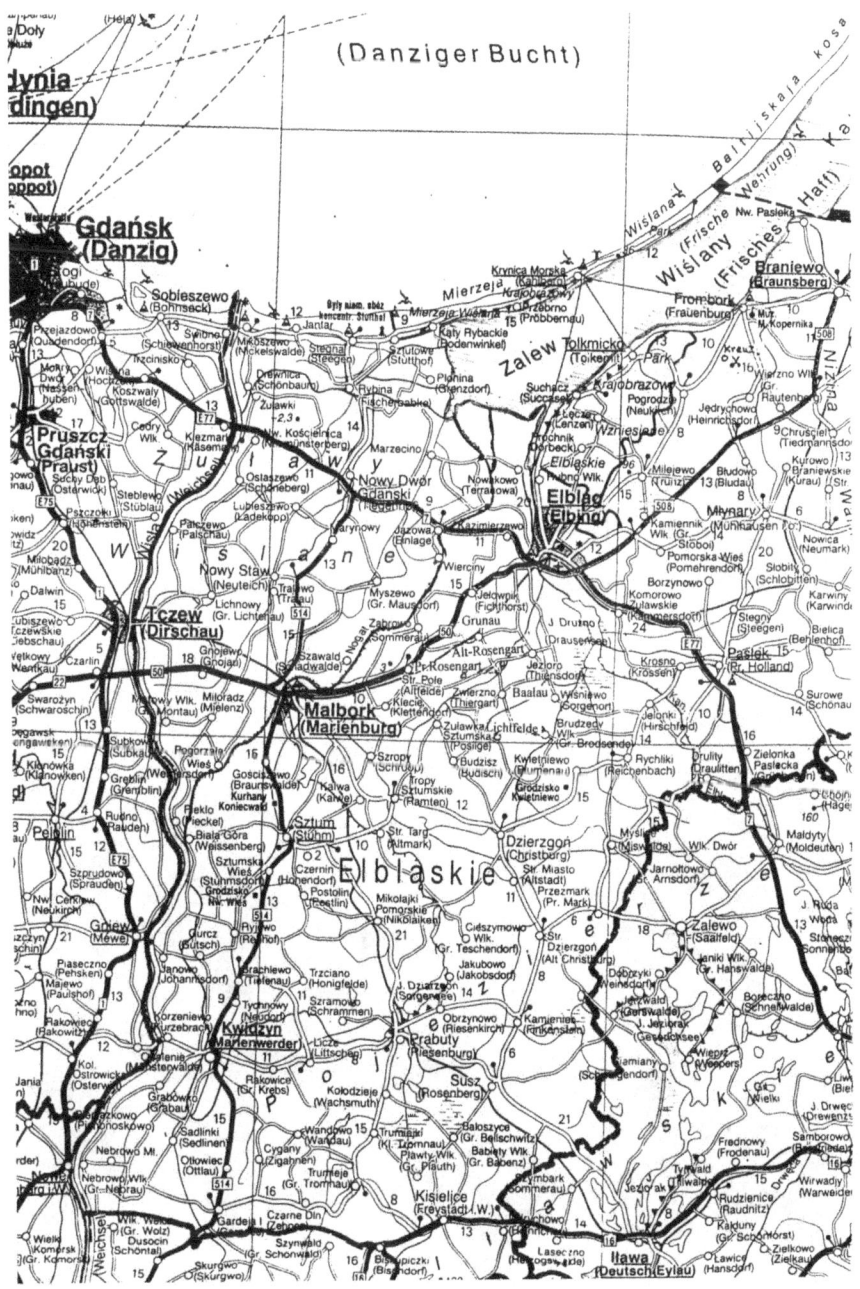

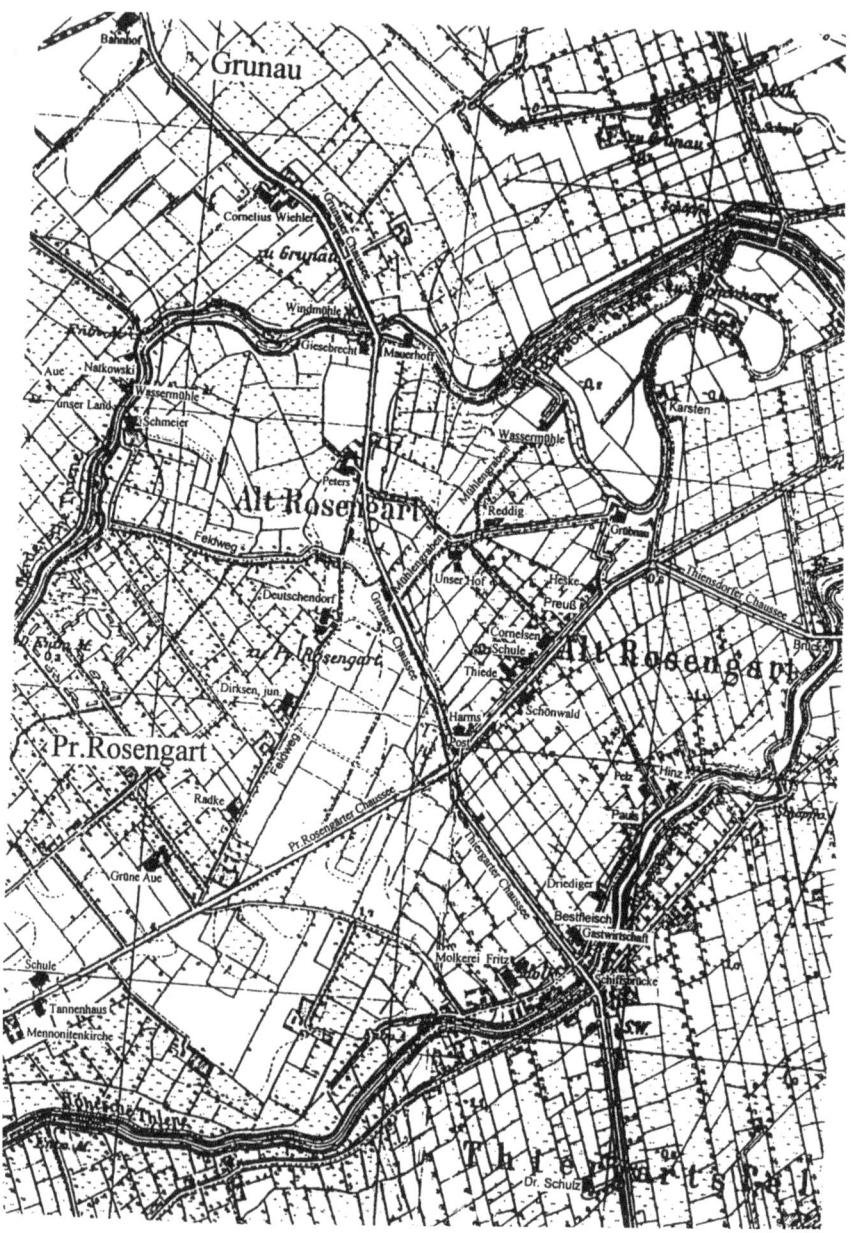

About the Author

Helmut Lemke was born in 1926 in West Prussia, Germany and attended a boarding school in the city of Marienburg. He served in the army on the eastern front during the last year of the war, was wounded and after his recovery searched for his mother in his homeland then occupied by the Russian army and under Polish rule. He lived as a refugee in East Germany, fled to West Germany and studied in theUSA and in Braunschweig where he got his degree in architecture. In 1955, he immigrated to Canada, worked as an architect in Vancouver and later as German and art instructor. He married Hildegard and they had three children. Helmut and Hildegard were both active in youth work and congregational affairs in the Mennonite church. They spent one year in Bielefeld, Germany where Helmut taught in an art college. Now retired, he is volunteering as a director of the More Than a Roof Mennonite Housing Society." Both Helmut and Hildegard are involved in art – painting and sculpture - and like to travel.

CPSIA information can be obtained
at www.ICGtesting.com
Printed in the USA
BVHW070606270121
598815BV00001B/40